DECOLONIZING FEMINISMS
Piya Chatterjee, Series Editor

Transnational Testimonios

The Politics of Collective
Knowledge Production

Patricia DeRocher

UNIVERSITY OF WASHINGTON PRESS
Seattle

UNIVERSITY OF WASHINGTON PRESS
www.washington.edu/uwpress

LIBRARY OF CONGRESS CATALOGING-IN-PUBLICATION DATA
Names: DeRocher, Patricia, author.
Title: Transnational testimonios : the politics of collective knowledge production / Patricia DeRocher.
Description: 1st Edition. | Seattle : University of Washington Press, [2018] | Series: Decolonizing feminisms | Includes bibliographical references and index. |
Identifiers: LCCN 2018004858 (print) | LCCN 2018019829 (ebook) |
   ISBN 9780295743929 (ebook) | ISBN 9780295743905 (hardcover : alk. paper) |
   ISBN 9780295743912 (pbk. : alk. paper)
Subjects: LCSH: Collective memory. | Transnationalism. | Feminism. | Indigenous peoples. | Narrative inquiry (Research method)
Classification: LCC HM1033 (ebook) | LCC HM1033 .C645 2018 (print) | DDC 909—dc23
LC record available at https://lccn.loc.gov/2018004858

Portions of this book originally appeared in "Testimonio and Its Travelers: Feminist Deployments of a Genre at Work," in *Pushing the Boundaries of Latin American Testimony: Meta-morphoses and Migrations*, edited by Louise Detwiler and Janis Breckenridge (New York: Palgrave Macmillan, 2012), and are reproduced with the permission of Palgrave Macmillan.

Cover illustrations from Wikimedia Commons: (*foreground*) traditional mola with geometric pattern, photo by Stefan Laube; (*midground*) detail of Chinese vase from Owen Jones, *Examples of Chinese Ornament* (S. & T. Gilbert, 1867); (*background*) glazed ceramic tile work, Tomb of Hafez, Iran, photo by Pentocelo

For Quinn
May you know more expansive futures

The truth, these stories are nothing but story, bits of string, odds and ends found here and there, embroidered together to make something new . . . If, in the course of my inventing, I have inadvertently stumbled on the truth, *perdónenme*.

—SANDRA CISNEROS, *CARAMELO*

Contents

Preface

> Those who authentically commit themselves to the people must
> re-examine themselves constantly.
>
> —PAULO FREIRE, *PEDAGOGY OF THE OPPRESSED*

During my second year of college teaching, I assigned Toni Cade Bambara's "The Lesson" in an introduction to literature course at a predominantly white liberal arts college outside Burlington, Vermont. While on the plane back from visiting the University of Minnesota, Twin Cities, where I had just been accepted as a PhD student, I started to grade a student paper that responded to an essay question I had formulated on the significance of Bambara having her child narrator speak in black vernacular English.

We had spent significant time discussing language politics in the course, generally, and I had also provided students with a piece of literary criticism specifically discussing Bambara's language choice in the short story. So I found myself absolutely horrified when I began reading an essay that argued that Bambara's purpose was to illustrate that the little girl "was not very intelligent." My stomach dropped: *What had I done (or not done?) as a professor to allow this student to provide such a violent misinterpretation of Bambara's work?*

It was also during this time that, after teaching my college courses in the morning, I would head over to work as a facilitator at an after-school program at a local elementary school. Organized by a local community center that serviced a number of New American families, mostly of color, the "melting pot program" included the goal of helping students "assimilate" into US culture. Looking back, I can see how this logic permeated the ways in which many of the school counselors and teachers engaged with students. I remember the gym coach matter-of-factly commenting on how half of the students wouldn't finish high school, and one of my supervisors informing a young black student that his language was "incorrect." But mostly what I saw were children passionate about life, sharing their cultures and languages with each other, taking out the globe and looking to see where their friends were from. I remember one of the older students commenting that the next time the art teacher treated him like that, he was going to "pull a Rosa Parks"; and I remember the time I sat silently swinging next to an emotionally distraught student from the Republic of Congo after the principal had told him that his belief in animal spirits—a part of his Luba epistemology—was "wrong." The next day I would start my morning with a room full of socially privileged white college students, disproportionately groggy and uninspired, slouched in their chairs, waiting for class to end so they could go play their video games.

The juxtaposition of these social spaces was deeply troubling to me—how was it that these schools, just minutes away from each other, could be such worlds apart? What would it take for the students sitting in my college classroom to really *see* and *hear* the child narrator in "The Lesson," who so reminded me of the joyful children who greeted me every afternoon? What would it take for the children in the after-school program to gain cultural access to the world of the college classroom that my college students took for granted?

Feeling defeated, I leapt down the proverbial rabbit hole. *What, exactly, does literature do, anyway?* I wondered. *How does it act on the world?*[1] When I first entered a doctoral program with a strong social science focus, literature seem peripheral. And yet, as I took courses in history and public policy, I noticed how the role of narrative remained front and center in everything we discussed. Narration was everywhere, all around me, all the time. When I stumbled upon my first testimonios, they seemed to provide the structural "answer" I was looking for. Testimonios—creatively shaped stories that refer outwardly to actual life events—were narratives that intentionally resided at the nexus of the discursive and the material. At the time, I interpreted testimonio as an acknowledgment of the limits of art in social justice projects, and as privileging the documentary, rather than how I now see it: as a definitive assertion of cultural work being integral to social justice platforms.

These conundrums and experiences are what planted the seeds for what has become this book, and what have informed the questions I have sought answers to in the ten years since. While this book focuses on polyvocal feminist testimonios, it is the political, theoretical, and philosophical questions they raise that led me to them in the first place, and that allow me a tangible focal point in which to ground the epistemic questions that I continue to grapple with in my academic and personal lives. It is their insistence of engaging with the politics of representation, and their recognition of the centrality of the cultural imaginary to consolidate or disrupt social inequalities, that I find so compelling.

At a fundamental level, I understand polyvocal feminist testimonio as a form of transnational feminist praxis that strategically performs epistemic translations by providing a textual bridge between practitioners and readers of vastly different social worlds. In contrast to traditional testimonio, primarily aimed at reaching a northern audience, I understand these works to be a form of "connected activism" (Medina 228) that are epistemically useful to the practitioners themselves while *also* seeking out horizontal South/South relationships and northern readerships.[2] Practitioners' commitment to reaching multiple audiences necessarily deepens the epistemic reach of testimonios, a reach furthered by multivoiced narrative frameworks that create productive "epistemic friction" (23), a form of dialogic interaction between differently socially situated subjects that helps to expand the epistemic worlds inhabited by both practitioners and readers. This polyvocal narrative strategy models in textual form the possibility of what Medina terms a "kaleidoscopic consciousness" (200), or an opening up of our epistemic worlds that allows us to "read" the same event through different social lenses. As I argue in the pages that follow, the cultural work that these texts accomplish are at once theoretically and methodologically complex and grounded and pragmatic, interrupting dominant flows of knowledge production. They also necessitate my own working across borders, most notably in relation to the multiple audiences for this book.

Before I speak about whom I envision these audiences to be, I want to address the power relations involved in being a white northern academic publishing a book on a life-writing form predominantly employed by writers from the Global South. Writing this book threatens to rein-state the violence of the power relations it seeks to critique, and I do not wish to sidestep this reality.[3] While I do my best to "speak with" (Nagar 83), I cannot undo the position in which I am located in relation to these texts, nor can I place myself outside of the power relations with which they engage. Even then, I want to complicate the assumption that testi-monios are written only by authors of color or subaltern voices. The truth is that these power relations are more shifting and complex, especially across national boundaries and the discursive racial categories that such imagined borders reinforce.

While the authors of the Argentine testimonios *The Little School* and *A Single, Numberless Death* enjoy class and racial privilege in their home country, as soon as their bodies and texts enter the North American con-text, they are positioned as geopolitically other and nonwhite. Similarly, the *testimoniadoras* in *Telling to Live: Latina Feminist Testimonios* experience processes of racialization and marginalization in the US context, but as US academics, they also experience educational, class, and geopolitical privilege. That is, as the writers' bodies and words traverse nation-states and readerships, they simultaneously traverse racial paradigms and epistemes. As such, my analyses intentionally bring attention to the sociocultural norms and hierarchies governing the particular social land-scapes that the texts inhabit while also allowing for shifting power rela-tions between particular texts and audiences. Finding a precise language to adequately speak to these shifting sets of cross-border dynamics has been a central challenge of this project to account for power imbalances between readers and texts while also accounting for multiple, often hor-izontal, readerships, and without narrowly assigning readers or writers a fixed set of racial signifiers or epistemes. This is a challenge the cultural workers with whom this book dialogues know quite well, as they have placed their hopes, tears, and labors into their works so that such cul-tural bridges *might* be formed. A politics without guarantees.

In many ways I did not want to write this book. It would have been much easier not to. It is always easier to stay soundly within our own epis-temic worlds, to not do the internal work. To not recognize how oppres-sion and ignorance and bias and power and privilege live in our hearts and minds. Easier to not confront the ugliest parts of our being. But at the end of the day, this is willful ignorance—an active, invisible form of epistemic violence. A choosing to stay stuck, an opting for the status quo, even when we know it to be wrong. It is easy, and lazy, to stay in this space. It is dangerous and terrifying to leave it. I have buried multiple versions of myself in the process of writing this book and I hope to bury many, many more.

This book moves in multiple directions, with many different pieces. It is exploratory, raising questions on the political possibilities of feminist testimonios more than providing definitive answers. Mostly, I hope to move current dialogue around testimonios forward and to compel readers to read and interpret the texts themselves—and to enact a just response that feels organic and personally meaningful.

To get to it, then, this book is for different audiences. First and foremost, it is written out of respect and with a sense of responsibility—in acknowledgment and admiration of, and gratitude for—the labor of the cultural workers who took the time and energy to construct these works, which have helped me to realize the depth of inequity that the historicity of my body has helped to maintain. My training is deeply indebted to women-of-color feminisms, particularly the work of Barbara Christian, and I therefore understand these feminist testimonios as *already* theorizing beyond the shallow way that academic writing is able to accomplish. This book is not by any means a worthy "thank you," but it is an offering.

This work is also offered as an epistemic bridge for those working in academia who would like to break out of their limited disciplinary and social worlds. This book is, in part, for other academics, educators, and privileged subjects who are trained and encouraged to encounter these feminist testimonios from an arrogant posture and who want to see and understand beyond the epistemically impoverishing constraints their training and/or privilege have allowed. It is my hope that this book will provide useful skill sets for other ways of hearing and interpreting these works, in the spirit of the academic work of M. Jacqui Alexander, Paula Moya, and José Medina, who have shown me that a rigorous intellectualism can simultaneously be a practical, ethical, and heart-opening exercise.

Finally, this book is written in the spirit of public intellectualism, in the vein of bell hooks and others who recognize that degrees are not synonymous with intelligence and that organic intellectualism is alive and well outside the walls of the academy. For this reason, this book is in part dedicated to my community college students at SUNY Adirondack, from whom I learned so much and who humbled me many, many times. I continue to carry these lessons with me.

Through the process of writing this book and in sharing its insights, I have been alternately told it is not "academic enough" and that it is "too academic." This criticism used to cause me much frustration, but I see now that such responses are proof that I'm doing *exactly* the kind of work I want to be doing. At its core it is about radical humility and making ourselves vulnerable to each other, listening in more ethical ways, overcoming our fear of asking questions, and being OK with not knowing the answers. In short, this book is for those who are ready to do the work. To open themselves, to come to recognize their own cultural blinders. To integrate the lessons of heart and head, the tangible and the abstract, the intellectual and the pragmatic. It is for those who wish to gain a greater recognition of the world we find ourselves in now, and to discover an ever deepening clarity about the type of world we want to usher in. Like the authors of feminist polyvocal testimonios, I offer this book in a spirit of grounded optimism and with the hope that its insights will reach the ears of others like myself, who cannot seem to stay within the lines.

I would not have been able to see this work as possible or valuable without the continued guidance, mentorship-turned-friendship, and patience of Richa Nagar, whose utter fearlessness and refusal to accept received dogmas and binaries—even and *especially* the reigning intellectually "sexy" academic paradigms of the moment—inspire me to follow her example. Thank you, Richa. Your fingerprints are all over this book.

Thank you to Nancy Welch, Omise'eke Tinsley, Shaden Tageldin, Valerie Rohy, Glen Elder, Edén Torres, and Carey Kaplan, each of whom has contributed so much to my political and intellectual journey. To Gopi Kinnicutt, Amy Kaminsky, Kim Beekman, and Beth Mausert for helping me reconnect my mind and body through a heart-centered yoga and meditation practice; it has reenergized my academic work. To the Pino family, who allowed me to hold a solitary writing retreat at their camp to finish this book, and for enabling me to see outside of my own epistemic bubble at a young age. To Lois Pino, especially, for continually reminding me of my epistemic growth (often painfully!), and for modeling that an alternative form of whiteness is possible. To Papoo and Papa, to whom I owe my education and so much more. To my parents, Tim and Elizabeth Connolly, for always allowing me to follow my own path and for enabling pathways into other epistemic worlds beyond the homogenizing tenor of our small town. To the editorial team at the University of Washington Press for all their constructive feedback while holding my vision for this book. To Brae, for breaking my heart wide open and teaching me the beauty and freedom of love without guarantees. And to Quinn, who arrived in this world at the very beginning of this project, and whose own burgeoning kaleidoscopic consciousness inspires me daily.

As an undergraduate, I once turned in a paper arguing that idealism is the only worthwhile form of pragmatism; my teacher informed me this was a paradox in need of revision. This book is for those who understand.

Transnational Testimonios

INTRODUCTION

An "I" That Is "We"

Revisiting the Epistemic Potential of Collective
Truth Telling

> Once, when I told her I liked to listen to her *historias*, she laughed
> and asked me if I had ever heard the saying, "*Cuéntame algo, aunque
> sea una mentira*" (Tell me a story, even if it's a lie). In a more serious
> mood, she would often wonder aloud whether the gringos would
> believe her *historia*—not because what she had told me wasn't the
> true story of her life, but because she feared that an understanding
> of what she had told me called for a leap of empathy that she
> suspected the gringos might not be able, or willing, to make. No,
> she finally decided, the gringos would never believe what she had
> told me.
>
> —RUTH BEHAR, *TRANSLATED WOMAN*

> If one looks at the history of post-Enlightenment theory . . . the
> person who *knows* has all the problems of selfhood. The person who
> is *known*, somehow seems not to have a problematic self. These days,
> it is the same kind of agenda that is at work. Only the dominant self
> can be problematic; the self of the Other is authentic, without a
> problem, naturally available to all kinds of complications. This is
> very frightening.
>
> —GAYATRI SPIVAK, "QUESTIONS OF MULTI-CULTURALISM"

YEARS AFTER RECEIVING THE NOBEL PEACE PRIZE IN 1992 FOR HER
activist work on indigenous Guatemalan land rights, Rigoberta Menchú
found herself the center of political controversy regarding the veracity
of her book, *I, Rigoberta Menchú: An Indian Woman in Guatemala* (1983). If

the publication of North American anthropologist David Stoll's *Rigoberta Menchú and the Story of All Poor Guatemalans* (1999) sought to complicate the politics of any one person speaking for the truths of an entire community—as he suggested Menchú's text attempted to do—then the *New York Times*'s reduction of Stoll's argument to a two-column exposé replaced Stoll's already misdirected attempt at intellectual rigor with journalistic vulgarity.[1] As a result, Menchú's international reputation quickly shifted from reputable "truth teller" to "deceitful woman." The ensuing knee-jerk distrust of Menchú's narrative account rehearses well-known colonial and patriarchal scripts in which the testimony of an indigenous third world woman subject became all too easily displaced by the countertestimony of a white male scholar from the northern academy.

In a follow-up interview to her *New York Times* incrimination, Menchú unapologetically defended her narrative with the following seemingly simple assertion: "*I Rigoberta Menchú* was a testimonial, not an autobiography" (Aznárez 110). While this distinction seems self-evident for Menchú—that testimonio and autobiography are dissimilar genres with divergent goals and modes of representation—this difference was clearly not apparent to the majority of the *New York Times* North American reading public. What, then, does it mean for Menchú to defend her truth claims by arguing that her book was a testimonial and not an autobiography?

In essence, Menchú was accused of representing others' experiences as her own; of constructing a composite narrative that wove together several people's life events and integrated them with her own life story. For Menchú, this is nothing to deny; instead, she argues, "The history of the community is my own history. . . . I am the product of a community" (Aznárez 110, 113). Menchú's response addresses one of the central tenets of testimonio, whereby a narrative "I" is called upon to represent the experiences of the "we," in which the narrator speaks as a member of an oppressed community or social group who utilizes the genre to bring attention to a collective social problem. True to traditional formulas of this writing form, the experiences of several community members are "grafted" onto the narrative body of the central speaker. Thus, while Stoll claims to have "caught" Menchú in a lie, his accusation refuses to recognize the intentional rhetorical shaping of her narrative account. In so doing, Stoll ignores the performativity of Menchú's life narrative as an intentionally crafted text and reduces it to positivist evidence.[2]

On a textual level, the dismissal of Menchú's text signals a lack of knowledge of testimonio as an established narrative form, and ignorance that alternate forms of self-representational practices exist outside of dominant western autobiographical paradigms. The outcry that followed Stoll's questioning of the "facts" of Menchú's story illustrates the North American reading public's deep investment in, and internalization of, autobiography as the quintessential form of life writing, as well as a disregard for the level of artifice present in any autobiographical act. But beyond this seemingly benign unfamiliarity with the genre and principles of testimonio, the discrediting of Menchú's account speaks to a more troubling deep-seated cultural chauvinism that refuses to engage with knowledge producers on their own terms when these terms fall outside of dominant western epistemes.

To return to the opening question—what it means for Menchú to defend her truth claims by arguing that her book was a testimonial and not an autobiography—I argue that were testimonio and autobiography to enjoy equal recognition for their intellectual and literary merits (as "memoir" and "autobiography" seem to do), Menchú would not need to articulate such a distinction. But this is not the case. Nor is it the case that these narrative forms are "simply" alternate preferred ways of writing the self. Rather, these different forms of life writing are constructed out of divergent philosophical lineages and theories of subjectivity, thereby yielding different political effects. While autobiography has been traditionally utilized to convey western bourgeois narratives of the "self-made man," testimonio is firmly rooted in liberation struggles in the Global South.[3] In short, and as illustrated by the fallout of Menchú's text, the concept of life experiences and understandings of the self as in constant relation to community formations proves largely illegible for a citizen body deeply entrenched in individualist epistemes, as does a more subjective, flexible model of truth-value for an audience groomed within a juridical model of truth that favors objectivity and concrete fact.[4] Menchú's insistence on her book being understood as testimonio and not autobiography thus confronts more than an arbitrary disagreement on its proper genre description. It signals the cultural currency of literary works and the level of trust readers place in them to reinforce their understanding of foundational cultural and ideological configurations such as "self" and "truth." In other words, it signals an interpretive impasse between vastly different epistemologies and worldviews.

The misrecognition of Menchú's text therefore serves to consolidate and reinforce dominant western ideological and representational practices by accusing her of doing autobiography "wrong." But to counter in Menchú's words, "It is not a question of believing my own truth or someone else's; I'm simply saying I have a right to my memory, as do my people" (Aznárez 116). By narrating her account in terms of collective memory, Menchú stakes a claim in how testimonio can be utilized to advance social struggle.[5] From Menchú's perspective, Stoll's fact checking misses the mark; or rather, the wrong facts are being checked. While she is raked over the coals, indigenous Guatemalans continue to lose more land, struggle to access education, and seek adequate political representation. Meanwhile, on the opposite end of this epistemic divide, by deflecting blame onto Menchú, Stoll enables northern readers to sit comfortably in their first world bubbles, unaffected and blameless, claiming victim status for falling prey to the fictional ruse of this third world troublemaker.

A highly politicized scandal at the time, the Rigoberta Menchú controversy continues to be discussed and debated in undergraduate classrooms as well as between scholars in the realms of testimonio, literature, and human rights. Too often, discussion of Menchú's text, both in terms of its formal qualities and in relation to its subsequent controversy, stands in metonymic relation to all discussions concerning testimonio. This textual fetishization has kept criticism on testimonio at a standstill, rehearsing the same questions and directing inadequate attention to less well known—and perhaps more rhetorically and politically complex—testimonial works. Additionally, undertheorized concerns over unequal power relations between an assumed (subaltern) testifier and (first world) documenter and audience—accompanied by the dwindling evidence that the genre will directly lead to tangible and immediate social change—has led to a series of articles denouncing the subversive potential of testimonio. Although these concerns merit careful attention, I agree with Kimberly Nance, who suggests that "declarations of testimonio's triumph and reports of its demise . . . [are] premature and [reveal] more about the genre's ability to frustrate literary and cultural critics than about testimonio itself" (Nance 5). Nance addresses, if indirectly, the fact that many testimonios are not written for an academic audience, nor are they meant to be contained within an academic context. Rather, as texts that emerge from a specific cultural context and with focused political intentionality, testimonios are not purist in form, content, or political-theoretical allegiance, a reality that serves to confound scholars who are trained to "master" and "dominate" the meaning of a text and/or to engage with creative works in discipline-specific ways.

Indeed, rather than engaging with the social justice work these narratives set out to accomplish, scholarship on testimonio has become increasingly apolitical and out of touch with the writing form's activist intentions. As Eva Paulino Bueno argues in "Race, Gender, and the Politics of Reception of Latin American *Testimonios*," "The study of *testimonio* has been transformed into a game of mirrors in which North American academics who write, speak, and publish on the subject assume the positions of spokesperson . . . determining which book is worthy of study and why" (118). In so doing, such debates sidestep the pressing discussions that need to be had around complex power dynamics between readers and text, and how these texts mean differently, and unpredictably, depending on the particular racial and geopolitical relations that emerge between the authors of testimonio and those who choose to read the book. For instance, how might Menchú's text mean differently when read by indigenous activists struggling for land rights in the North American context, versus being assigned as a first-year seminar text at Harvard? And even then, how can we ever render static the fluid power dynamics involved in texts connecting with audiences in unexpected ways?

While paying homage to the influential reach of Menchú's text, I seek to break through current scholarly stasis with a reminder that testimonio did not begin or end with *I, Rigoberta Menchú*. As stated, my own interest in the Menchú controversy is as a cultural event that offers rich insight into larger debates that testimonio raises on the relationships between memory and truth, the politics of knowledge production, and the possibilities and foreclosures of bridging epistemic worlds. But while I evoke Menchú's narrative and public berating to introduce some of the central themes and tensions underpinning this book, this is also where I put her case to rest. The remainder of the book turns specific attention to contemporary feminist polyvocal testimonios, an umbrella concept for a hybrid body of work that utilizes life-writing practices to deliver intersectional, macrolevel social critique in the form of first-person plural narrative accounts.

These works at once share a deep affinity with Menchú's text even as their representational methodologies are continually revised to gain traction and legibility in activist and northern circuits, circumventing some of the foundational interpretive impasses that led critics to question the veracity of Menchú's account. This book argues that practitioners of contemporary feminist testimonies are more than writers; they are textual activists who employ writing as a social tool.[6] By bringing into focus the varied landscape of contemporary feminist testimonios I deliver an analysis of the rhetorical and imaginative tropes they utilize to paint richly textured representations of gendered subjectivity in order to document current inequities and to imagine more egalitarian futures. Such intentional craftings allow them to traverse multiple audiences, some rife with tenuous racial and geopolitical power asymmetries, others offering a more horizontal, analogous mapping of power and privilege with the truths they put forth.

As such, this book more broadly considers the politics of subjective truth-claims in knowledge production: *Whose knowledge counts as knowledge? Whose truths are believed and whose truths are discounted, and why? Is it possible for readers and writers with conflicting experiences, perspectives, and worldviews to ever bridge such epistemic divides?* Specifically, this book conceptualizes the power relations at play when socially marginalized subjects utilize alternative life-writing paradigms to perform socially lived theory and how multiple, differently positioned audiences come to interface with such texts. I employ the framework of "life-writing practices" in place of the western notion of "autobiography" (Smith and Watson 2010), and maintain a focus on "testimonio" as a resistant form of life writing.

As the opening epigraph from Behar and Spivak highlights, such narrative accounts run the constant risk of being interpreted within a reductionist paradigm by racially and geopolitically privileged audiences in which the truth-claims put forth by the speakers (read as "authentic" marginal social subjects) are either uncritically believed as transparent, uncomplicated narrative truths of life-as-it-happened, or alternately, wholly dismissed at the attitudinal whim of geopolitically privileged reading audiences who make the willful choice to remain uninformed on global political issues and their entanglements with them. As such, this book works to disrupt this narrow interpretive model by moving beyond the "true/false" binary in order to complicate the ways we understand the power-laden relationship between speaker, reader, and text in contemporary feminist testimonio by reframing this *interpretative impasse* as an *epistemic impasse* wherein social actors from disparate worlds struggle to see and hear each other's truths.

Corresponding with the "deliberative" strand of testimonio (Nance), the strategic adoption of a "many-voiced" framework is one of the central rhetorical strategies undertaken by contemporary practitioners of feminist testimonio in order to call attention to the crafted "staging" of their representations (Shank and Nagar), and to refuse to accept the one-dimensional position of "native informant." Such frameworks sidestep the representational impasse of the Menchú controversy by making visible the plurality of speakers and experiences the works negotiate and allow practitioners of feminist testimonio to boldly insert themselves into the fraught terrain of knowledge production. Through their employment of hybrid and experimental representational practices that highlight how truth claims are always socially situated, they challenge ready-made assertions over whose truth claims count as "knowledge," and establish themselves as knowledge producers in their refusal to be read as noncomplex, "authentic" third world subjects.

Engaging the diverse fields of transnational feminist thought, literary studies, autobiography studies, Latin American studies, and Caribbean studies, this book performs a "countertopographic" (Katz) comparative discursive analysis to understand how contemporary feminist literary writers and activists mobilize testimonial narratives to bring attention to desired social issues. The primary texts I engage with are from a range of geopolitical sites, including Argentina, Haiti, India, Jamaica, Trinidad, and the United States. Some are collaborative and activist in intent, such as the Latina Feminist Group's *Telling to Live*, the Sangtin Writers' *Playing with Fire*, and the Sistren Theatre Collective's *Lionheart Gal*. Some, such as Shani Mootoo's *Cereus Blooms at Night* and the corpus of Edwidge Danticat, are more fictional in nature. Others, such as Nora Strejilevich's *A Single, Numberless Death* and Alicia Kozameh's *Steps under Water*, intentionally blur the line between fiction and nonfiction, mixing and matching the imaginative with the documentary. I attempt to trace some overarching representational patterns and methodologies in these various strands that become visible when these pieces are read alongside of each other. In highlighting how these practices enter the contested terrain of knowledge production by fostering epistemic bridges that bring practitioners and readers from different social worlds into critical contact, I hope to focus more academic attention on the theoretical and methodological contributions of such works, and to encourage readers to cultivate a more epistemically responsible reading practice.

In short, through the lens of feminist polyvocal testimonio, my book engages with questions of storytelling, epistemic translation, knowledge, and power, while arguing that narration and storytelling are vital tools for reimagining transnational feminist politics and enacting more egalitarian futures. It posits that to contribute to a more democratic mode of social knowledge production we need to take a deeper look at why and how people employ stories to interpret social truths based on their own experiential knowledge rooted in their daily lives, and how such practices contain suggestions for how these narratives can intervene in epistemological impasses between North and South. In turn, the book suggests that even socially responsive academic theories such as postpositivist realism must not simply "create" interpretive rubrics for translating experiential-based narratives into reliable social knowledge, but must listen carefully to how people are *already* employing such practices.[7] What stories choose to highlight is intimately connected to the social interventions they seek to make and what the storytellers' experiences have allowed them to see, and this partial perspective is not something to be "overcome" in the pursuit of knowledge—it is rather that which allows us to understand at all.

A note on the layout of my book. You will notice that there are four distinct parts. Part 1 is dedicated to contextualizing academic debates about testimonio and exploring the epistemic importance of feminist polyvocal testimonios. Parts 2, 3, and 4 work closely with feminist testimonios themselves. By placing these discourses alongside of each other without any facile reconciliation, I seek to echo the spirit of polyvocal feminist testimonios, which encourage epistemic friction by bringing disparate worlds into proximate contact, and which are articulated in different language registers for different audiences and contexts.

Part 1 opens with "Situating Testimonio: A Spirit of Resistance in Textual Form," which provides a working definition of testimonio. The chapter situates this writing project in relation to the fields of Latin American studies and autobiography studies to contextualize the scholarly trajectory surrounding it. Chapter 2, "Feminism, Epistemology, and Experience," brings testimonio into dialogue with feminist theory debates on partial perspective and situated knowledges (Haraway), postpositivist realist identity theory (Moya), the epistemic value of experience (Scott), and epistemic responsibility (Medina), enabling a more flexible, expansive understanding of testimonio as a methodology and writing project in the service of social justice platforms.

Chapter 3, "Constructing Feminist Transnational Bridges through Polyvocal Praxis," provides a working definition of feminist testimonio as modeling an epistemically responsible methodology that bridges disparate social worlds to cultivate what Medina terms a "kaleidoscopic consciousness" in its readers and practitioners (74). This chapter documents the overarching rhetorical tropes and narrational strategies feminist testimonios employ to articulate macrosocial critiques in microsocial, affective registers through the avenue of marginal experience narratives. Such works draw on the epistemic privilege of socially marginalized actors to disrupt dominant social narratives in order to produce more complex, less false social knowledge. Most notably, this chapter speaks to their "polyvocal" narrative strategy as a central means of establishing a dialogic praxis.

Part 2 opens with "'Co/Labor/Actions': Polyvocality, Pedagogy, and Praxis," where I engage with the dialogic methods and rhetorical practices that feminist activist polyvocal testimonios utilize to stage their political interventions. I articulate how feminist collaborative activist testimonios at once embody and enact their political visions through dialogue and co-narrational strategies that privilege a process-based approach. In so doing they insert themselves into the layered landscape of the politics of knowledge production and social movements as a form of "connected activism" (Medina 228). The specific works engaged with in this section are the Latina Feminist Group's *Telling to Live: Latina Feminist Testimonios* (2001), the Sangtin Writers' *Playing with Fire: Feminist Thought and Activism through Seven Lives in India* (2006), the Sistren Theatre Collective's *Lionheart Gal: Life Stories of Jamaican Women* (1986), and Beverly Bell's *Walking on Fire: Haitian Women's Stories of Survival and Resistance* (2001).

In part 3, "Testifying to the Politics of the Imagined," I move away from activist deployments of the genre to articulate how and why feminist literary authors translate historical events into the realm of fiction and other hybrid creative writing forms. I argue that the strategic use of testimonio as a rhetorical narrative framework—positioning the reader as witness to a fictional narrative testifier—undermines a mindless, capitalist consumption of politically motivated literary texts by replacing a unidirectional model of entertainment with a bidirectional social pact. Specific texts include Nora Strejilevich's *A Single, Numberless Death*, Alicia Kozameh's *Steps under Water*, Alicia Partnoy's *The Little School*, and Shani Mootoo's *Cereus Blooms at Night*.

Part 4 supplements the comparativist model of previous sections with a "deep dive" into the multiple writing forms that Haitian American writer Edwidge Danticat utilizes to generate epistemic bridges between multiply situated audiences. This geopolitically rooted and sociohistorically situated section opens with "Retransmissions: Reading across Languages, Genres, and Readerships with Danticat's 'Fakelore,'" and attends to the continued importance of multilingual cultural workers such as Danticat in the face of colonial legacies and neocolonial conditions through discussions of *Krik? Krak!*, *Behind the Mountains*, and *Brother, I'm Dying*. As a self-described "dyaspora" who finds herself between cultural worlds and epistemes, Danticat testifies to the possibility of creating interpretive bridges between vastly different social worlds, and the necessity of taking aim at the cultural imaginary to intervene in contemporary social realities.

The postscript, "Countering Restriction with Expansion: Cultivating Kaleidoscopic Counterpublics," links these textual explorations to the contemporary social stage, including the lived landscape of Burlington, Vermont, where I make my home. Here I make the case for understanding feminist polyvocal testimonio as enacting a decolonial ethos that cultivates feminist counterpublics (Alvarez) by encouraging readers to practice internalized "epistemic friction," which can pave the way for a kaleidoscopic consciousness (Medina).

PART I

Telling Stories, Writing Praxis

Decolonizing Knowledge Production

CHAPTER 1

Situating Testimonio

A Spirit of Resistance in Textual Form

> When the times changed, you changed too. . . . That's *teknik*,
> craftiness.
>
> —VITA TELCY, *WALKING ON FIRE*

TESTIMONIO IS A GENRE AT WORK. AS A VARIANT OF WHAT TRINH
T. Minh-ha calls "Third World literary discourse," testimonio claims to be
not exactly an "art for the masses," but an "art for the people, by the people,
and from the people" (252). Minh-ha's words highlight how the principles
and functions of Latin American testimonio more broadly correspond
with first-person plural social justice writing projects in their differing
contexts, struggles, and forms. As such, this chapter calls for an expansive understanding of testimonio that transcends specific formal qualities and trades in a definition of what it *is* for *what it does and why*. Beyond
its classification as a genre in which a member of an oppressed group
attempts to convey an urgent social problem, testimonio offers a sustained situational analysis of how larger power structures are felt and
experienced at the level of marginalized social actors.

Testimonio therefore offers one particular way, or *methodology*, of telling a story about how the social landscape actively shapes and affects
the personal lives at the center of a narrative account. More than a laun-
dry list of narrative must-haves, testimonio shares a commitment: a utilization of first-person plural narratives to relay a macrosocial critique
in a microsocial, affective register. As a culturally resistant writing

project, testimonio recognizes creative writing as vital to social justice projects. It asserts that change begins with the cultivation of a critical consciousness and attitudinal shifts, and inspires its readers to begin these processes of attitudinal adjustment and to open up to the possibility of a more just world. As such, testimonio is nothing less than a hybrid textual praxis for those who use the written word as cultural weapons to rearrange well-worn bourgeois narratives and replace them with radical social visions of justice for all. In this way, testimonio is a spirit of resistance in textual form; it embodies the creativity and ingenuity of social actors who hold little formal power and yet who actively reject a vision of themselves as powerless.

Testimonio is not for doctrinaires. It provides no easy, formulaic solutions; it offers instead partial truths and the articulation of complex realities. It rejects all "pure" political or aesthetic platforms in favor of a tactical approach. It breaks its own rules in an effort to resist categorical stasis and confounds those who seek to bind it with ready-made definitions. Testimonio is therefore necessarily flexible; its varied forms and functions mirror the resourcefulness of its writers and enable it to take the shape of divergent textual forms and to articulate a diverse array of liberatory platforms. Caren Kaplan has aptly identified testimonio as an "out-law genre," one that "enables a deconstruction of the 'master' genres, revealing the power dynamics embedded in literary production, distribution, and reception" (208). As such, it resonates with sustained efforts by marginalized social groups to hybridize modes of autobiographical telling to decolonize these writing forms from the inside out. And yet, in its enactment of a hybrid textual politics, it distinguishes itself from other writing initiatives; it is "a project of social justice in which text is an instrument" (Nance 19).

The current proliferation and diversification of testimonio exemplifies one manifestation of what Chela Sandoval terms "the methodology of the oppressed," defined as a "process of taking and using whatever is necessary and available in order to negotiate, confront, or speak to power—and then moving on to new forms, expression, and ethos when necessary" (*Methodology* 28). Rooted in the "technologies of semiotic reading, deconstruction of signs, meta-ideologizing, differential movement, and moral commitment to equality" (180), the methodology of the oppressed resists rigid ideological identification and fosters revolutionary potential. Testimonio's insistence on navigating treacherous North/South divides and trafficking in dominant paradigms attests not only to a fierce insistence on a bidirectionality of power espoused by differential consciousness, but also to an unflinching resolve to utilize dominant circuits to "speak to power."

How Has Testimonio Been Defined?

Testimonio "proper" has been deemed the quintessential example of resistance literature.[1] Any account of this writing form must simultaneously address its formal structural qualities and its unflinching political vision. Recognized as a distinct literary genre in Latin America since the 1970s, testimonio is a hybrid form of writing that blurs the boundaries of politics/narrative, fact/fiction, and individual/collective; as such, it defies normative literary classification.[2] As an alternative to autobiography, testimonio offers a way of seeing the communal in the private and allows its authors to assert knowledge claims and articulate political visions on behalf of their social groups without sacrificing the specificities of individually lived experiences. With a definitive pedagogical impetus, the writing of testimonios provides a historical archive as seen "from below" and depends upon a witness/listener in its purpose and form. By holding the reader accountable, testimonio makes a cross-border readership a vital part of the process in gaining recognition for the lives of marginalized people and their stories—often by prompting the reader to take direct political action in solidarity with their cause, or applying the book's lessons to their own political struggle—while simultaneously refusing full access to the lives it narrates.

One of the most important political and stylistic aspects of testimonio is its hybrid positioning, which allows it to effectively confound several western binaries. Marianne Hirsch and Valerie Smith assert that the counternarratives that unfold within the framework of testimonio "emerge out of a complex dynamic between past and present, individual and collective, public and private, recall and forgetting, power and powerlessness, history and myth, trauma and nostalgia, conscious and unconscious fear or desires" (5). Testimonio's paradoxical qualities force it to maintain a between-worlds space: it confronts macrosocial flows of power through the telling of intimate, microsocial details of people's

daily lives; it disrupts sequential temporality by insisting on the coexis-
tence of the past and present; it utilizes personal experience to sharpen
an understanding of collective histories. This push-pull between the
individual and the collective, fact and fiction, the microcosm and the
macrocosm, has also led testimonio to occupy the periphery of normative literary classification, having been referred to as "socioliterary"
(Nance 18), "extraliterary" (Beverley, "Margin" 42), "antiliterary" (Beverley,
"Margin" 42), and as an "out-law genre" (Kaplan 208).

While definitions of testimonio abound, one now-classic description
is articulated in Latin American literary critic John Beverley's landmark
"The Margin at the Center: On *Testimonio*," which defines it as "a novel or
novella-length narrative in book or pamphlet . . . form, told in the first
person by a narrator who is also the real protagonist or witness of the
events he or she recounts, and whose unit of narration is usually a 'life'
or a significant life experience" (30–31). Many scholars identify testimonio as a genre that "gives voice" to the (presumed illiterate) subaltern
through the mediation of an editor, anthropologist, or other intermediary. Linda Maier's extended definition highlights how "mediated" testimonio is only one possible form. Maier includes works narrated by a
person who belongs to an "oppressed, excluded, and/or marginal group
and who speaks/writes as a member of that group," through which the
individual "I" becomes responsible for representing the experience(s) of
the "we" (5). Although Maier defines this variation as "direct" or "eyewitness" testimony (6), in several instances testimonios are written by
"eyewitness" authors who also partake in "mediated" forms of testimony
by placing their own experiences in dialogue with experiences of those
who share their social positionality or set of experiences.

Regardless of whether the narrator is the direct or indirect author of
a given testimonio, its political intentionality is definitive and "has to
involve an urgency to communicate a problem of repression, poverty, sub-
alternity, imprisonment, struggle for survival" (Beverley, "Margin" 32).
Broadly speaking, testimonio is concerned "with a problematic collective
social situation in which the narrator lives" (Beverley, "Margin" 33). It is
this focus on the collective that separates testimonio from other forms
of life writing; the collective ethos of testimonio decenters western epistemologies that privilege the rigid individualism of the Enlightenment
"I."[3] Similarly, Hirsch and Smith assert that while such narratives

"represent individual identity as shaped by membership in one or several groups," they nevertheless focus on a "singular story [so that] they can better highlight difference and particularity of context, eschewing generalizing and homogenizing tendencies of identity politics" (7). The individual "I" within the narrative frame is thus a rhetorical device to organize the composite experiences of members of a social group into an integrated narrative account.

The use of first-person plural, or an "I" that is "we," evokes "an absent polyphony of other voices" (Beverley, "Margin" 34), leading this formulation to heavily rely on metonymy.[4] Because the "I" is held in close tension with the "we," it is used to relay the typicality, rather than uniqueness, of a situation. In this configuration, the narrative-I occupies a paradoxical position in which it simultaneously does and does not position itself as a paradigmatic life (Spivak, "Three Women's Texts" 9).[5] While use of the first-person plural disrupts individualist logic, it also does not completely abandon the notion of the individual. Rather, the use of first-person plural as the narrative referent "constitutes an affirmation of the individual self in collective mode" (Beverley, "Margin" 35). Because testimonio grounds itself in the particularities of an individual's life experiences, it simultaneously recognizes the power of aggregate accounts to broaden its extent of social significance.

For instance, in the Argentine testimonio *A Single, Numberless Death* (*Una sola muerte numerosa*), author Nora Strejilevich attests to the disappearance of a particular political prisoner: "There seemed to be no one around when they plucked her from the bus and shoved her into the car. Same old story. In broad daylight, in the middle of downtown, in the bloom of her youth. Only in Olga's case, the one they wanted to pluck from the bus was me" (93). The narrator's account, conveyed in an offhand, matter-of-fact tone, calls attention to the pervasiveness of military disappearances during the Dirty War, showing how an individual account is meaningless without understanding it in relation to the "we." While the narrator is careful to name Olga and to testify to her individual story, the simultaneous tactical narrative normalization of the atrocity reminds the reader that there were many Olgas. Each had her own individual account yet the accounts eerily mirror each other.

In contrast to these traditional forms, there are also some traditional testimonios that reject the use of metonymy, and replace the first-person plural with a polyphonic splicing and interweaving of different narrative accounts. This "intercutting" of voices allows speakers to remain individuals while also being a part of a collective chorus (Schaffer and Smith 177). Within this multivocal structure, several narrators occupy the text, sometimes named and sometimes anonymous, often conveying contradictory social information and rendering the "absent polyphony" present. The effect is a collective resonance in which such testimonios position culture as a contested terrain. The similarities and divergences between individual accounts enables a three-dimensional understanding of sociohistorical conditions in a situated context. Polyphonic testimonio therefore offers itself as a "contradictory assemblage" (Schaffer and Smith 80) that allows for an overarching common story to emerge through accumulation; truth through repetition. It is this focused use of polyphonic resonance that becomes an intentional epistemic strategy in feminist polyvocal testimonio.

In her discussion of Bakhtin's notion of discursive heteroglossia, Irene Matthews suggests that the polyphonic resonance of all forms of testimonio can be understood as initiating a "heterobiographical pact" that allows for the "exist[ence] of multiple personas as well as multiple narrative-points-of-view in the final product" (92). As an act of cultural resistance, testimonio has proven itself a useful tool in disrupting simplistic representations of the Global South in which cultures are all too often positioned as static, unchanging, and monolithic.

Finally, testimonio is a fundamentally pedagogical writing project. Traditionally, it has been thought to confront and motivate action in a socially privileged, northern audience through a situated analysis of oppression in the Global South, serving as a textual component of a larger social justice project. Its "success" has been measured through actualized social change (Nance 13). While my own work complicates this picture, arguing that its pedagogical intervention is meant to also connect activists located in other geopolitical spaces and struggles, the paradigm of witnessing remains useful for highlighting how testimonio evokes a sense of social responsibility in its readership, and for transforming what could be a mindless consumption of testimonio into a relationship in which the reader feels an obligation to form a reciprocal social pact.

These are the standard qualities of testimonio that have been typically addressed by Latin American literary critics. But critics within autobiography studies also have an investment in understanding its structural components. As my discussion of Menchú suggests, the lines between "autobiography" and "testimonio" are fluid yet fraught, causing academics great discomfort when charting the literary and political terrain that (dis)joins them.

"Contiguous Categories": Testimonio as a Mode of Life Writing

While critics such as Beverley have asserted that autobiography and testimonio are not the same, others, such as Doris Sommer, have argued that they should be understood as "contiguous categories" (110). Such ambivalence articulates how autobiography and testimonio are "sister" forms of life narrative but also overtly antagonistic to each other's core representational principles. They must be considered relationally—not only in aesthetic but also in political terms—but despite their dialectical relationship, they do not have equal recognition or ideological value.[6]

As coexistent forms of life writing, autobiography and testimonio both call upon personal memory as their "primary archival source" (Smith and Watson 7). However, "There are crucial distinctions in *how* these forms narrate a life" (5). As the recent turn in autobiography studies shows, all autobiographical telling involves varying degrees of narrative performativity, as authors create a narrative self through an intentional shaping of congregate life experiences, regardless of a text's attempts at concealing its own artifice. Through their conveyance of "real" life events, all forms of life writing are also permeated with "oral residue," through the translation of verbal happenings into a written mode (Smith and Watson 76). What differs is how they construct their relationship with the reader: "Life narrators address readers whom they want to persuade of their version of experience" (Smith and Watson 7). It is therefore *how* and *what* they tell and *for what purpose* that differentiates one form of life writing from the next.

One common way of imagining the relationship between these two forms of life writing has been to categorize testimonio as a marginal variant, or subset, of "true" autobiography. However, as the Menchú controversy indicates, this formulation privileges a particular way of conveying a life story—namely western bourgeois tales of individualism and upward mobility. One of the most readily available and recognizable forms of autobiography is the bildungsroman, or novel of development, in which a protagonist undergoes a professional or personal journey that often equates to social and economic upward mobility (epitomized by *The Autobiography of Ben Franklin*).[7]

This easily recognizable format is rooted in Enlightenment values in its privileging of an individualistic rags-to-riches ethos that attributes the protagonist's success to his reliance on rationality and individual ingenuity. My masculine encoding of the protagonist is not incidental. The very social assumptions and progressions that underpin what was long thought to be a "universal" plot structure have until recently excluded female protagonists, since upwardly mobile women were long confined to the domestic, and the limited social mobility among poor women disqualified their life stories. Diverse racial and geopolitical positionalities among women further explain why the bildungsroman historically has not been hospitable to translating the trajectory of women's lives into textual form. While the twentieth century has indeed given rise to a number of women's bildungsromans (Nawal el Saadawi's *Woman at Point Zero*, Maxine Hong Kingston's *Woman Warrior*, Edwidge Danticat's *Breath, Eyes, Memory*), these adaptations have often inverted the canonical trajectory of the genre by highlighting women's limited opportunities for social mobility, while taking liberties to fictionalize biographically true events.[8] While Enlightenment thought has undoubtedly shaped certain strands of life writing, such critical interventions by women writers signal that autobiography neither began nor need end with this sociohistorical phenomenon. As Smith and Watson assert, "If we recall the diverse modes of life narrating by marginalized, minoritized, diasporic, nomadic, and postcolonial subjects through the history of life writing, the focus on liberal individuality as both the motive and achievement of autobiographical writing is insufficient" (203).

Smith and Watson suggest instead reframing "autobiography" from a single genre to a more pluralized understanding of a range of autobiographical *acts*.[9] In their formulation, autobiography becomes not so much a monolithic literary genre as "a set of shifting self-referential practices that, in engaging the past, reflect on identity in the present" (1). In paying homage to the numerous feminist and postcolonial critics who have in recent years sought to destabilize the understanding of autobiography as a singular and geopolitically specific phenomenon—one that has enabled all autobiographical acts lying outside of the culturally imagined "west" to be read as mere copies of a "civilized" original—Smith and Watson destabilize the hegemony of the term "autobiography" by replacing it with "life narrative," understood as "an umbrella term that encompasses the extensive array and diverse modes of personal storytelling that takes experiential history as its starting point" (7). Within their paradigm life narrative is further broken down into "life writing" and other artistic mediums that engage with autobiographic acts in an effort to highlight the range of forms and functions involved in self-referential cultural productions. Such discursive refinement clarifies the relationship between autobiography and testimonio. Reconfiguring "autobiography" into the less overdetermined "life writing" positions us to see how it has never been as stable a category as it would seem. This destabilization brings into view a web of interconnecting modes of self-referential speech acts that are not ranked on a hierarchical scale of ideological value.

Understanding life writing as a set of diverse self-representational practices not only gives due credit to the plurality of life-writing forms in existence, but also positions critics to better see where and how various strands of self-writing *overlap*. While we might characterize a particular piece of life writing as autobiographical bildungsroman, it might simultaneously exhibit qualities of testimonio and ethnography. In other words, all autobiographical acts engage with hybrid strategies and rhetorics, so while different modes of address are understood to be dominant in specific strands of life writing, they are often employed *in combination* with defining characteristics of another.

This "polyglot" effect (Behar 17) is of critical importance to my own work since only one of my primary texts self-consciously refers to itself as "feminist testimonio."[10] The feminist life-writing projects with which I engage are rather alternately referred to as (traditional) testimonio, postcolonial bildungsroman, historical novel, (auto)ethnography, or life history. While these descriptors are no doubt useful for literary critics' categorization purposes, an unfortunate common effect is to cultivate a "one or the other" mentality that downplays the interconnections between different modes of life writing, thus stifling productive conversations across textual forms. The call for a both/and approach that acknowledges how forms of life writing span several subcategories is especially apt for utilizing the discursive category of "feminist testimo-nio" as an enjoining descriptor to yoke together texts that seem formally distinct. It provides a means of bringing them into co-conversation in order to identify emerging patterns that remain sublimated when read through the lens of normatively assigned genre categories.

To return to a consideration of testimonio and liberal autobiography as two interrelated modes of life writing that at once parallel and prob-lematize each other, one of the defining characteristics is *how they imag-ine subjectivity*. Testimonio is centrally preoccupied with relationships (Sommer 120). These relationships vary in scale and scope and include exposing interlocking social systems of power by conceptually linking public and private, self and collective, past and future. While traditional liberal autobiographical accounts frame their protagonist as a unique, exemplary, and atypical figure, in testimonio the overwhelming *typicality* of the speaker is definitive (107). Testimonio's depiction of an unexcep-tional (which is not to say noncomplex) character is of crucial importance to reminding its readership that the speaker is addressing a collective social problem in which the individual's experiences are not unique. In this sense, testimonio is profoundly democratic in a way that liberal autobiography can never be. By embodying the radical notion that any "I" is worthy of playing a central role in the portrayal of a complex, problematic self, thus strongly resonating with Avery Gordon's notion of "complex personhood" (4), testimonio actively writes against the roman-ticized and oversimplified representations of marginalized people's lives.

Liberal autobiography and testimonios also *use* experience differently. While experience within liberal autobiography is utilized to achieve per-sonal resonance, to define the personality traits of the narrator in order to sharpen a depiction of his or her character strengths and weaknesses, the use of experience in testimonio achieves an impersonal effect (Som-mer 109). Whereas the "self" is the defining subject matter in liberal autobiography, in testimonio, the self is called upon to bring attention to the collective social situation in which the speaker is located. In testi-monio, the use of personal experience becomes a *vehicle*, rather than the point of focus.

This impersonal bent is derived from the fact that "we," as readers, are not encouraged to self-identify with the speaker. Rather, as a writing form that anticipates substantial power differentials between the speaker and reader of the text, identification is discouraged, and possibly dangerous. Testimonio "always signifies the need for a general social change in which the stability of the reader's world must be brought into question" (Beverley, "Margin" 41). The active positioning of readers as interpretive outsiders problematizes the reader's usual authority to judge the text.

The gaze of the narrated-I also differs between these writing forms. If what defines one form of life writing from another is *whom* life narrators wish to address and *why*, then the ways in which they direct their readership's gaze cannot be overlooked. It is through the central narrator's eyes that we enter a text's imaginary world, so where the narrator is looking determines what we are able to see. Whereas memoir directs attention to the people and events surrounding the narrator (Smith and Watson 274), liberal autobiography attempts to depict a rich inner life of its main character by including internal ruminations about life events. Though memoir and liberal autobiography use different methods, the ultimate effect of both is to keep attention focused on the autonomous individual at the center of the narrative. The "I" is the centerpiece of the text; the "I" provides the narrative with internal coherence. In contrast, even as testimonio uses the life trajectory of its narrator(s) to affectively appeal to its readership, it always encourages its readers to look outward and around—beyond, behind, below, and above the speaker—to understand how their lives fit into the larger social landscape. In this formulation, the narrator is positioned as the *relayer* of the textual message, rather than its embodiment.

Finally, the *intentionality* driving each form of life writing most clearly distinguishes between liberal autobiography and testimonio. While all narratives are necessarily pedagogical, of the two only testimonio is deliberately so. In its appeal to pathos it invites the reader to become affectively cognizant of a specific instance of social injustice, doing its best to awaken the reader. Testimonio is therefore better understood as a "project of social justice in which text is an instrument" rather than as a self-contained work (Nance 19). While liberal autobiography ultimately serves as a form of entertainment in which the reader is openly invited to consume and absorb the narrator's story for his or her own purposes, the rhetorical framing of testimonio refuses to allow the reader to forget the social urgency propelling the penning of the text. True to its namesake, testimonio addresses witnesses, not just a readership. The very nature of the testifier-witness dialectic suggests a reciprocal social pact, an ethical engagement of two consensual parties, to "bear witness" to a social truth. While the testifier might gain closure through the telling of the narrative, responsibility is in turn shifted onto the witness to form a just response to this social information.

"Truth" Versus "Truth-Value": Beyond Objectivity

A predominant concern has been the political efficacy of testimonio, specifically, whether its radical ethics are compromised by engaging northern readerships. It is true that the ways in which testimonios navigate a conservative/radical tightrope entail difficulties. It is inevitable that testimonios will at times steer off course; that the balance of power sometimes tips the wrong way, and that some works are more effective than others. I doubt that any practitioners would suggest otherwise. It is important to recognize, however, that testimonios' use of dominant narrative paradigms is often intentional, serving to decolonize them from the inside out. Testimonios might appeal to what they know a first-world publisher and audience might want, but rather than "selling out," they are often working strategically within recognizable liberal paradigms to articulate a more radical social agenda.

This trafficking in co-optable language and narrative tropes can be understood along the lines of Chela Sandoval's claim that decoding is a necessary skill for decolonized consciousness, since this method positions one to both participate within and to "break" with the dominant ideological logic, ultimately allowing the subject to "identify, develop, and control the meaning of ideology" (43). In the context of testimonio, the employment of dominant tropes and story lines testifies to the ability of its authors not only to decode dominant scripts for their own purposes, but also to *reencode* them through hybridized writing strategies that allow their radical political platforms to "pass" as liberal paradigm, and to in turn gain access to northern publishers and readerships. Rather than consolidating and reinforcing dominant power structures, such efforts confound and rework them.

If testimonio is a genre "at work" that makes use of the realm of representation to call attention to epistemic injustice by taking aim at the cultural imaginary, what is it that makes these microsocial critiques of macrosocial power structures "work" at all? What is the epistemological relevance of storytelling? And what is the relationship between experience, storytelling, and social knowledge? How do even the most fictionalized stories create meaning out of the seemingly mundane details and "raw" material of our daily lives? Finally, how specifically does testimonio, as an experiential-based socioliterary genre, engage the "problem" of experience?

Strejilevich compellingly takes up such questions in the sphere of witness testimony in her article "Testimony: Beyond the Language of Truth," where she articulates an important differentiation between legal depositions that privilege unmediated fact and objectivity and witness testimony, which is subjective and intimate, complete with ambiguities and disruptions: a "witness account that is not allowed to voice the intimate, subjective . . . should not be called testimony, but rather, a deposition" (703). Strejilevich's differentiation between "testimony" and "deposition" takes issue with the narrow ways in which the justice system uses witness testimony as evidence, despite its inescapable narrative component. Her critique echoes Joan Scott's warnings against "the evidence of experience," and argues that what society stands to learn from witness testimony is firmly rooted in its intimate, subjective mode of address.

Far from tolerating the disruptions and digressions of subjective testimony in order to glean from it concrete names, dates, and locations—the heralded facts upon which a legal conviction is predicated—her insights demand a rethinking of the type of knowledge witness testimony enables. She argues that the substance of testimony—the understanding, perspective, and analysis it provides—can be true even if and when it gets the concrete details wrong, and therefore that its unique contribution to truth resides *precisely within* its subjective framework. Strejilevich's insight is relevant to critiques of Menchú's account because of its deviation from "official," fact-based accounts. Strejilevich further interrupts the assumed equivalence of "truth" with "objectivity" through her suggestion that "by falling into the snare of objectivity testimony betrays itself . . . testimony should stress just truthfulness, not objectivity" (709).

Strejilevich is not alone in pointing toward a more expansive understanding of "truthfulness" that falls outside the paradigmatic confines of unmediated objectivity, and that therefore might aid in more productive frameworks for understanding the epistemological relevance of experience. Her assertion that testimony can convey truth even when it gets the facts wrong is reinforced by Alicia Kozameh in the preface to her own Argentine literary testimonio, *Steps under Water*: "The substance of the story, of every episode, is real; it happened. Either I myself or other *compañeras* lived it. I have, however, replaced names or possibly details that in no way affect the essence of what occurred" (xvi). Kozameh's careful word choice, of asserting how the "substance of the story" is "real" and that her alteration of names and details "in no way affect[s] the essence of what occurred" mirrors the subtle, but key, differentiation between "truth" and "truth-value" that I am concerned with. Whereas juridical models of truth argue that "the devil is in the details," within Kozameh's logic, the details are secondary to the "substance" of what the narrative conveys. While the objective facts (read: evidence) provide *knowledge* of a given account, it is only through a subjective account (read: experience) that we begin to *understand* what it means.

Smith and Watson likewise argue that life narrative, as a self-referential practice, "redefines the terms of what we call 'truth' . . . [since] it resides outside a logical or juridical model of truth and falsehood" (17). Life narrative utilizes subjective memory as an archival resource to convey the author's perceived truth, and the author's truth is itself responsive to contextual social locations, experiences, and worldview. Insofar as memory is a shifty and shifting resource, and life-writing practices are always performative, testimonio is utilized to effectively convey to its readers the authors' situated interpretation of events, and thus offers truth in a subjective register—truth that is rooted in cognitive understanding and epistemic knowledge rather than fact-based objectivity.

Considering the recognized "truth-value" of life stories for generating social knowledge *generally*, I propose, might also aid us in *specifically* considering how testimonio as methodology carefully constructs experiential-based narratives to convey more accurate analyses of power from the perspective of those most marginalized. In Medina's language, testimonios articulate epistemologies that nudge both practitioners and readers toward a "kaleidoscopic consciousness" in which people are able to shift between epistemic perspectives and registers, not dissimilar to Sandoval's notion of the clutch.[11]

Given testimonio's commitment to serve as a counternarrative that contests dominant renditions of history from the standpoint of the oppressed, I propose that it be viewed as a writing praxis that serves as an applied example of postpositivist realist theory, a body of thought that understands experiences, like identities, to be simultaneously real and constructed, contextual, and relational, for the purpose of epistemic wholeness, therefore offering social "truth-value," even as testimonios are always socially situated, theoretical mediations of objective "truth."[12]

CHAPTER 2

Feminism, Epistemology, and Experience

But how does one know truth when one finds it? Truth isn't a property of an event itself; truth is a property of an account of the event. As such, it has to be perceived and processed by someone, or else it couldn't be framed in language to count as an account at all.

—KAY LANE SCHEPPELE, "TELLING STORIES"

Our experiences do not have self-evident meanings, for they are in part theoretical affairs; our access to our remotest personal feelings is dependent on social narratives, paradigms, and even ideologies.

—SATYA MOHANTY, "THE EPISTEMIC STATUS
OF CULTURAL IDENTITY"

QUESTIONS ABOUT HOW TO FRAME, UNDERSTAND, AND DRAW UPON experience and identity have long plagued postcolonial and feminist scholars.[1] Conceptual and definitional imprecision about what, precisely, "experience" *is* has no doubt fueled these debates. My own working definition of "experience" argues that our experiences are always both "real" and "constructed," at once referring to actual, outward, objective events, but always necessarily filtered through our subjective lens as embodied subjects, and further shaped by language and available social narratives as we attempt to convey our experience to others. While experiences refer outwardly to actual events in the world, experience itself is always a narratively crafted account of the event—interpreted within, processed within, and therefore affected by our locations within our worldscape.

If experience at one time constituted the mainframe of activist feminist consciousness-raising efforts through the assertion that the "personal is political," it is now often considered suspect at best, irrelevant at worst. Shifting theoretical trends and the increasing professionalization of gender and women's studies have no doubt contributed to its bad reputation. Further, the binary between essentialist and postmodernist perspectives on experience has been perpetuated by overly simplistic, careless interpretations of the nuanced arguments made by feminist standpoint theorists and postmodernists who have dared to stake claims on the uses of experience.[2] These oft-caricatured renditions of qualified, careful arguments have led to a gradual retreat from the subject of experience, leaving the dominant currents of feminist theory with the unsophisticated conclusions that essentialism is "bad" and postmodernism is "good," with, of course, a caveat reserved for the necessary evil of "strategic essentialism." However, even in the canonical postmodernist feminist texts that are called upon to discredit experiential knowledge claims, the arguments do not so much dismiss experience as qualify how it must be worked with to yield reliable social knowledge.

Responding to trends in social history projects that strive to offset received historical narratives through the countertestimony of marginalized social actors, Joan Scott warns against historians interpreting testimony and archival accounts as representative of an unmediated "real" (776). Scott's reservation is less with the evocation of experience in scholarship and more with the terms through which it is engaged. Social historians' refusal to critically engage with experiential narrative accounts—to let them "speak for themselves"—Scott argues, leads to the configuration of "experience" as "evidence for the fact of difference, rather than a way of exploring how difference is established" (777).

Scott contends that social historians have tended to call upon experiential accounts as positivist counterevidence—as accumulated social facts strewn together in narrative form—without considering the interpretive practices involved in the telling and crafting of the account, rather than recognizing experience as an account of an event filtered through an interpretive lens that people utilize to make sense of the material and causal conditions of their daily lives, and how these conditions correlate with social institutions and relations of power. Likewise, Nance suggests that critics of testimonio "have agreed more or less politely not to criticize *testimonio* seriously as text, and/or to substitute either admiration for its producers or suspicion of their motives for any politically engaged textual analysis of the product" (12). Both Scott and Nance argue that the epistemological value of experience is lost without a serious, focused attempt to understand how power structures actively inform the ways that socially located speakers understand, feel, and narrate their life experiences. It is how we *read* and *interpret* testimonio as a self-consciously crafted form of experiential-based social knowledge that holds the most epistemological potential.

Similarly, in "Can the Subaltern Speak?" Spivak warns against taking testimony as signaling a "pure" form of consciousness, understood as an essentializing and patronizing form of engagement, suggesting that the silences—what the narration does *not* narrate—are vital components (81). Spivak also emphasizes how any attempt to engage with the "subaltern other" on behalf of "benevolent" academics perpetuates a degree of epistemic violence; there are no uncompromised spaces from which to assert knowledge claims. "Being heard" is fraught with contradictions.

Scott, Nance, and Spivak remind those working with experiential knowledge claims to hold narrated individual experiences in close tension with the larger structural forces that produce and enable those experiences. As Scott suggests, it is "not individuals who have experience, but subjects who are constituted through experience" (779). This idea is not incompatible with Wendy Brown's point that politicized identities are both "product of and 'reaction' to" existing forms of power and domination, and are artificial social groupings that congeal in relation to socially imposed (outside) conditions (402). Without further interrogating what experiential accounts mean—and why they have been told in a particular way to achieve their desired effects—scholars miss an opportunity to decode these narratively encoded events, an interpretive process that yields a much richer analysis than when they are taken at face value. Such decoding more broadly affords a critical opportunity to understand the complex contestations of knowledge and power that are enabled through the narration of experience.

Although their points of intervention differ, none of these scholars contest the idea that claims of experience must be interpreted, worked through, and placed in dialogue with other voices and social forces in order to foster understanding of them in relation to the whole. Scholars attempting to purge experiential knowledge claims from the feminist project miss this more nuanced reading. As Scott herself states,

"*Experience* is not a term we can do without . . . It is so much a part of everyday language, so imbricated in our narratives that it seems futile to argue for its expulsion" (797). These thinkers do not fully discount experience; rather, they differ in regard to what precisely the epistemic value of experience is and how to engage in the delicate balance of critically engaging with and learning from, without wholly discounting, experience-based accounts. In this sense, the immediate theoretical/institutional contexts that these scholars are writing from/to/within largely determine their line of argument.

While these cautionary tales provide a much-needed warning on how less careful processing of experience can lead to the production of faulty knowledge claims, the real problem is that none go on to articulate a theoretically cautious yet pragmatic vision of *how* to derive epistemic value from experiential claims. As an interdisciplinary feminist literary critic who reads stories as narratively coded forms of social knowledge, and who recognizes experience as an essential tool that offers inspiration and insight for these accounts, I find the current terrain of the feminist experience debates to be, quite simply, unsatisfying. I suggest we take a closer look at what experience *can* contribute to more accurate social knowledge and how it must be *processed* to reach its potential contribution. This undertaking is motivated by a desire to work against the field's academic/activist divide and to renew feminist theory's relevance to social justice struggles. As Stone-Mediatore argues, "Our new distrust of experience-oriented narratives risks a dismissal of such texts that is just as epistemologically and politically dangerous as the earlier positivism. In fact, despite academic critiques of experience, many social struggles . . . continue to rely on stories of experience to bring public attention to their concerns" (1). The proliferation of polyvocal feminist testimonios is a powerful case in point.

In my journey to arrive at a more complex understanding of the epistemological relevance of experience I have found the emerging body of postpositivist realist theory to be a theoretically nuanced yet pragmatic body of thought that draws upon productive pieces of feminist standpoint theory and postmodernist critiques to articulate its own negotiated position on the question of experience. This negotiated standpoint allows postpositivist realist theory to recognize experience as simultaneously real and constructed: it is real insofar as it refers outwardly to actual events and conditions in the material world; it is constructed in that the telling of an experiential event must be communicated within a narrative form, which can only ever serve as a socially situated interpretation of an objective event.

Satya P. Mohanty's "The Epistemic Status of Cultural Identity" is most often credited with laying the foundation of this body of work. Explicit in his goal to interrupt the essentialist/postmodernist debate on experience, Mohanty makes the following bold proposition: "What if we gave up both radical perspectivism and the dream of a 'view from nowhere,' in order to grant that all the knowledge we can ever have is necessarily dependent on theories and perspectives? We might then be able to . . . understand how theory-laden and socially constructed experiences can lead to a knowledge that is accurate and reliable" (48). Mohanty frames knowledge as a human enterprise, and as such always socially entrenched, confined to existing ideas on how to create knowledge and inherited interpretive paradigms for understanding our world. For him, this realization does not void the search for more accurate depictions of social relations. Rather, it is a necessary step in order to shift social relations of dominance to mutually beneficial relations between people from different social locations: "It does not urge us to give up the job of interpreting the world (in the interest of changing it) but instead points out how the possibility of interpreting our world accurately depends fundamentally on our coming to know what it would take to change it, on our identifying the central relations of power and privilege that sustain it and make the world what it is" (53). Insofar as dominant social scripts mystify the relations of power that perpetuate systemic inequalities, Mohanty argues that oppositional social movements and knowledge production such as testimonio—or what Medina terms "epistemologies of resistance"—are necessary to produce more accurate sociohistorical understanding.

If we are ever to use our experiential knowledge for such ends, we must first understand what, precisely, "experience" is. As Paula Moya articulates, experience is "the fact of personally observing, encountering, or undergoing a particular event or situation . . . Experiences are not wholly external events; they do not just happen. Experiences happen to us, and it is our theoretically mediated interpretation of an event that makes it an 'experience'" ("Realism" 81). Since we ourselves are socially situated beings, inevitably bound to our partial perspectives, any account we provide of an experiential event will necessarily be affected by our social location and can only be conveyed through available narrative structures. Hence experiences, like identities, are both "real" and "constructed"; while they refer to objective events, they can only be articulated through subjective modes of communication. Even when we try to solely give the "facts" of a situation, what we choose to include or exclude as factually relevant will be subjectively decided upon depending on our social location.[3]

Moya's perspective has much to do with where postpositivist notions of identity and experience are coming from: scholars whose geopolitical, ethnic, gendered, and sexual locations place them on the social margins, and who because of this, experience identity as something *very real* in how it influences their ability to conduct their daily lives. While this realness is not in relation to a biologic determinism, it is real in the sense of causal relations. Though identity may in fact be socially constructed and policed, indexical and relational, it nevertheless gives way to "real"—as in felt, experienced, and actualized—*effects*. Insofar as racialized class systems, heternormative matrices, first world assumptions, and gendered divisions of labor acutely inform the lives of social actors who fall outside the provisions of these arbitrary but powerful and consequential rules, experience, as causally related to identity formation, will continue to matter to those who are ostracized because of their social location.

Within the framework of postpositivist realist theory, social "identity" is understood as necessarily *constitutive* of our life experiences; it does not predate them. One of the theory's core principles is that humans do not have stagnant and innate characteristics based on social group. Rather, social groups are understood as developing in response to imposed social conditions. Identity is not something we "are," but is a causal relationship between people and things: "What we 'know' is intimately tied up with how we conceptualize the world and who we understand ourselves to be in it. Our conceptual frameworks are thus inseparable from how we comprehend ourselves in terms of our gender, culture, race, sexuality, ability, religion, age, and profession—even when we are not consciously aware of how these aspects of ourselves affect our points of view. Our identities thus shape our interpretive perspectives and bear on how we understand . . . our everyday experiences" (Moya, "Mobilizing" 102).

Moya, like Strejilevich, suggests that because our social locatedness affects what and how we see, and what and how we see is causally linked to the life experiences we have from our social locations, we should treat our experiences as "epistemic resources" rather than trying to overcome our subjective stance ("Mobilizing" 96). Understanding how social location affects our worldview enables us to reframe experiential accounts as events that shed light on our relationship to power.

Cloaked in the language of "identity," these principles work toward a more nuanced understanding of what aspects of experience are useful, including a reconsideration of what constitutes "standpoint" in standpoint theory.[4] In *Whose Science?* (1991), Sandra Harding argues that for a "position to count as a standpoint, rather than as a claim—equally valuable but for different reasons—for the importance of listening to women tell us about their lives and experiences, we must insist on an objective location—women's lives—as the place from which feminist research should begin" (123). It is not necessarily "women's experience" that leads to social knowledge, or what she terms "strong objectivity," but rather the self-consciously assumed *standpoint* achieved through an analytic processing of the experiential "raw material" derived from the perspective of women as subjects.

A critical standpoint, then, is a *learned* perspective; it is not something we innately possess, no matter what our subject position. Whereas individual women's opinions and experiences would constitute a *claim*—valuable as an initial interpretation of an event in their lives—it is through a collection of several women's truth claims and systemic analytical processing of them in relation to their varied contexts and social locations that a *standpoint* begins to materialize. In Mohanty's words, "Since 'experience' is only the raw material for the kind of political and social knowledge that constitutes a feminist standpoint, it cannot guarantee or ground it" (53). However, without it we would be unable to articulate a feminist standpoint at all.

Postpositivist realist theory asserts that one's social location does not determine the experiences one will have, thus reinforcing how social identities are *multiply informed*—an important corrective to earlier models of standpoint theory that lacked an intersectional approach—and how the development of a critical posture is a fought-for perspective. While it may be true that marginalized subjects are less resistant to coming to critical consciousness because they have more to gain and less to lose than dominantly situated subjects, who structurally benefit from others' exploitation, critical consciousness is necessarily a learned, epistemic posture. The more we understand the systemic workings of power, the more able we are to understand how the realities of our daily lives correspond to our entangled location(s) within these relational webs. As Medina argues, while there is no ontological guarantee, socially disadvantaged subjects are in the ironic position of being epistemically privileged—the seeds of consciousness are planted in their need to understand the power relations that ensure their survival (73). Such critical experiential accounts by marginalized subjects are potentially more epistemically valuable due to what their relationship to power enables them to see and know, and how they can use this knowledge to contest oppressive dominant cultural scripts. As Freire asks, who is "better prepared than the oppressed to understand the terrible significance of an oppressive society?" (45). Experience's epistemic use-value is therefore largely dependent on our ability to recognize how larger structures of power inform our daily realities and our proximity to or distance from dominant social structures.

Postpositivist realist theory sees experience as a *potential* resource, which recognizes that our personal interpretations of experiential events may be flawed due to insufficient information or lack an understanding of structural relations of power. As socially situated beings it is probable that our understanding of certain life events changes based on our development of critical consciousness or upon receiving previously unknown information that propels us to rethink our interpretation of an event. As Carolyn Steedman argues, our interpretation of life events might also be altered precisely through the very act of telling: "Visions change, once any story is told; ways of seeing are altered" (22). This is why Satya Mohanty argues that experience can "lie" to us just as it can reveal; it is not innately good or bad. The shifty and shifting nature of experiential knowledge claims might make some scholars skeptical of experience as a valid epistemological resource, but experiences usefully reflect the dynamic nature of power; power structures themselves are not static, but always in a relational state of flux. Since the development of critical consciousness is a continual process, alterations in our ways of seeing should be both expected and welcomed.

Experience-based narratives therefore remain a vital resource in articulating knowledge claims about one's world and in taking a self-conscious stance against social processes beyond one's control. While not the sole meaningful source of epistemic knowledge, experience remains a significant one, especially for social subjects who do not have access to formal education and who have been relegated to the status of being objects of study by academic "experts." "When we treat experience-based narratives as mere ideological artifacts," writes Stone-Mediatore, "we reinforce the disempowerment of people who have been excluded from official knowledge production, for we deny epistemic value from a central means by which such people can take control over their own representations" (2). This is what we lose sight of when scholars assign themselves as sole interpreters of others' experiences and assume that the research and archival subjects with whom we engage lack the tools to provide critical interpretations of their own experiences: "When scholars focus on criticizing 'experience,' we alienate our work from these practical struggles," Stone-Mediatore continues. "We may address others' stories as sites for our deconstructive analysis, but we forfeit learning from them and building theories responsive to them" (1).

Such arrogant postures reinforce the notion that the academy is the sole site of knowledge production, perpetuating distrust for the knowledges produced within its faction by those locked without. To avoid furthering the fissure between the academy and activism, we need to carefully consider the interpretive processes necessary for processing the sociopolitical truth-value of experience. When we as scholars consider how people make use of experiential narratives to assert knowledge claims in their daily lives, we begin to realize how they themselves *already* understand experience as a theoretically mediated event and epistemic resource that can be used to call attention to an unjust social order so that they can negotiate, analyze, and reinterpret power relations in their daily lives. Indeed, we might find that theoretical debates on the uses of experience are far less sophisticated than the ways in which people utilize experience in daily practice and in the creation of social knowledge outside the academy.

If the truth-value of experience lies in its interpretation and not in the specific event it narrates, we must be vigilant in conceiving interpretive processes that can aid in the extraction of truth-value from a given experiential narrative. In other words, if positivist frameworks overestimate and postmodernist frameworks underestimate the ability of an individual to communicate a reliable interpretation of experience, post-positivist theory argues that we must rethink experience as at the crossroads of the microcosm and macrocosm; we must consider how it is possible to self-consciously process, analyze, and interpret our memory-based experiences even as we recognize how we are constituted by them. In our recognition of experience as both "real" and "theoretically mediated," we must consider *what types of interpretive practices are most likely to contribute to more accurate social knowledge that highlights how dominant power structures are maintained.*

Testimonio, in which marginal experience narratives serve as a form of storytelling capable of conveying objective social truths in subjective registers, capitalizes on the ability of stories to relay qualitative and relational perspectives on the world; they provide an in-depth, situated analysis about how it might be to live in the world within a specific social location. Just as one person's interpretation of a life event might drastically differ from another's, so the narrative viewpoint espouses a particular worldview at the expense of others, and as such provides us with a three-dimensional understanding of how the world looks from that chosen perspective. If the narration of an experience comprises a translation of a life event, then testimonio recognizes how creative *retranslations* can open up new social possibilities and bring the promise of more just futures sharply into view.

Telling Stories: Translating Experience into Social Knowledge

How is it possible for marginal experience narratives, as subjective interpretations of events, to produce accurate social knowledge of how power operates? From my perspective as a literary scholar, it seems self-evident that experience can only be conveyed through available narrative conventions, and as such, can only ever be communicated *as* story. And yet, while we know that storytelling—in the forms of parable, folklore, myth, history, and fiction, to name a few—has always been and continues to be utilized as a way of communicating and passing down social truths, a common association with the term "story" is "lie." Whether scolding a child for "telling stories" or attending a storytelling session where one expects to hear larger-than-life, fabricated tales, there is a societal perception that "story" equates to "untruth."

Stone-Mediatore argues that there is a "long-standing opposition between story and truth. This opposition is presupposed by both empiricists who seek to eradicate narrative from knowledge proper and by poststructuralists who deny the possibility of knowledge on the grounds of its ineluctably narrative character" (5). In short, it seems that "storytelling," like "experience," has earned a bad reputation. The question is, if stories—like experiences—are one of the main ways we make sense of the world, how does it follow that these seeming "untruths" can prove themselves a reliable source for generating social truth-value?

In an academic atmosphere that privileges unmediated objectivity and rational thought, the subjective and interpretive registers involved in storytelling continue to marginalize narrative truth telling from knowledge "proper." While the academic dismissal of stories does not prevent us from telling them or understanding them for the social truths they put forth—we have always told, and will continue to tell stories in our daily lives—it *does* limit the amount of care and attention we give to how we read and interpret stories and for what purpose. In other words, while stories remain a core interpretive device for the human experience, they are not adequately theorized in their epistemic contributions to social thought.

Stone-Mediatore is right to call attention to the widespread suspicion over the ability of subjective, narratively coded discourses to produce reliable social knowledge in academic realms; yet we cannot ignore the diverse platforms and contexts outside of the academy that increasingly recognize and depend upon marginal experience narratives to arrive at historical and social truths. As Smith and Watson make clear, we are in the midst of a life-writing boom; as Schaffer and Smith's *Human Rights and Narrated Lives* makes more clear still, many of these life-writing projects are directly taken up in the realm of social justice platforms by utilizing marginal life narratives to catalyze social change. Contemporary uses of life narrative range from the legal arenas of truth commissions, courtrooms, and human rights investigations, to multimedia campaigns such as Black Lives Matter, It Gets Better, and We Are the 99%, to fictionalized autobiography and graphic memoir, such as Marjane Satrapi's *Persepolis*.

In the legal realm especially, there has been a marked, if gradual, shift toward recognizing the integral relationship between social stories and truth. Attorney Kay Lane Scheppele asks, "How are people to think about the law when their stories, the ones they have lived and believed, are rejected by courts, only to be replaced by other versions with different legal results?" (2080). As she argues, this shift toward making visible the narrative frameworks involved in legal depositions is causally related to the opening up of law schools to increasingly diverse peoples, necessarily expanding the social experiences of the "we," many of whom come from social locations that have been systematically marginalized through legal rulings, and many of whom have been consequently told that their experiences are "untrue" because of their deviation from dominant legal paradigms. Scheppele calls attention to the negative effects of a narrowly juridical notion of truth espoused by the courts, especially in pluralistic societies: "In rethinking legal narratives, the first step is to realize that the presence of different versions of a story does not automatically mean that someone is lying and that a deviant version needs to be discredited. Stories can be told many ways, and even stories that lead to very different legal conclusions can be different plausible and accurate versions of the same event" (2097). Scheppele's statement is also useful for reflecting on why and how the "true/false" binary at work in the Menchú controversy is ultimately inadequate for understanding the truth-value of her intentionally constructed narrative account.

And yet, despite these incremental shifts toward recognizing the central role of narrative in progressive sectors of rights-based activism and political and historical thought, a general distrust of storytelling and subjective knowledge prevails. Even in the realm of life writing, where memories are explicitly worked with to fit into a narrative framework, there remains a profound misconception that truth can only be located in the factual event and not in one's interpretation of it.

Postpositivist realist theory's claim that one's experience of an objective life event can only ever be expressed and understood as a theoretically mediated interpretation, or as a subjectively situated narration of said event, provides a productive bridge for considering how storytelling contributes to social knowledge. If we can only ever arrive at objective social truths through subjective means (since knowledge seekers are necessarily socially situated beings), it follows that stories can help us realize more accurate social knowledge precisely through their self-consciously subjective perspectives and narrative organization. We then need to consider how the story-based narrative structure conveys social truths that other written forms do not.

This is what Stone-Mediatore means when she argues there has been inadequate attention to the contribution of narrative to political thought: "Marginal experience narratives contribute to political thinking and political life precisely in their function as 'stories,' that is, as experience-rooted but creatively reproduced narrative texts" (6). To contribute to a more democratic mode of social knowledge production we need to take a deeper look at why and how people employ such stories to interpret social truths based on their experiential knowledge. In other words, we need to take the storyteller seriously: "When the storyteller tells the event as a story, *she draws our attention to certain relationships and qualities that are not given in the facts* but that we might find to be relevant to the phenomenon of our world. The story is an invitation . . . to 'look at it this way.'" (37, my emphasis). The intentionality of a story determines its potential contribution to political thought, and the way it conceives of the relationship between subjectivity and objectivity, truth and truth-value. Even responsive academic theories such as postpositivist realism cannot simply "create" an interpretive rubric for translating experiential-based narratives into reliable social knowledge, but need to listen carefully to how people are *already* employing such practices through their life-writing efforts.

In "Methods of Oral Testimony," Moema Viezzar argues that "ideology has 'flesh and bone': it materialises in the work and living conditions" (73). In other words, the objective reality of power relations manifests itself in the subjective, situated contexts of people's daily lives. If this is true, it seems we also need a "flesh and bone" form of theorizing capable of documenting and resisting its material and contradictory effects. Experiential-based storytelling provides one such method for delivering social critique. More specifically, the storytelling methods utilized by testimonio draw upon marginalized experience narratives to provide a situated "theoretical account of our current social and political arrangements" by providing perspective from the bottom of the social order looking up (Mohanty 54).

Indeed, even within the academy, marginal experience narrative has been reclaimed as a central tool of consciousness raising and ideology formation. Women-of-color feminists have increasingly turned toward creative theorizing and hybrid writing forms that cut across disciplines, knowledge registers, and fiction/nonfiction divides. Feminist writers such as Gloria Anzaldúa and Cherríe Moraga have been particularly lauded for their efforts to claim hybrid forms of life writing as self-consciously resistant modes of knowledge production that can contribute to less biased social knowledge.[5] Moraga and Anzaldúa's coedited collection, *This Bridge Called My Back: Writings by Radical Women of Color*, utilizes "chronicles" of daily life events in order to "present a political analysis in everyday terms" (xxiv). As Brent R. Henze argues, this self-conscious interpretation of life events enables narratively crafted experiences to serve as "'political analyses,' presented in the 'everyday terms' of regular experience" (240). Life-writing practices that utilize testimonial accounts to comment upon and intervene in objective social relations move beyond evaluating experiences as "bits of social and political theory" in order to utilize them to actively stage sociopolitical interventions.

For instance, in *Borderlands/La Frontera: The New Mestiza*, Anzaldúa's utilization of marginal experience narrative as a form of political analysis becomes increasingly experimental in structural form. As Inderpal Grewal asserts, "Anzaldúa sees the structure of her book as a metaphor for the new consciousness she represents. The duality of form and content becomes as inseparable as bone and flesh, with the boundaries of chapters spilling into one another. The languages, voices (her mother's, her aunt's, her grandmother's), genres, and disciplines (autobiography, anthropology, history) all merge" (248). These fragmented and experimental story-based framings of marginal experience narratives are not incidental; they are critical for interrupting received knowledges, reworking representational paradigms, and rethinking the world from the perspectives of those most exploited: "When writers . . . use their writing to explore unregistered or systematically obscured experiences of resistance to social norms, they do not just destabilize received representations of the world" (Stone-Mediatore 9). They instead pen resistant imaginations and futures.

Within this logic, the narrative form becomes a crucial factor for how the social information housed within the narrative will be received. Our experiences may only be available to us through well-worn narrative tropes and plot structures, but marginal experience narratives that play with received forms consciously mix and match styles and genres to reorder and rethink what is possible. Thus, the metaphoric structure of *Borderlands* is representative of the new consciousness Anzaldúa hopes to bring forth through her work. It not only reinforces the extent to which we can "rework" existing social paradigms by self-consciously breaking the rules, but also highlights how textual practices can provide one powerful way of arriving at reconceptualized understandings of social relations.

The life-writing project of testimonio puts this theory into action through its story-based, theoretical mapping of the meanings of people's daily lives within a varied sociopolitical landscape, and thus highlights how narrative can contribute to political thought. As a memory-rooted, creative life-writing form, testimonio resides at the intersection of experiential-based narrative and storytelling practice, and hence at the intersection of discourses concerned with the truth-value of experience and stories. The storytelling methodologies espoused by testimonio are utilized for more than story's sake; they are constitutive of a form of grounded theorizing that allows its practitioners to articulate macrosocial political analyses and critiques in microsocial registers. These meaning-making practices, while rooted in the subjective elements of daily life, are utilized in order to reflect on objective social relations, and thus to resonate beyond their immediate narrated circumstances. While the story-based approach is the *method*, testimonio is never "just" a story. Its experiential-based, concrete drama adds an affective dimension to social knowledge that insists upon an embodied, situational reckoning with the information it houses. By working against abstraction such narratives reinforce how these social problems are not just to be pontificated upon, but rather, how they affect real people, in real time, and thus require real solutions. Testimonio offers a powerful textual example of how people largely locked out of structures of power are ahead of the game in recognizing the importance of narrative to the production of more accurate historical knowledge. The oppositional consciousness of testimonio attests to the power of storytelling by refusing to limit the account to the facts, and to focus instead on the sublimated or unexplored effects of a social experience.

In "My Experience in the Theatre Collective Sistren," Jamaican theater director Honor Ford-Smith describes the collective's experiential-based storytelling methodology as staking a claim in "what it means to deal with the world as creative individuals, rather than as victims or objects" (49). Further: "Our business is story telling. We tell stories over and over again about our grievances in order to expose abuses and to challenge the existing situation" (25). As such, storytelling is Sistren's preferred mode of delivery for voicing social critique and imagining more just, alternative paradigms. The collective's stories provide the group with a useful framework within which to situate and articulate social critique and political analyses. There is cultural and historical precedent for this as well, as the Sistren Theatre Collective notes: "*Lionheart Gal* draws on a legacy of tale-telling which has always preserved the history of Caribbean women . . . These tales encode what is overtly threatening to the powerful into covert images of resistance so that they can live on in times when overt struggles are impossible or build courage in moments when it is" (Sistren xv). As defined by Sistren, to "storytell" is to recognize storytelling as a resistant mode of praxis capable of communicating social truths that other writing forms are either incapable of conveying at all, or capable of conveying only in registers that are not safe. It is thus the inherent *creativity* of testimonio's storytelling methodologies that lends itself to representing nuanced depictions of marginalized experiences and realities, and for articulating social knowledge that is useful for rethinking power dynamics in everyday life. Testimonio is unrestricted by rigid journalistic expectations, which allows for the imaginative element that provides the power to think beyond, to see differently.

The ideological power of resistant life storytelling is exemplified in Carolyn Kay Steedman's *Landscape for a Good Woman: A Story of Two Lives*, where she interweaves autobiographical elements of her own life and those of her mother in order to shed light on working-class lives in South London in the 1950s. Steedman's text explicitly identifies the types of interpretive processes that are necessary to use experiences to counter dominant accounts of history. Steedman's text is therefore self-consciously about interpretations. As she suggests, the life stories her mother told her constituted "a form of political analysis . . . that allows a political interpretation to be made of her life" (6). She reinforces the potential of drawing upon one's own memory archive in order to encode a form of social analysis out of one's particular social situation. As she suggests, her book is particularly "about lives lived out on the borderlands, lives for which the central interpretive devices of a culture don't quite work" (5). Recounting the disillusionment she personally experienced when reading accounts of working-class lives that did not reflect her own reality, she recalls coming to a point where she decided to create her own. Steedman provides a relational interpretation, since the meaning of her childhood cannot be separated from its intimate, if vexed, relationship with her mother. As the title suggests, she is most interested in understanding her position within her existing social landscape, and more generally how our social landscape affects what stories we tell.

Steedman's central preoccupation with interpretation further develops the idea of story-based narration as a critical tool for working with personal memory to comment on objective social conditions. Echoing Strejilevich and postpostivist realist theory, she argues that a life event is not significant in itself; rather, the way we remember and make use of the event provides its potential contribution to social knowledge: "The point doesn't lie there, back in the past, back in the lost time at which they happened; the only point lies in interpretation. The past is re-used through the agency of social information, and that interpretation of it can only be made with what people know of a social world and their place within it" (5). Steedman insists that the truth-value of experience lies in what we do with it: how we use it to create meaning, and what type of meaning we seek to create.

And yet she goes further than the work of postpositivist realist theory and Strejilevich in her detailed claim to memory work as an important tool for counteracting the limiting social narratives imposed on those living on the margins of society. Her central interest is in exploring the pragmatic and tactical side of memory work, in which she suggests we "comb through" our memories, forward and backward, thus illuminating the causal relations between them (21). This combing through time is a way of creating emotional distance from the original memory, broadening our scope to explore the social landscape that informed a particular event, and to realize how more recent contexts and experiences continue to inform our current understanding of the event. In testimonio, the narrator "attempts to create bridges between 'here' and 'there' through the narration of *what might not be told as a theory but as an insight*. It is for this reason that a poetic voice might be needed to tell the story" (Strejilevich 704, my emphasis).[6] The stories conveyed in testimonio might not connect all of the dots, but the dots they do connect are meaningful and purposeful, more deserving of being understood as a fragmented yet grounded form of theory. As Latina feminist Aurora Levins Morales powerfully articulates in *Telling to Live*, testimonio is the process of "making theory out of the stuff in our pockets, out of the stories, incidents, dreams, frustrations that were never acceptable anywhere else" (32).

It is the situated, embodied form of social knowledge that provides testimonio's force, closely resounding with Sandra Harding's notion of "strong objectivity" growing out of collective marginalized knowledge claims. True understanding cannot be derived through mere cerebral exercise, but rather through a reckoning with the messy details of daily life and the conflicts that emerge between heart and head. The experiential quality of testimony makes its contextual, situated, "concrete" drama an exceptional contribution to social knowledge, one that prides itself on a felt, cognitive understanding of an event rather than mere reduction of its meaning to facts and figures. Through its intimate mode of address, by taking observations down to the concrete, contradictory, and complex level of lived experience, testimonios encourage readers to reason with more than their intellect; testimonio allows a means of affective connection through an ability to position readers to see through the eyes of others who reside in different cultural and material worlds.

Travels and Feminist Translations: Reconsidering the Theoretical Terrain of "The Real Thing"

As Linda S. Maier and Isabel Dulfano note in *Woman as Witness: Essays on Testimonial Literature by Latin American Women*, testimonio has been saturated with women's voices since its inception as a contemporary genre (2). Two paradigmatic testimonios—*I, Rigoberta Menchú* and *Let Me Speak! Testimony of Domitila, a Woman of the Bolivian Mines*—feature women's testimonies and were edited and translated by women, not to disregard the innovative contribution of feminist oral historian Margaret Randall.

It is ironic, then, that as more women literary writers and activist women's groups have come to utilize the genre for their explicitly feminist creative and political work outside of an immediate Latin American context, testimonio has been declared to have run its course. Georg M. Gugelberger's anthology *The Real Thing: Testimonial Discourse and Latin America* provides a retrospective on the "rise and fall" of testimonio within the northern academy, juxtaposing Beverley's optimistic and much-cited opening essay "The Margin at the Center: On *Testimonio*" (1989) with his more somber "The Real Thing" (1995). In an authoritative voice offering the final words of the collection, Beverley states, "The moment of testimonio is over" ("Real Thing" 280–81).

But if the testimonial moment is "over," why would US-based Latina feminist scholars employ testimonio as a methodological framework for grappling with the sociohistorical and material differences that are often swept under the rug in an effort to cultivate camaraderie between Latina feminist academics? Why would impoverished Haitian women actively seek out a US-based oral historian to recite stories and poems of their particular struggles and modes of resistance?[7] Why would a group of working-class Jamaican women use testimony and people's theater to address poor women's issues thirty-five years after the original group was formed and twenty-five years after constructing a written account of its founding members' stories?[8] And why would a group of village-level Indian NGO activists encourage their fellow *sangtin* positioned within the North American academy to undergo a (linguistic, conceptual) translation of their collective writings and reflections in book form?[9]

The point for Beverley, as an academic, is that "new forms of political imagination and organization are needed; that, as in everything else in life, we have to move on" (282). This claim is not entirely different from Chela Sandoval's insistence that the "methodology of the oppressed" need rely on tactical, flexible maneuvers as a way of resisting political stasis and stagnation. But if the testimonial moment is "over," how does Beverley account for the ways in which testimonios continue to emerge in new geopolitical sites and in increasingly diverse structural forms? And why must these "new forms" necessarily be categorized outside of the category of testimonio? Indeed, Beverley remains conspicuously silent regarding how his scholarship came to cement the paradigmatic "rules" of the genre. Beverley's identification of testimonio as a distinctive genre worthy of literary attention (for a mostly northern academic elite) was a valuable contribution, but his (now) canonical categorization serves a much less radical function in our current social landscape and is unable to account for the ways in which the genre has transformed itself—or rather—has been transformed by those who seek to use its pedagogical force for their own political and creative needs.

Edward Said's explication of the theoretical tensions between "original" and "copy" are relevant:

> In an essay ("Traveling Theory") written several years ago, I discussed the ways in which theories sometimes "travel" to other times and situations, in the process of which they lose some of their original power and rebelliousness . . . the first time a human experience is recorded and then given a theoretical formulation, its force comes from being directly connected to and organically provoked by real historical circumstances. Later versions of this theory cannot replicate its original power; because the situation has quieted down and changed, the theory is degraded and subdued, *made into a relatively tame academic substitute for the real thing*, whose purpose in the work I analyzed was political change. ("Reconsidered" 436, my emphasis)

Said's gloss on his original line of argument strongly resonates with Beverley's insistence that it is time to "move on." Indeed, in "The Real Thing" we hear an almost identical sentiment when Beverley states that while testimonio was at one time "intimately linked to international solidarity networks in support of revolutionary movements or struggles around human rights, apartheid, democratization . . . detached from these contexts, it loses its special aesthetic and ideological power" (281). In both Said's and Beverley's musings, there is legitimate concern over how far radical ideas can "stretch" before losing their integrity and oppositional consciousness. Clearly, attentiveness to the social situatedness of a text is of central importance. But as Said concedes in a radical reenvisioning of his original essay, this perspective also forecloses the possibilities of theories "sparking" and igniting passion in readers removed from the immediate context of conception, but who perhaps reside in situations with parallel sociopolitical circumstances, thereby allowing the theory to grow fertile roots on seemingly foreign soil. Might it, for instance, be possible that testimonios reach other activist audiences, thus sparking a "chained action" (Medina 313) effect in concert with other social movements?

In revisiting his argument, Said fathoms the possibility of "an alternative mode of traveling theory, one that actually develop[s] away from its original formulation . . . [and] flames out, so to speak, restates and reaffirms its own inherent tensions by moving to another site" (438). By the end, Said completely retracts his earlier argument, telling his readers instead that the "point of theory . . . is to travel, always to move beyond its confinements, to emigrate, to remain in a sense in exile. . . . This movement suggests the possibility of actively different locales, sites, situations for theory" (451–52).

Said's revised understanding of traveling theory is useful for contesting Beverley's argument that "the moment of testimonio is over" on several levels. In a literal sense, testimonio continues to take root in new geopolitical spaces. These migrations are engendering new possibilities for the formulaic construction of this mode of life writing as it becomes utilized by differently located groups and applied to their social issues. Academic analytical frameworks and tools for understanding testimonio must also "travel" in order to do justice to this developing body of work.

To return to Said's articulated tension between "original" and "copy," I propose that we need to question the productivity of a teleological, lineage model of origins in the first place if, in fact, the point of theory *is* to travel, and theory is *always already* traveling. It is not insignificant that the contemporary genre of testimonio, as we currently understand it, emerged in a dynamic Latin American social landscape marked by cultural revolutions, dictatorships and *los desaparecidos*, and struggles for land rights and legal recognition. Yet, it need not be *contained* by this context; to do so would be to ignore the broader political possibilities it engenders. Indeed, testimonio is often understood as "belonging" to Latin America because the Casa de las Americas created a prize category for it in 1970 (Nance 2).

By limiting our understanding of testimonio to a specific geopolitical site, or to a list of imposed genre conventions, we risk ignoring the underlying *ethos* and political and cultural realities that define this flexible, grounded writing form. Rather than marking Latin America as the rightful "owner" of this form of life writing, the creation of the Casa de las Americas prize category and the subsequent development of Latin American testimonio criticism speaks to the hybrid writing projects' sustained success, proliferation, and timeliness within the varied Latin American climate in which a particular strand of this larger first-person plural life writing project emerged. While it may serve as a paradigmatic example, we need not consider it the only geopolitical site to utilize a first-person plural life-writing project, filtered through the life lens of a marginalized subject to deliver grounded social critique.

In truth, various forms of testimonial literature have remained on the margins of life writing in English since the sixteenth century (Beverley 280), serving both conservative agendas in the forms of travel writing and nation-building texts, and progressive abolitionist platforms.[10] Recent books such as Sharmila Rege's *Writing Caste/Writing Gender: Narrating Dalit Women's Testimonios* further complicate understandings of testimonio as mere cultural imports—troubling any easy understanding of "original" and "copy"—by illustrating how *dalit* (lower caste affiliated) Indian women have been "doing" testimonio without calling it as such, or in fact ever hearing the term. With narrative accounts ranging from 1981 to 2003, these texts mark a simultaneous congruence with contemporary Latin American testimonios, rather than an "application" of Latin American testimonio to the postcolonial Indian context.

While Rege's book attaches the Spanish signifier "testimonio" to the selected *dalit* narratives with no formal qualification, Kavita Panjabi's "Probing 'Morality' and State Violence: Feminist Values and Communicative Interaction in Prison *Testimonios* in India and Argentina" explicitly addresses why testimonio should be understood as a writing methodology by-for the oppressed that extends beyond Latin American national and ideological borders: "Focusing on the 'microsocial' worlds of women's . . . experiences, they enact critiques of the 'macrosocial' patriarchal oppressive states, elaborating upon the ways in which women's bodies become one of many sites of state control" (155). Panjabi's formulation of a comparativist reading between Indian and Argentine texts specifically locates feminist testimonio as a form of textual praxis capable of illuminating transnational flows of power and its gendered effects in women's daily lives.

Rege and Panjabi call for a broader conceptual understanding of testimonio as a textual practice emanating from a range of geopolitical sites that self-consciously employ the Spanish signifier to discursively, politically, and conceptually align their elsewhere-located-projects with the liberatory Latin American social movements that have employed testimonio as part of social justice platforms, a maneuver that taps into the already established cultural currency the Spanish term yields. Utilizing this signifier to refer to geopolitically and structurally diverse first-person, social justice–focused literature builds upon a well-established, widely recognized, and respected socioliterary platform while simultaneously performing a powerful symbolic gesture of countertopographic (Katz) postcolonial solidarity that works to trace a South/South political trajectory. Such discursive alignment attests to a hybrid textual politics that works from within to reenergize already established writing forms rather than directing efforts to uncover nonexistent "pure" alternatives.[11]

In this way, I utilize the term "testimonio" as a fabricated lens to yoke together differently manifested first-person plural narratives with a social justice impetus to make visible what cannot be seen when these narratives are kept in isolation on the basis of genre and country of origin.[12] Utilizing the term "testimonio" to signal a "glocalized" (Vigil 5), or "translocal" ethos (Alvarez 1) moves us to a "point of origin" model that draws upon Chandra Mohanty's comparativist framework to highlight epistemological interconnections between sites with overlapping histories, even as these histories have different manifestations in contemporary social landscapes. It serves as a discursive gesture that destabilizes a dependence on physical and national borders by placing emphasis on epistemological and historical *interconnections* and enacts a necessary risk by charting alternative cartographies and communities of co-travelers that rely upon epistemological and political points of overlap. By creating a textual bridge to link together readers with social actors from different geopolitical sites, epistemologies, situations, and perspectives, testimonio brings disparate worlds into critical proximity, a proximity that privileges intimacy even while distance is maintained. It is a practice in *epistemic translation*, a translation of the speaker's world to an audience who occupies quite another.[13]

This glocal, or translocal, ethos is particularly well illustrated by activist feminist testimonios that emanate from outside Latin America and employ culturally specific language, metaphors, and folklore to firmly anchor themselves to the cultural spaces from which the narratives emerge. For instance, linguistically, *Telling to Live* straddles English and Spanish. *Lionheart Gal* translates Jamaican Creole into a written mode. *Playing with Fire* and *Walking on Fire* serve as translations from Hindi and Haitian Creole, with key phrases expressed in the original languages. Metaphorically, *Playing with Fire* uses the metaphor of "monsoon clouds" to address the weight of the tears the women experienced when sharing their stories (9). In *Walking on Fire*, Bell utilizes a locally resonant simile to describe the conditions of poor Haitian women: "Popular snacks in Haiti are *peze souse*, squeeze and suck, frozen pops . . . The *istwas* (storytellers) in this chapter are told by women being consumed like a *peze souse*" (24). In addition, *Lionheart Gal* and *Walking on Fire* heavily rely on Jamaican and Haitain folkloric traditions to illustrate their points. As such, geopolitically diverse practitioners of testimonio do not merely "apply" a uniform notion of testimonio. They alter and translate the form to resonate with their immediate situations and needs.

These varied translocalized utilizations of this resistant writing form speak to the renewed and innovative ways it is "sparking" with geopolitically diverse activists and authors who see its promise and epistemic value. In the following chapter I turn to address an emerging strain of this writing project: feminist polyvocal testimonios.

CHAPTER 3

Constructing Feminist Transnational Bridges through Polyvocal Praxis

> Bombarded by another's language and culture, we play out our resistance to the siege, fighting in vain against the artillery of reality with phrases as our only weapons.
>
> —NORA STREJILEVICH, *A SINGLE, NUMBERLESS DEATH*

> Feminist criticism, we should remember, is a mode of *praxis*. The point is not merely to interpret literature in various ways; the point is to *change the world*. We cannot afford to ignore the activity of reading, for it is here that literature is realized as *praxis*. Literature acts on the world by acting on its readers.
>
> —PATROCINIO P. SCHWEICKWART, "READING OURSELVES"

AS A BRIDGE CONCEPT, FEMINIST TESTIMONIO EXPANDS UPON THE work of foundational testimonio while refusing the mass erasure of women's subjective experiences across disparate geopolitical sites, cultural contexts, and material conditions. If testimonio has been mainly concerned with questions of political economy and the lived effects of globalization in the daily existence of marginalized social actors generally, the feminist lens brings into focus multiple simultaneous dimensions of embodied subjectivity in an effort to further contextualize how effects of globalization are differently experienced by distinctly gendered bodies even within comparable class and regional locations. My concept of feminist testimonio is deeply steeped in an intersectional politics and US women-of-color feminisms. However, within each feminist testimonio the meanings of women's political awakenings are always context specific and intimately connected to a politics of location, causing texts to differently inhabit the label "feminist."

As Olga Benoit argues in Beverly Bell's *Walking on Fire*, "Feminist means becoming a woman politically" (186). In this sense, the descriptor "feminist" denotes a text's self-conscious awareness of the interconnectedness of social inequalities and grants particular attention to the specific ways that gendered cultural oppressions and material poverty attach themselves to women's bodies in different geopolitical locales. While "women" remain a constant subject of focus in these various texts, none consider this gendered positioning in isolation from national, ethnic, racial, class, religious, and sexual affiliations, among others. As such, feminist testimonios espouse a deeply intersectional methodological approach through their understanding of how intersecting axes of social power inform people's lived realities and through their documenting the effects of individual strands of institutional power structures as these materialize in the threaded complexities of women's daily lives.

There are two major strands of feminist testimonio: literary and activist. Although some feminist testimonios span both categories, I contend that this basic demarcation speaks to larger trends in the format, function, and goals of feminist testimonio. Many literary writers now employ a testimonial framework in their often historically grounded "fictions" (Edwidge Danticat, Nawal el Saadawi, Shani Mootoo), but so too do activists and political women's groups outside of the literary sphere (Rigoberta Menchú, Sistren Theatre Collective, Sangtin Writers) employ testimonial writing to more directly stage political interventions. Indeed, even within these examples the lines between the literary and nonliterary are blurred. As the previous section explores, while all narratives are simultaneously real and imagined to different degrees, both the "literary" and "activist" forms of feminist testimonio remain committed to the creative *and* political. This blurring of the (non)-imagined, as illustrated through testimonio writings at large, is essential for disrupting elitist western notions of "art for art's sake" and in explicitly linking the imagined to the political. Feminist testimonios rewrite and redirect basic tenets of testimonio even as they build upon them, importantly reenvisioning and reenergizing the testimonial genre by utilizing it as a methodological tool to realize the creative and political visions of women writers and activist women's groups in their socially situated contexts.

Feminist testimonios are thus best understood as political weapons that take aim at the cultural imaginary to challenge the center-periphery worldview of dominantly positioned social actors. They formulate epistemic bridges that invite readers to work through "epistemic friction" (Medina) so that differently racialized and geopolitically located readers alternately are asked to find overlaps between the social struggles of the authors and their own, or to become defamiliarized with their own internalized worldviews and open themselves to other ways of being. Practitioners of feminist testimonio are more than writers; they are word warriors who employ the written to enact a tactical-textual recruiting method that draws upon a focused rhetorical deployment of pathos to affectively connect with readers who occupy different cultural and material worlds in order to bring these worlds into critical proximity. As such, the descriptor "feminist" more broadly signals an egalitarian and politically motivated mode of inquiry, attuned to power differentials in knowledge production and complex politics of difference.

Taking Aim at the Cultural Imaginary: Linking the Discursive to the Material

For scholars to question the literary and political merit of testimonio at a time when it is a vibrant medium for transnational women writers under the reasoning that it no longer "works" participates in the well-worn masculinist argument that women's contributions are not central to literary canons or political revolutions. There is also a more biting, diffuse masculinist undertone at play: the assumption that cultural resistance—such as creative writing and theater—does not serve an important epistemic function in and of itself. Rather, so this thinking goes, cultural resistance is only meaningful if it directly, tangibly translates into resistant political action in the "legitimized" forms of strikes, boycotts, and armed revolutions.

As a culturally resistant writing project, testimonio recognizes creative writing as an integral component of social justice platforms. However, while traditional testimonio has employed writing as a means to a political end, feminist testimonios take specific aim at the cultural imaginary by intervening in dominant modes of representational practices and by engaging with multiple audiences. If foundational testimonios have privileged "action" in physically combative forms of resistance and recruiting readers to join them, feminist testimonios place equal weight on altering a reader's political consciousness and worldview—an "action" defined by an epistemic shift.

Feminist testimonios acknowledge the labors of writing and reading, remembering and dreaming, as political *work*. Of course, women-of-color feminisms have argued this for years. As Trinh T. Minh-ha argues, this focus on the labors of telling and writing is of central importance to challenging dominant definitions of what counts as cultural resistance. Contemporary writers such as Edwidge Danticat have suggested the same.[1] In fact, life writing has long been a central forum for articulating struggles as women writers have employed various autobiographical practices to literally write themselves into cultural being.[2] Feminist uses of testimonio merely extend the ways in which women writers use life writing to "convert their marginality into a creative site of cultural production" (Schlau xix).

The motivation to recognize writing as cultural work solidifies how the discursive and the material are inextricably linked and how flexible, multidimensional modes of resistance must be recognized in the too often masculine realm of "struggle" and "revolution" that continues to privilege the material. Medina not only articulates his own indebtedness to women-of-color thought but also suggests that the social imaginary is largely responsible for the continuity of epistemic injustices and that "imagination is not a luxury or privilege, but a necessity" (268). For Medina, "The imagination is an exercise in perspective-taking, a way of inhabiting spaces and relating to others that connects up with our actual world, establishing a bridge between our world and other possible ones that we may want to build" (255). Unchecked, the cultural imaginary collaborates in reinforcing dominant epistemes and ideologies. Therefore, it is only through the cultivation of "resistant imaginations" that actively contest dominantly received paradigms that more just futures are possible. Medina's philosophical trajectory gives epistemic validity to these smaller interpretive shifts, suggesting that such internal psychic effects often serve as catalysts for self-actualization.

As Sara Ahmed suggests, politics, like fear, is future oriented (65); but testimonios largely depend upon reengaging and working with memory in order to differently frame how cultural events have been dominantly narrated, since contemporary "contact is shaped by past histories of contact" (7). Feminist testimonios view experiential writing as "work" and "labor" through an articulation of processes of "memory work" and "dream work." Jean Franco argues that "memory work" is a "productive activation of memory enabling it as a political weapon" in which it is "not just memory but social and collective memory that is seen as resistant to the dominant narrative" (237). From this perspective, feminist testimonios are sites of "active remembering" that write against the silencing of unofficial, marginalized accounts of history (Hirsch and Smith 13).

But "memory work" is no easy task. As the phrase suggests, it is laborious; it is work that is marked by strong internal and external resistance. In *A Single Numberless Death* Strejilevich documents the very real challenge of memory work as she grapples with complex emotions during her struggle to be officially recognized as a political prisoner by the Argentine government. This struggle—coupled with the severely uneven power relations between herself and government officials—triggers for her the memory of the military breaking into her home: "That must be the reason nothing ever happens to them. The Joint Commander entered our house through the main door, and no one thought anything of it. These men are speaking with the voice of experience. We, however, seem like petty thieves, amateurs unfamiliar with the basic rules of impunity: act in broad daylight, without worrying about covering your tracks" (Strejilevich 37).

The military (public sphere) invades the narrator's home, and the homes of many other political prisoners (private sphere); the Joint Commander has the authority to walk through the "main door" without fearing repercussions. The ability to access and terrorize the private lives of Argentine citizens comes from his unquestioned "experience," experience that places him on the "right" side of hegemonic history, while the victims and the survivors must continue to prove their right to existence in the forms of counternarratives and legal proceedings, all the while being unable to move past trauma-induced physical and psychic disruptions in their personal lives. As Strejilevich's account suggests, memory work is not luxury or choice. It becomes a mode of survival, a way to act in the present moment without being paralyzed by the oppressive structural forces that must be faced.

But if memory work is a tool of survival, the crafting of testimonial narratives becomes a creative, politically engaged act that directly challenges unidirectional life accounts in the realms of history, ethnography, and literature. Memory is not elicited simply for memory's sake. It is utilized to recognize traces of the past in the present; it is called upon to imagine more egalitarian futures. Indeed, the simultaneity of looking back to look forward is present in all of testimonio: "If testimonio is an art of memory, it is an art directed not only toward the memorialization of the past but also to the constitution of more heterogeneous, diverse, egalitarian, and democratic nation-states, as well as forms of community, solidarity, and affinity that extend beyond or between nation-states" (Beverley, "Introduction" 24).

Feminist testimonios simultaneously enact dream work through an articulation of their expressed desires for just futures. Collections such as Beverly Bell's *Walking on Fire* implicitly highlight the social function of hope; the speakers articulate their political motivations through a felt desire to not have their children give up on their dreams as they have been forced to do. Other collections, such as the Sangtin Writers' *Playing with Fire*, self-consciously saturate the text with a palpable tension *between* memory and dream work. As the Sangtin Writers make clear, the labor of memory work allows its participants to dream of an otherwise, in this case a targeted "otherwise" in the form of a people's movement that does not reinstate social hierarchies in its organizational framework.

Likewise, while many literary manifestations of feminist testimonio look toward the future for its protagonists and readers, this opening is always drawn in stark contrast to the life outcomes of other characters or the acute pain of a protagonist's past experiences. In Shani Mootoo's *Cereus Blooms at Night* this presents itself in the delicate, unlikely friendship that develops between an elderly woman patient whose history of sexual violence remains both manifest and absent in her subsequent muteness, and a gender queer nurse who is only truly "seen" by his seemingly broken patient. In the framework of Mootoo's novel, this unique friendship develops outwardly from their felt "shared queerness" (48), suggesting that the relationship these characters develop cannot be separated from the social violence both have experienced.

Thus in *all* manifestations of feminist testimonio, "memory work" cannot be thought of in isolation from "dream work." While activist and literary manifestations might err on one side (documenting existing gendered conditions) more than the other (imagining social alternatives), the functions of memory work and dream work are *complementary*.

Beyond "Recognition": The Forging of a Bidirectional Social Pact

Some have understood the project of traditional testimonio as naïvely placing its transformative potential in the hands of the reader—leading some to call it a "pedagogy of the unoppressed" (Nance 49). Feminist testimonios, however, fiercely insist on a bidirectionality of power that refuses to yield all interpretive power to the reader. Indeed, in feminist testimonio the labors of writing, memory, and dream work are reframed to hold meaning for the participants/writers/tellers themselves long before their words reach a reading audience.

Feminist testimonios' reframing of "work" and "labor" is integral to how they destabilize the widely held unidirectional interpretation of the witness-testifier paradigm. Literary criticism on testimonio has served to overemphasize the power differentials between presumed first world reader and third world text, often foreclosing the possibility of a text's ability to successfully navigate this terrain. Meanwhile, trauma studies have oversimplified the paradigm, placing too much power in the witness's capacity to heal the trauma of the testifier.[3]

While the testifying process can aid in confronting trauma by acting as a catalyst in the healing process (even as it often triggers psychic and somatic stress, as explored by Strejilevich and Kozameh), I am wary of attempts to frame the usefulness of testimonio in terms of its cathartic effects, wherein an outside party "bears witness" to the story and rewards the testifier with "recognition."[4] In the words of Kelly Oliver, "Recognition is the soft currency with which oppressed people are exchanged within the global economy. In this way, recognition, like capital, is essential to the economy of domination" (23). Recognition, seen from this perspective, is the process by which marginalized people garner attention from dominant culture(s) for the sake of inclusion and affirmation of existence.

Within this logic, the "work" of testimonio is equated with having the speakers from the Global South gain "recognition" and visibility from readers in the North. While this paradigm of recognition appeals to, and is often utilized by, the assimilationist model of mainstream multiculturalist efforts, it does not properly represent the goals of the feminist testimonio project, which seeks to build a voluntary, cross-border alliance one reader at a time. Thus, the witness-testifier model is not utilized in feminist testimonio to make the speaker visible for visibility's sake, but to bring the speaker's situation into view so that it can be changed for the better, by asking more racially and geopolitically privileged audiences to connect their authors' struggles to their own, and by destabilizing the accepted worldviews of more racially and geopolitically privileged audiences, thereby generating productive epistemic friction.

Activist testimonios do so by claiming political worth in the labors that collectively comprise a given text, not merely the audience's reading of the project's final published form, as explored further in part 2. In this way, activist feminist testimonios highlight how the "work" begins long before individual testimonios reach a reading audience and will continue after the product has reached its final published form. Because the practice of testifying necessitates that the speaker forge connections between events and understand the interconnections and interdependencies between people and places—propelling them to a broader understanding of their own situation more fully—it not only allows one to testify for the sake of closure, self-understanding for individual fulfillment, or gaining "recognition" from a readership, but also as a means of further *sharpening one's political lens*, of understanding how one's own life fits into various sociopolitical landscapes and global power structures.

Feminist testimonio's modeling of a bidirectional understanding of the witness-testifier paradigm, which gives weight to the mutuality and interchangeability of "witness" and "testifier" in a given exchange, echoes Megan Boler's notion of "collective witnessing" (176), as well as with what Susan Sánchez-Casal and Amie A. Macdonald term "communities of meaning" enabled through "identity contingencies" (113). Such communities of meaning "cultivate a diversity of socially embedded truth claims out of which epistemic wholeness develops" (Sánchez-Casal and Macdonald 3). This dynamic, reworked interpretation of the witness-testifier paradigm illustrates how feminist testimonios utilize the writing project to textually encode their works in ways that encourage a *dynamic dialogic process* between practitioners of a specific testimonio project in order to build horizontal coalitional alliances both between practitioners and with disparate reading audiences. Whether accomplished through the effective use of a testimonial framework in fictional narratives or through detailed descriptions of the methodological processes that underpin activist accounts, a bidirectional, dynamic model of collective witnessing that encourages dialogic processes of exchange raises the stakes for readers and tellers alike, encouraging a blurring of critique and grounded engagement, of reflexivity and alliance work, thereby moving readers from positions of critical reflexivity to postures of political alliance and solidarity.

It is no accident that dialogue remains a staple of consciousness-raising efforts. From Freire, to social organizers, to classroom projects committed to social justice struggles, to Medina's call for a kaleidoscopic consciousness, to the collaborative feminist activist testimonios discussed at length in part 2, the dialogic relationships of listening and telling, asking and answering, remain a significant component of transforming social knowledge claims into more epistemically whole knowledge. By working with people from other social locations, we are prompted to see issues from a multiplicity of perspectives, in turn leading us to better understand the situatedness of our own perspective on an event or social issue, and ideally, to gain a broader understanding of our world and our racial and geopolitical locations within it. Whether realized through members of a collective engaging in situated exchanges, conducting interviews with those of parallel social circumstances, placing different narrative voices alongside each other within the narrative frame, or posing questions to a reading audience, dialogue remains a central way in which these works utilize subjective knowledge claims to comment on objective social situations.

Indeed, if it is true that "dialogic praxis is pushed to the margins" in mainstream academia (Nagar and Swarr 8), then it is also true that feminist testimonios intentionally position the dialogic processes that have enabled them to produce social knowledge front and center within the narrative frame. To reference the influential methodology of Margaret Randall, dialogue is not just about the act of telling; it is just as much about *listening*, and particularly *listening to those who have been historically silenced* (60). Adds *griyo* and former Haitian Minister of the Status and Rights of Women Lise-Marie Dejean, "If you want decentralized power, you must begin by sitting with people and listening to them" (Bell 160).

The epistemic importance of experience is not in its claims to unmediated, or "pure," forms of consciousness, or as "evidence," but rather in its ability to illustrate how structural flows of power play themselves out in the crevices of daily life. With this in mind, I propose that feminist testimonio's ability to bring different, but not quite disparate, voices into conversation offers an important way to think through how narrative form significantly determines how experience matters in knowledge production. One of the central ways feminist testimonio achieves this is through the cultivation of polyvocal narrative frameworks. Such intentional crafting moves beyond the polyphonic quality of traditional testimonio in that it models, through diverse means and methods, an epistemic commitment to attend to multiple social truths through processes of dialogue and epistemic revision, for the purpose of crafting more epistemically whole knowledge.

Polyvocality as an Epistemic Aesthetic of Representational Resistance

While traditional testimonios have employed an "I" that is "we," contemporary feminist testimonios often incorporate many voices and subject positions, creating a polyphonic effect. This polyvocal structure mitigates the genre's reliance on metonymy by allowing speakers to be explicitly named and identified within the body of the text.[5] In such works, individual narratives become meaningless without grappling with the overlaps and departures between them. This is especially true when differently positioned speakers relay conflicting and contradictory accounts of the same events. Through heterogeneity of experience, fragmented truth claims subtly emerge, claims that then need to be pieced together and worked through in order for epistemic wholeness to more thoroughly materialize. This form of testimonio is not interested in providing ready-made solutions or unproblematized truth claims, and most directly correlates with Kimberly Nance's description of "deliberative" testimonio, in which hesitations and contradictions are rhetorically employed to comment on the limits of memory to convey social knowledge (32). Such polyvocal frameworks interrupt narrow reader assumptions of testimonio providing an unadulterated access to "truth" (as evidenced by the Menchú controversy) by highlighting the possibility of coexisting social truths.

To be clear, discussions of polyvocality as a distinctly feminist ethics have existed for decades.[6] Kathleen Martindale, a feminist philosopher and ethicist, described a commitment to polyvocality as "hearing the differences in and among women," conceding that *realizing* this commitment in practice is no easy task (258).[7] Polyvocality in feminist testimonio should be understood as a form of realized praxis, a modeling of the politics of difference it espouses. Indeed, Latina scholar Ariana Vigil proposes that we understand polyvocality as modeling a decolonial affect that writes against received European histories and power structures (77). This intentional strategy can be understood as a resistant aesthetic that serves as an important form of disidentification (Muñoz 4).

Hybrid writing styles such as polyvocal testimonios thus do more than simply "add" perspective. Their collage-like, fragmented narratives allow room for the backward and forward processing of interpersonal memories involved in producing a historical account and model the possibility of a kaleidoscopic consciousness in their very structure. Through this narrative framework multiple truth claims emerge—claims that often contradict each other—and yet it is through this multiplicity that we are able to hear important linkages and continuities between sets of experiences, which collectively realize a cautious standpoint.

But *how* they employ polyvocality and to what *effect* largely depends upon whether a given feminist testimonio is literary or activist in intent. For instance, polyvocality in literary testimonios (which may be referred to as the testimonial novel, historical fiction, or postcolonial bildungs-roman) is often achieved either through the form of a short story cycle or through shifting the narrative perspective of individual chapters by alternating between characters. Activist feminist testimonios—which may be referred to as (auto)ethnography, oral history, or life history—achieve a polyvocal effect by either dedicating an entire chapter to individual speakers' life stories or by braiding together several speakers' stories around individually themed chapters. This collective resonance openly positions culture as a contested terrain while highlighting how the similarities and divergences between individual accounts enable a three-dimensional understanding of sociohistorical conditions in a situated context. Through the heterogeneity of experience and perception, fragmented truth claims subtly emerge, claims that then need to be pieced together and worked through in order for epistemic wholeness to more thoroughly materialize.

The effect of both utilizations of polyvocality is to provide a dynamic, multivoiced framework that necessarily interrupts homogenous, monolithic representational practices and heads off the interpretation of socially marginalized speakers as noncomplex, "authentic" subjects. Still, feminist literary and activist *uses* of polyvocality differ. While literary strands tend to employ polyvocality as a way to raise theoretical and epistemological questions on the subjective nature of memory and historical accounts, it is the contestation and diversification of dominant cultural narratives that by in large remain the focus; the stories themselves enact the meaning. In contrast, while feminist activist testimonios are also in the business of "multiplying the narrative," they take care to articulate the collaborative methodologies that underpin their projects, which are attentive to the possibilities and foreclosures of differently positioned women coming together to work around collectively defined sets of social issues. As such, while both feminist literary and activist testimonios reframe the genre through polyvocal structures, their motivations and methods for doing so differ.

Cultivating Communities of Meaning through Dialogic Exchange

As the Personal Narratives Group argues in *Interpreting Women's Lives*, "In the face of women's life stories, the search for Truth requires truths" (263). By undercutting the notion that any single narrated experience can provide an objective, unmediated, version of "Truth," polyvocal testimonios embody a theory of partial perspective, insisting that while our lived subject position necessarily informs what and how we know, our experiential knowledge must be brought into dialogue with others in order for it to have meaning beyond ourselves. By interlinking individual women's life stories and positioning these truths alongside each other in the narrative frame, polyvocal feminist testimonios structurally allow for a larger, collective "Truth" to cautiously emerge.

Through their innovative, polyvocal, story-based narrative frameworks, testimonios offer new avenues for considering the epistemological relevance of experience. By insisting on the truth-value of experience narratives while also insisting that an individual account's truth-value is not fully realized until it is brought into sustained dialogue with others, polyvocal feminist testimonio insists that social meaning-making is a collective process that benefits from the epistemic diversity of its meaning makers, a distinctly decolonial ethos. In so doing, it embodies an expansive coalitional politics that extends its dialogic methodology to readers who no doubt occupy different social and material worlds. By understanding the theoretical significance of testimonio's story-based methodology to deliver social analysis through marginal experience narrative, we are reminded of the necessity of destabilizing narrative's relegated position as existing outside of knowledge proper.

Furthermore, the "piecing together" of different perspectives and viewpoints through the juxtaposition of experiential stories works to move from the articulation of knowledge "claims" to a more worked-through, fought-for social "standpoint." It is through a collection of several women's claims, and a systemic analytical processing of them in relation to their varied contexts and social locations, that a standpoint begins to materialize. The polyvocal frameworks of feminist testimonio, and the contradictions and complexities that accompany such a representational practice, thus reinforce how a standpoint can only begin to materialize through sustained attempts to work through the contradictions and complexities that arise from the social differences present in interpretive communities.

The polyvocal frameworks of feminist testimonios provide what Moraga calls a "theory in the flesh" account of postpositivist realist theory's assertion of the need to work through social difference for the purpose of better understanding ourselves and each other, and for the purpose of allowing epistemic wholeness to materialize. Such interbraidings of experience encourage practitioners to recognize the partiality of their own knowledge claims. This mode of reflexivity requires that participants take seriously the knowledge claims produced by others, and make room for these "competing" worldviews in their intellectual and emotional processing. As practitioners engage in this process, which necessarily expands their epistemic worlds, the practice extends itself to readers, who are asked to sit with the epistemic friction the testimonios cultivate.

In other words, polyvocal feminist testimonios recognize that in order to transform an experience from an insight into a potential source of social knowledge, they must enter into *sustained dialogue* with those who are poised to listen; readers/listeners, in turn, must question the text's meaning and from their own situated perspective *for the shared commitment of producing more accurate social knowledge.* It is through this process of self-conscious dialogic interaction that a claim is put forth into the world to be worked on and turned into a more objective depiction of itself. This is precisely what motivates Strejilevich to conduct interviews of others' experiences of the Dirty War: "I needed to hear other stories coming from the same place in order to complete my own. . . . All of these unfinished stories became a choir that opened the key to my own despair" (711).

While Strejilevich began her narrative interpretation with her own voice—with what she knew or thought she knew of her experience—she came to realize that her own experience needed to be supplemented by other voices to fill in the gaps in her knowledge and the memories that lay beyond the grasp of her understanding in order to produce a more accurate historical account of her experience. Through this process, she came to realize that her political imprisonment during the Dirty War cannot be fully understood without placing it in dialogue with the accounts of others from the "same place." Although this phrase is initially left unqualified, she later clarifies its meaning: "former prisoners, former disappeared, families of the disappeared, activists, friends of my brother and cousins who are still missing, and people *who just happened to live there at that particular time*" (711, my emphasis). Through this qualification Strejilevich highlights how wide-ranging groups of people can become entangled in webs of meaning-making through historical circumstance; there is nothing assumed or pre-given in this assemblage of interviewees. While there are no doubt vast ideological, social, and material differences between them, within this context, they are each other's "own people."[8]

Hearing accounts of those personally affected by similar events allows her to let her guard down, and she willingly becomes part of a community of knowers. This affective dimension brings her to her next step of comprehension, to access emotions that she previously could not reach—those that did not seem safe to acknowledge—and that give way to painful, yet necessary, release. Yet this dimension also attests to Strejilevich's prioritized shift from subjective toward more objective forms of understanding, reinforcing postpositivist realist theory's assertion that objectivity can be achieved only through a multiplicity of processed subjective experiences. While each individual account is "unfinished" on its own, when placed in resonance with others, a multivoiced "choir" emerges that helps each individual narrative become a more complete story—a kaleidoscopic consciousness. By working with an interpretive community to revisit the past in order to garner more of a historically accurate perspective on it, we gain a fuller perspective.

In other words, Strejilevich was not looking for ready-made, one-dimensional "answers" from those with whom she conducted interviews. Rather, she wanted to engage with others who had parallel experiences in order to come to a sense of resolution that could only occur through an *opening up* of her private interpretations to epistemic friction, to see how they converged and diverged with others. By entering into this interpretive community Strejilevich shapes her "inklings" and "hunches" into knowledge claims, working those vague but gnawing feelings that she "knew" but couldn't quite articulate into sites of knowledge. Integrating her personal memories and interpretations with those of others, she locates stories that reciprocate, validate, and "decipher her own echoes," an act that provides order and materiality to her recollections and that boast a fuller interpretive meaning of her political imprisonment. It is through dialogue that she arrives at a more accurate analysis of how her own personal experience elucidates the Dirty War as historical event.

Strejilevich's discussion thus highlights the epistemic function of polyvocality in feminist testimonio, speaking to why one would seek out others to better tell one's own story, and more theoretically, how entering into dialogue with an interpretive community from similar social locations and positionalities can provide a crucial step for transforming personal experience into relatable and reliable knowledge of social relations.[9] Such interpretive communities are what Sánchez-Casal and Macdonald mean by "communities of meaning," which are forged through the intersection of "social location, cultural identity, epistemic standpoint, and political convictions" (11). As such, communities of meaning are also "communities of knowing," or "places where people discover some commonality of experience through which they struggle for objective knowledge" (11). Such interactions broaden a shared commitment to epistemic responsibility and friction, and pave the way for a kaleidoscopic consciousness.

For instance, Beverly Bell's *Walking on Fire* and Margaret Randall's oral history accounts complicate the dialogic interaction seen in *Lionheart Gal* and *Playing with Fire* by yoking together different perspectives of women who occupy similar social situations within a fragmented narrative frame, thus formulating a "community of meaning" through the juxtaposition of narrative voices. Or, as with the diverse storytelling methods employed by Edwidge Danticat, practitioners also utilize archival accounts, expound upon intergenerational family histories, or seek out collaborators to reflect on a sanctioned social topic, as illustrated by her edited collection of essays, *The Butterfly's Way: Voices from the Haitian Diaspora in the United States*.

While in some polyvocal testimonios this dialogic interaction is "imagined" in the sense that one writer or editor establishes a polyphonic frame out of collected interviews or a world of fictional characters, in activist polyvocal feminist collaborations this dialogic quality reflects the group dynamics that inform the text. In both instances, a diverse range of narrative perspectives is highlighted as a resource that contributes to more epistemic wholeness, especially when engaged in a dialogic fashion. Regardless of how they are configured, all polyvocal feminist testimonios deeply reflect Freire's insistence that dialogue not be understood as mere conversation for conversation's sake (understood as polite, uncritical discourse), but rather as a focused engagement with one another's ideas and truth claims in order to arrive at a more objective and better understanding of the topic at hand[10] By working through and across social differences—and by starting with those differences that have been most materially and ideologically marginalized—these texts show that such exchange can contribute to more accurate social knowledge through situational and relational interplay.

As Ford-Smith recounts in an afterword to *Lionheart Gal* penned in 2005, "This commitment to dialogue and to small-scale coalition and collaboration across what is now called difference was the ethical centerpiece of the early work of Sistren, and of this collection . . . It would not have been possible without a commitment to this process over a protracted period of time" (296). Similarly, the Latina Feminist Group argues that "to write and theorize about a range of Latina experiences . . . required being in sustained dialogue with one another" (9). The importance of sustained intragroup dialogue is reiterated by *Telling to Live*'s assertion that "sharing can begin a process of empowerment" (1). Such reflections touch on key components of solidarity work in transnational feminist praxis: trust and radical vulnerability.

These passages reflect central principles of both Freirean dialogic methodology and postpositivist realist theory, especially in how a group's collective goal of more epistemically whole knowledge cannot exist without individual input and reflection. As Brent R. Henze argues, agency itself is a dialectical process: "Far from conflicting with the formation of a true collectivity, individual agency facilitates the process; and the resultant collective has greater potential for liberatory political transformation" (237). Polyvocal feminist testimonios reinforce this sentiment insofar as the collections could not exist without individual accounts and reflections, and yet the individual accounts become epistemologically meaningful only through the work of group interpretation. The effect is more "multiple," or "connected," subjectivity than seamless collectivity.

This commitment to dialogic process is also found at the level of individual narrative accounts. As Claudette Phene suggests in *Walking on Fire*'s "A Little Light": "When you get into an organization, you change completely. What makes you change? I come to see you, know you, share ideas. That allows a change in both of us" (Bell 115). In "Veteran by Veteran," the narrator recounts the pedagogical function of sharing experience in a group setting: "Me haffi tek me own time and find nobody force notten pon me. Di only way me could a get exposure is by mixing meself wid odder people. Me gather experience from dem, den me go one side and tink bout plenty tings dat puzzle me" (Sistren Theatre Collective 157). Here, dialogue is configured as a necessary component in the democratic production of social knowledge, and hence a valuable alternative to the top-down and rote memorization tactics the narrator encountered in a school setting. By working through her own experiential knowledge base and putting it into dialogue with others, the narrator highlights how she seeks out others' social truths and formulates her own conclusions by situating her truth in relation to theirs.

This continued inward/outward movement between individual reflection and group discussion, and moving through and across individual accounts, parallels Freire's insistence that praxis can be constituted only through the fluid motion of action and reflection—that each is meaningless without the other. As Henze argues in relation to the figure of "Alice," a member of a feminist consciousness-raising group, "Alice's life adds to [its] collective pool of resources. The group framework becomes more effective as it is tested on an increasing range of experiences, leading it to become better able to help Alice interpret her experiences; she understands better, she has more to offer back to the group, and so the cycle continues" (245).[11]

Insofar as feminist testimonio offers itself as a forum for dialogic exchange, it highlights how knowledge production is a collaborative endeavor that benefits from the collective amalgamation of the subject positions, experiences, and skill sets of those involved. But while the dialogic processes of feminist testimonio recognize all experiential knowledge claims as epistemically valuable, they do not understand all experiential knowledge as epistemically equal in value.[12] Rather, in feminist testimonio the conversation begins by placing the knowledge and insights of marginalized social actors at the center of the exchange, interrupting and inverting academic paradigms that "relegate the nonacademic collaborators as the second tier of knowledge production" (Nagar and Swarr 8). In so doing, practitioners of feminist testimonios both address and actively reject "how dialogic praxis is pushed to the margins" (8) in academic settings and claim themselves as primary knowledge producers who in turn invite their readership to learn from what their experiences and social positions have enabled them to know. Rather than glossing over the radical power asymmetries involved in the writing, publishing, and reading of testimonios, they incorporate discussions of these power differentials into their very narrative frameworks, proactively shaping the terms of conversation and exchange.

As a human process, this dialogic approach is certainly vulnerable to error. As Freire argues, "Dialogue cannot exist without humility . . . How can I dialogue if I always project ignorance onto others and never perceive my own? . . . How can I dialogue if I am closed to—and even offended by—the contribution of others?" (89). Medina similarly calls for an "epistemic humility" in such dialogic processes (23). Nevertheless, through a sustained outward/inward movement, such collective meaning-making allows individuals to do the personal work of decentering their own worldview as it simultaneously solidifies for them how their worldview has been shaped by their sociopolitical positionings. While the process has no guarantees, it does enable the possibility of participants coming to consciousness through recognizing the systemic relations that define their "limit situations" and working with others to change them (Freire 99).

The process of working through multiple situated "truths" to arrive at a better historical understanding of "Truth," of engaging with chosen "communities of meaning," also resonates with Wendy Brown's claim that the possibility of progressive identity politics is enabled by moving from the concept of "being" to that of "wanting" (407). Rather than recognizing identities *as* things, polyvocal testimonios allow us to reconceptualize social location as manifested in contextual relationships *between* people (Hames-García 110). Such a political posturing rejects fixed, rigid identity categories—without discounting asymmetrical power relations based on social location—in favor of coalitional platforms premised on shared political/intellectual goals. Joan Scott's warning about experiential accounts is premised on the neglect of historians to "piece together" different experiences that would enable to us understand how different articulations refer back to differing social positionings within "the same economy" (779); the insistence of polyvocal feminist testimonios (as realized versions of postpositivist realist theory) on weaving together individual experiences for the purpose of "epistemic wholeness" acknowledges the centrality of Scott's concern while simultaneously building on it to consider that different experiential knowledge claims do, in fact, represent fragments of the "same economy."

Through their commitment to epistemic friction, polyvocal feminist testimonio "entails a theory of how group interests can expand" (Hames-García 127). By utilizing personal experience for impersonal ends, polyvocal feminist testimonios pave the way for progressive coalitional politics in their recognition of history as a collective, rather than individual, enterprise. They create a dialogic interplay so that the differences are not only allowed to present themselves, but to prove themselves as vital resources in working toward a collectively defined goal. In so doing, these works enable a transnational feminist politics of location, a coalitional exercise that Kaplan defines as "a practice of affiliation . . . [that] identifies the grounds for historically specific differences and similarities between women in diverse and asymmetrical relations, creating alternative histories, identities, and possibilities for alliances" (139). By espousing a politics more akin to "wanting" then "being," polyvocal feminist testimonios consider how and in what form certain marginal experience narratives will help them to get there, and mobilize a dialogics of experiential tale-telling to truth-tell social realities in story-based form.

In the next section, I emphasize that these projects are first and foremost for themselves. However, as writing projects, they are also meant to interface with an audience. While I have discussed at length how polyvocal strategies are meaningful to the practitioners themselves, and even for charting South/South trajectories, they are, of course, also read by racially and geopolitically privileged readers. Here I attend to the ways in which they anticipate how they will be perceived by such readers and in so doing set the terms for their exchange.

Staging Cross-Border Feminist (Reading) Alliances as Transnational Feminist Praxis

As Stuart Hall has laid out for us in his theoretical mapping of the complex practices of encoding and decoding cultural texts, there is certainly more than one way a text can mean, and readings of the same text can without doubt span a progressive-reactionary spectrum. As Hall explores, the author's encoding of a particular cultural text comprises only a partial (though significant) aspect of how a text signifies; the situated and power-laden relationship between text and audience is a critical component in how a text will be read and understood. This is especially true in a North American cultural landscape in which hegemonic white, middle-class scripts continue to comprise the unmarked, normative backdrop against which the accounts of all homogenized "others" are read and understood. The process of decoding, as demanded by story-framed analysis, demands moving from the realm of the abstract to the concrete.

The concept of decoding is a good reminder that narration is a dia-logic mode of communication that seeks to communicate its truths *to* someone.

Feminist literary criticism has long recognized the activity of reading—understood as the dialogic interaction of reader and text—as a central site of ideological struggle. As counternarratives that contest the terms of the social and aesthetic through the cultural contexts in which they emerge, feminist testimonios are first and foremost "for themselves," and yet they perform important cultural work that offers profound pos-sibilities for cutting through pervasive individualist and first-worldist modes of thought. Feminist literary criticism is itself a mode of praxis that takes seriously the "worldly" situation (Said 1983) in which readers and texts come to interact, prompting readers to grapple with how our individual and relational histories affect our interactions with the texts we read. However, the project of feminist testimonio, as a socioliterary writing project, necessitates a convergence of feminist literary criticism and transnational feminist theory in order to properly articulate the scope of its aesthetic and political dimensions: "How we read testimonio (and how diverse 'we' are) holds as much power as the question of how this genre is produced" (Kaplan 124).

The "risky business" of testimonio—given all the extraliterary and institutional factors working against its actualization—is well paired with transnational feminist critique. Transnational feminist praxis oper-ates on a comparativist model that in Chandra Mohanty's words seeks to provide "a way to theorize a complex relational understanding of expe-rience, location, and history such that feminist cross-cultural work moves through the specific context to construct a real notion of univer-sal and of democratization rather than colonization" (238). Mohanty's framework privileges relationality, in which tension, mutuality, and co-implication are foregrounded as a way of calling attention to moments of intersection and divergence of interwoven women's histories. The practice of sharpening one's ability to see interpersonal and inter-place-based webs of relation corresponds with what Cindi Katz has referred to as "countertopographies," a conceptual framework for mapping the inter-dependencies and intersections between one's own subject position and the global processes that forge unlikely connections between seemingly disconnected spaces and people.

As Nagar and Swarr argue, "Claiming more spaces for dialogic praxis necessitates constant renegotiations and retheorizations of power through alliances, languages, and critiques that disrupt dominant logics and imaginaries" (18). Taking seriously the notion that everyone can be a potential ally, the decolonial ethos of feminist testimonios enacts a cross-border solidarity rather than a sisterhood model by utilizing the texts to create a textual bridge that brings differently positioned global actors into contact without glossing over the radical asymmetries of power between them. Feminist testimonios prompt their practitioners and readers to ask, "How is it that we know and understand how we are formulating our opinions? How do we arrive at certain conceptualizations of the world?" (Elenes 695). Such processes of extended critical reflexivity necessitate that speakers and readers make room for "competing" worldviews in their intellectual and emotional processing of testimonio, which catalyzes the individual work involved in decentering our worldview as well as raising our consciousness about how our worldview has been shaped by our sociopolitical positionings.

Mohanty's comparativist framework is central for considering defensive decodings of feminist testimonio by geopolitically privileged reading audiences, since, as she argues, "The existence of Third World women's narratives in itself is not evidence of decentering hegemonic histories and subjectivities. It is the way in which they are read, understood, and located institutionally that is of paramount importance . . . the ways we read, receive, and disseminate such imaginative records is immensely significant" (78). Mohanty's point reminds us that testimonio is not a foolproof project. Despite careful rhetorical crafting, northern readerships will inevitably perpetrate varying levels of epistemic violence on the texts. For a racially or geopolitically privileged reader, having one's epistemic blinders removed can prove jarring, to say the least, especially when paired with repeated appeals to act in solidarity with those they might view as unalterably "other." To guard themselves, socially privileged readers may institute a series of defense mechanisms to mitigate the potential risk of having their worldview challenged.

Latin American testimonio scholar Kimberly Nance considers such defensive reading tactics in *Can Literature Promote Justice? Trauma Narrative and Social Action in Latin American Testimonio*. Nance refers to two of the most prevalent defensive posturings as "forwarding" and "fusion" (53). Forwarding refers to the process through which readers shift responsibility onto someone else, or tell themselves they are not the proper addressees (53). Fusion, by contrast, is the process through which readers ignore substantial material differences between the worlds they and the speaker inhabit. While forwarding evades responsibility by shifting the blame, fusion is accomplished through overidentification: "We're both victims in one way or another, and reading this book helped me to deal with my own oppression" (54). The risk of honest self-reflection and the internalized effects of individualist cultural grooming no doubt fuel these forms of disengagement.

"What is needed," writes Medina, "is a *transformative but not shattering lucidity* that enables subjects to see how their whiteness [and/or privilege] has been constructed socially and historically vis a vis other identities and at the same time a lucidity that points in the direction of *new ways of inhabiting that identity*" (220); the intentional rhetorical crafting of deliberative testimonio is certainly up to the task. Nance outlines the ideal reader response for testimonio as a two-step process of interpellation. The first step is a reader's affective identification with the text through imagining herself in the same situation—by taking an "empathetic leap." The second, and most important, step is a reader's acknowledgment of their own subject position; they must assess their complicity with the situation described in the text, and identify what assistance they can provide.

This ideal reaction thus begins with empathy—making the "leap" to understand and emotionally invest in the narrator's situational analysis—and then moves beyond this as the reader acknowledges complicities and formulates a just response, which in Medina's terms could be as simple as working through epistemic friction and sitting with the discomfort. In actual practice, this twofold response no doubt proves much messier than in its theoretical formation. Indeed, Nance's model does not suggest that moments of fusion or forwarding will not occur within even an "ideal" reader's interpretive process, or that an ideal reaction will necessarily happen in a clear-cut linear fashion. Rather, what matters is that these momentary resistances are ultimately worked through—that the reader's ego, or what Medina refers to as "epistemic arrogance"—is ultimately sublimated through the reader self-electing to posture a cross-border alliance by choosing epistemic humility (23).

These various modes of reader response direct us to the importance of recognizing feminist testimonios as "staged performances" (Shank and Nagar) that carefully *anticipate* and *direct* readers through self-conscious modes of address. In other words, it is necessary to identify the forms of address employed by feminist testimonios that are intended to enact modes of "co-conversation" for the purpose of enabling relational and collaborative modes of democratic knowledge production.

The specific modes of rhetorical address utilized to nudge the reader in the intended direction therefore merit close attention. As my close readings in part 2 illustrate, it is through such careful consideration of feminist testimonios' rhetorically crafted appeals that we are better able to complicate the argument that testimonio perpetuates a liberal rather than transformative politics. As prime examples of deliberative testimonio, they reverse the anthropological gaze by offering a glimpse of how dominantly positioned readers are viewed through the lens of socially marginalized subjects (Nance 58).[13] It is no wonder then that this unflattering image is mitigated by appeals to recognizable tropes and plot structures so as to keep readers from utter disengagement—a push/pull between biting critique and comforting familiarity, and an offer to alternately inhabit dominant modes of being. As Sandoval's concept of the "clutch" suggests, such a trafficking in dominant paradigms signifies a narrative strategy rather than an uncritical adoption of such discourse; a working within to "break" with.

Through the "dear reader" approach, feminist testimonios groom their audiences as trusted—or at the very least, potential—friends in order to make their audiences consider themselves capable of intervening in the social problem at hand: "Speakers neither demand that their readers come precommitted nor that their allies be flawless . . . [they are] potential allies, educable and possibly of use in increasing the amount of justice in the world" (Nance 162). Through this process they pave the way for multiple audiences. Racially and geopolitically marginalized readers are invited to align their own social struggles with those articulated by the practitioners themselves. Racially and geopolitically privileged readers are invited to destabilize their worldview and understand the world from a different perspective. Insofar as such works might seem to treat their readers better than they deserve—as confidants, allies, *comadres*—it is important to recognize these speech acts as performative in the service of generating an epistemic bridge: "The description of the reader is not meant as an accurate or even complimentary reflection of the real reader; it is performative speech, seeking to make something happen by declaring it already has. The rhetorical strategy is to get readers to accept a certain definition of themselves so that they will then feel obligated to live up to it" (Nance 59). As such, feminist testimonios embody a delicate yet fierce balance of political generosity and focused intentionality by guiding readers through cultivated forms of rhetorical address that necessarily correspond with the specific forms and functions of individual projects and contexts. While in daily life the extent to which marginalized social actors are called upon to inform and educate dominant subjects serves to perpetuate asymmetrical power relations, feminist testimonios willfully and craftily engage in this pedagogical pursuit in an effort to reach as many potential allies as possible.

Again, however, the project of feminist testimonio is not simply an attempt to "reach" dominantly positioned audiences and win them over; it simultaneously claims a dialogic space that allows individual social justice projects to speak to and learn from each other. For readers who identify with collective movements, whether they are active participants or not, narratives coming out of a shared experience offer new avenues for activism and self-understanding, new models of remembering (Schaffer and Smith 27). Indeed, while conducting interviews for *Sandino's Daughters*, Margaret Randall was repeatedly informed of how texts emanating from the Cuban Revolution played a formative pedagogical role in the crafting of Nicaraguan revolutionary methods, including Randall's own *Cuban Women Now*, leading her to define *Sandino's Daughters* as "an important tool" (i).

The rhetorical and creative crafting, as well as the intellectual and political processes that inform and organize feminist testimonios, are as important to the political project of feminist testimonio as the end textual product presented to a reading public. No doubt, the incorporation of a testimonial narrative framework in literary deployments and the blurring of witness and testifier in activist deployments speak to how feminist testimonios carefully *anticipate* and *direct* the reader through its modes of address. Through these tactical maneuvers, feminist testimonios proactively encode their texts in ways that enact limits on the ways in which global audiences are able to interpret, or decode, their dialogic textual writing praxis.

Feminist testimonio is epistemically valuable not only because its multivoiced frameworks house different stories within the narrative frame, but also because these accounts tell different stories depending on the positionality of the reader. The "truth" that emerges is located between the expressed narrative and the interpretation readers take from it, enabling the possibility of expanding a reader's sense of "one's own people" and expanding the epistemic reach of their social world. By embodying core principles of postpositivist realist theory, and in addition to modeling coalitional alliances through collective meaning-making, polyvocal feminist testimonios provide a means through which "dominant group members [can] expand their sense of their own interests by attending to opaque interests" through recognizing interconnectedness and interdependencies with others (Hames-García 121).

While the diverse perspectives and narrative accounts allow for possibilities of greater epistemic wholeness as authors and readers from divergent worlds come into textual contact, the stories of testimonio— as a rule—always start from the standpoint of the oppressed, staking a radical claim that those most affected by power maintain a unique position to best understand and critique its workings. When readers respond justly to the narrative call of polyvocal feminist testimonio, it can be understood as a postpositivist realist exercise that asks us to consider the truth-value of the practitioners, to think from their perspective, even as we are unable to transcend our own.

Regardless of our personal racializations and geopolitical locations, by placing our worldview in dialogue with others—even in this imaginative, intangible way—we make conceptual room for the possibility of thinking beyond our own self-interests and ourselves, of entering other epistemic realms. As readers of polyvocal feminist testimonios, a responsible interpretive account might look something like this: "By supplementing my perspective with hers, I am enabled to make better-informed choices about my own actions—actions that resist or contribute to the oppression that I may only witness secondhand" (Henze 247). This self-reflexive response guards against what Kimberly Nance terms "fusion," or overidentification with the narrator, as well as unproductive disengagement, and replaces these interpretative responses with a responsible consideration of what the text enables us to know, and do, from our social locations.

While feminist testimonio's polyvocal representational practices do not guarantee that a reader will act responsibly in relation to the social information housed within the text, they serve as a potential means to move the reader toward what Medina refers to as "kaleidoscopic consciousness," or the ability of a person to understand the limits of his or her own epistemic world and to willingly and intentionally understand a situation from another's point of view. In more pointed language, it is a form of "epistemically virtuous double consciousness . . . that has epistemic counterpoints inside it and therefore, internal epistemic friction" (194). This perspective-taking exercise isn't about mastery, and it isn't an end goal that can one day be fully achieved. Rather, it is an imperfect, continual practice of consciously recognizing what one's social location has and has not allowed one to see, and to diligently work on perceiving the world through other epistemic perspectives.[14] This process might start with a privileged reader confronting his or her biases in the solitary act of reading. Maybe the reader takes the risk of engaging a friend or family member on the topic, eventually offering to let that person borrow the book. Perhaps the book alters the way this person sees those perceived as "others," or changes the person's purchasing patterns. Maybe it sparks an awareness of a social issue and causes the person to read another book, to move out, slowly but surely, of his or her epistemic comfort zone. There is no end to this work, no possibility of mastery. Rather, it is a continual process by which we uproot internalized biases and open ourselves to new ways of being. Ultimately, it is for the readers to decide whether they remain in willful ignorance or engage in a process of epistemic expansion. Testimonio is, after all, a politics without guarantees, an offering to its readers to see and be differently.

Through their self-conscious framings, both literary and activist strands of feminist testimonio teach their audiences how to better see and understand the asymmetrical interdependencies between themselves and the women's lives at the center of a given account, and to understand how these relational webs are connected to processes of globalization. Feminist testimonios should, therefore, be understood as an exercise in cultural translation that enjoins different cultural and material worlds by bringing diverse authors and readers into critical proximity, a textual cont(r)act that privileges intimacy even while distance is maintained. In its more nuanced goals, the work of feminist testimonio is as much invested in altering the worldview of its readers as it is in ending a specific instance of injustice. Or rather, feminist testimonio realizes that these effects are deeply entwined. By penetrating the cultural imaginary, they acknowledge and enact the interconnectedness of the material and discursive, and recognize how one's worldview directly affects one's actions within the world.

PART II

Transnational Translations

CHAPTER 4

Activist "Co/Labor/Actions"
Polyvocality, Pedagogy, and Praxis

> Seven women, seven lives, countless aspirations, worlds, dreams,
> and struggles. Sometimes, the threads of our lives get entangled
> with one another, and at others, they isolate themselves and
> scatter . . . What we have achieved in this first phase of our journey
> is difficult to describe—a self-confidence, a collective spirit, a deep
> respect for one another, and a much sharper vision to live and fight
> in a society whose chains burn us and ignite us to smash and break
> them. At the same time, only by suffering under the weight of those
> chains are we able to imagine new possibilities that allow us to chart
> the directions of our upcoming battles.
>
> —SANGTIN WRITERS, *PLAYING WITH FIRE*

SO MARK THE OPENING LINES OF THE SANGTIN WRITERS' *PLAYING
with Fire*, a collaboratively written narrative that interweaves nine testimonial voices—seven of which belong to village-level NGO activists in
Uttar Pradesh—in its exploration of a collective feminist methodology
through which to realize more egalitarian organizing efforts. The *sangtins'* penetrating words strongly resonate with a poetics of solidarity
articulated by polyvocal feminist testimonios that actively foreground
the material and ideological conditions that wedge themselves between
the felt realities and the hopes and dreams of the women located at the
center of their narratives. The multilayered tensions articulated in this
passage—between the individual and the collective, oppressive realities and the promise of liberated futures—remain a staple in such

works as they attempt to illustrate the effects of macrosocial power structures in women's daily lives while documenting the ways in which women actively struggle against processes of marginalization.

Published in 2006, the Sangtin Writers' *Playing with Fire* (itself an extended translation of the original Hindi version, *Sangtin Yatra*, published in 2004) is a fiercely committed and energized work that requires us to reconsider Beverley's claim that the moment of testimonio is over. This section looks closely at how contemporary feminist activist polyvocal testimonios at once utilize and re-create testimonio as a methodological tool to embody the creative and political visions of activist women's groups in their socially situated contexts. As articulated by the Sangtin Writers, "*Playing with Fire* does not so much document or reflect the theory and praxis of collaboration as it enacts them. Theory of collaboration is generated *as* praxis" (154).

Specifically, this section focuses on the processes of collective meaning-making such texts reflect through their intentional collaborative methods of co-creation, and how this enables them to at once model and enact possibilities for feminist coalitional alliance-building attuned to a complex politics of difference.

Rather than deliver close readings of individual narratives, this section attends to each work's structural scaffolding to illustrate how its polyvocal structure models the dialogic, collaborative ethos driving these writing projects, which generate an epistemic friction that renews and redirects the type of political work testimonios are capable of performing.[1] Their targeted representational interventions position them in the fraught terrain of knowledge production that frames marginal experience narratives as "raw material" in need of further "expert" analysis.

I work with a selection of testimonios compiled by activist women's groups from distinct geopolitical locations, all of which are outside of the immediate Latin American context: Sangtin Writers, *Playing with Fire: Feminist Thought and Activism through Seven Lives in India* (2006); the Latina Feminist Group, *Telling to Live: Latina Feminist Testimonios* (2001); Beverly Bell, *Walking on Fire: Haitian Women's Stories of Survival and Resistance* (2001); and Sistren Theatre Collective, *Lionheart Gal: Life Stories of Jamaican Women* (1986). A brief overview of each text's point of intervention and stated goals attests to testimonio's ability to traverse increasingly diverse cultural and political terrain.

The Sangtin Writers' *Playing with Fire* is set in the Sitapur district of Uttar Pradesh, India, an area thick with international development initiatives. The collective formed out of concern for how Nari Samata Yojana (NSY), the NGO that (at one time) employed eight of the nine Sangtin Writers,[2] reinforces social hierarchies along the lines of class, caste, and religion through bureaucratic practices that undermine the organization's stated efforts to "empower" underclass women, including undervaluing the contributions and labors of the village-level activists who consist *of* and work directly *with* the women the organization purports to serve.[3] One of the main critiques of the *sangtins* about the gap between NSY's theory and practice is that while it seeks to "empower" *dalit* women (lower caste affiliation), most of its employees are *sawarn* (higher caste affiliation).

The collective labors that produced the book took place over thirty-four months beginning in March 2002, and included in-person meetings as well as electronic correspondence (as a result of some members living on different continents). The collective discursively represent themselves as "*sangtins*," an Awadhi (an oral, local language of Uttar Pradesh) word meaning "of solidarity, of reciprocity, of enduring friendship among women" (Sangtin Writers xxiii). The original Hindi edition, *Sangtin Yatra*, translates as "a journey of sangtins" (xxiii). *Playing with Fire* marks one moment of a continuing journey of writing, dialogue, and organizing by reflecting on the limitations and possibilities of NGOs' ability to enact foundational social change, and seeks to reach "those who are invested in (or disenchanted by) the notion of 'empowering the marginalized'" (xxiii).

Lionheart Gal, created by the Sistren Theatre Collective, charts a complex picture of pressing social concerns faced by mainly black working-class Jamaican women. "Sistren" refers to the Jamaican Creole/Patwah term for "sisters." While the book was initially meant to provide a methodological overview of the collective's production processes, the project quickly transformed into a collection of members' life stories when their trajectories and themes proved too dynamic and multifaceted to be reduced to secondary evidence. Through this reconsidered focus, the editor and then theater director Honor Ford-Smith suggests the stories reveal the impact of development on women and "illustrate ways in which women can move from the apparent powerlessness of exploitation to the creative power of rebel consciousness" (xiii). The book's topics range from early motherhood to intimate partner violence, working and living conditions to critiques of education, political participation, and rebellion, thus thoroughly critiquing the idea that "women's issues" remain in the private sphere.

Beverly Bell's *Walking on Fire* continues a concern for "multiplying the narrative" and is aimed at complicating static, monolithic representations of Haitian women by focusing on the creative means of resistance Haitian women use to *bat tenèb*, "beat back the darkness" (xiiv). Similar to *Lionheart Gal*, this collection focuses on a number of social issues that, while not typically considered "women's issues," testify to the ways in which domestic and international policies destabilize women's struggles to maintain economic stability and cultivate dignified lives while simultaneously attesting to the "rebel consciousness" that keep these women's hopes and dreams alive. *Walking on Fire* differs from the other texts in that Bell does not write as an immediate member of a women's collective. Rather, Bell conducted interviews with women from several different organizations between 1991 and 1994. She incorporated thirty-eight of them in the book's final form, thereby providing a broad picture of the diverse ways Haitian women engage in resistance efforts.[4] Rather than discursively framing the life narrators as "interview subjects" or "research participants," Bell importantly refers to them as "*griyos*," a Haitian Creole term denoting a well-respected teller of Haitian history that actively blurs the boundary of "story" and "history," as well as "official" and vernacular accounts. These historical narrative accounts are termed "*istwa*" in Creole.

The Latina Feminist Group's *Telling to Live* at once lays genealogical claim to and stretches the idea of testimonio by bringing it into the unlikely realm of the US academy. The eighteen-member collective was first formed by a group of Latina academics in 1995 with the goal of working through important sociohistorical differences (ethnic, national, religious, linguistic, class, sexual, and US regional) that cut through the pan-ethnic configuration of "Latinas" in a way that often gets glossed over as a result of solidarity efforts. One of the book's central preoccupations is accounting for the simultaneous social privilege and marginalization—and resulting contradictions—the coauthors' experience as racialized subjects who nevertheless hold advanced degrees and teach in US postsecondary institutions. After a seven-year collaboration, marked by especially productive summer workshops in Baca, Colorado, the book emerged as an expression of the ways in which testimonio had become a central methodology used by members both to explore and share with each other and to theorize *latinidades*. Group members refer to themselves as "*testimoniadoras*," testifiers, of their *papelitos guardados*, guarded papers.

Of these four feminist polyvocal testimonios, all but *Playing with Fire* position the various women's narratives side-by-side within the narrative frame; *Playing with Fire* further complicates this polyvocal form by braiding together individual voices and interweaving the stories with a collaboratively generated comparative analysis within the body of a thematically framed chapter.[5] With the exception of *Walking on Fire*, these texts emerged as part of established collectives; they serve to document brief moments of much longer political journeys.

Each work also differently employs a decolonizing use of standard English by "bending" it to serve its immediate needs. That is, rather than utilizing English as a transparent, translational mediation device that waters down the forceful political message of the "original," these works use English to performative effect. *Telling to Live* straddles English and Spanish, at times depending on one language more than the other, more often fluidly interweaving the two. *Lionheart Gal* is written to represent the sounds and phrasings of oral Jamaican Creole. *Playing with Fire* is an English translation of the Hindi *Sangtin Yatra*, itself a translation from the Awadhi dialect that the autobiographers originally used in their diary reflections. *Walking on Fire* is an English translation from the Haitian Creole spoken during the interview process. These texts also employ culturally resonant metaphors that firmly anchor them to the cultural spaces from which their narratives emerge. Additionally, *Playing with Fire* and *Walking on Fire* directly insert themselves in ongoing debates on the politics of knowledge production. Both collections fiercely insist that the women at the center of the texts be understood as primary knowledge producers, proactively shaping the interpretive processes of readers who are poised to hear their testimonies as "raw material" in need of further "expert" analysis.

While the interventions of *las testimoniadoras*, Sistren, the *griyos*, and the *sangtins* take aim at different institutional structures as a result of their disparate social contexts, the broader implications of these projects nevertheless parallel with a centrally named goal of the *sangtins*, which is to "reshuffle" (to echo *griyo* Rosemie Belvius) the "expectations about who can produce knowledge; the languages, genres, and forms in which knowledges get produced; and how new knowledges gain relevance as they interact with different audiences" (Sangtin Writers xxvi). The life stories utilized by these texts therefore serve to challenge elitist modes of knowledge production by putting forth disparate formations of grounded theory, or, as Aurora Levins Morales suggests, a practice of "making theory out of the stuff in our pockets, out of the stories, incidents, dreams, frustrations that were never acceptable anywhere else" (Latina Feminist Group 32). In many ways each of these collections responds to Selitane Joseph's question and suggestion: "What did the big women's meeting in Beijing do for us Haitian women? We haven't seen any effects. Why don't they come and sit with us peasant women to see how we're living today?" (Bell 142). These staged textual dialogues invite the reader to listen to their ideas about how to address the particular issues they face as gendered subjects.

Of course, the accessible language and vernacularized sentiments of these "homemade theories" can deceptively mask their utilization of sophisticated structural framings and modes of rhetorical address as a means of entering into the uneven terrain of knowledge production. One productive way of calling attention to the performative aspect of feminist activist polyvocal testimonios is to differentiate between their "backstage preparations" (read: the political work informing but falling outside the narrative frame) and their "staged performances" (read: the material presented within the final textual frame). In "Retelling Stories, Resisting Dichotomies," Sofia Shank and Richa Nagar speak to the political salience of this interpretive approach:

> We highlight the importance of "backstage preparations" (the necessary conversations about vulnerabilities and experience, as well as their translations) and the "staged performances" or final scripts (those stories we actually decide to translate and tell) . . . Defined in this way, activist theater can be regarded as a political and theoretical platform that self-consciously engages with representation by deliberately constructing, framing, and performing any and every story. In so

doing, political theater and activism directly engage, utilize, and confront representation as a central concept that guides the action, and allow us to foreclose the concept of "direct access" to experience, or the idea of a transparent rendering of story. (9–10)

By considering feminist activist polyvocal tesitmonios in terms of "staged performances," we not only release ourselves, as readers, from unrealistic expectations to access unmediated truth claims through their narrative accounts, but are also better poised to understand their self-conscious use of representational paradigms to creatively rework power imbalances between practitioners and their reading audiences. Additionally, if as Shank and Nagar suggest, "spatial relationships are foundational in determining the ways in which representations are transmitted and performed," beyond the relationship between reader and text, we can consider how the spatial aspect of polyvocal frameworks actively performs a dialogic model for coalitional alliance-building across epistemic worlds.

As a prominent manifestation of their staged interventions, each text reworks the traditional model of the testifier-witness, allowing practitioners to take more control over how their representations will be received, and reclaiming the genre from a simplistic politics of recognition. Rather, they re-create and revitalize the political heft of testimonio to better suit feminist activist efforts in three main ways: a collaboratively established polyvocal framework attuned to a complex politics of difference; a process-versus product-based approach as evidenced by expansive methodology sections that document modes of dialogic engagement, especially between members of a collective; and an explicit pedagogical rhetoric that encourages readers to become potential allies and to incorporate the interpretive practices performed and modeled within the text into the reader's daily life practices.

The works are always first and foremost for themselves and the work the activists hope to accomplish. The polyvocal strategies range from the literal incorporation of several voices and subject positions to the inclusion of different textual mediums and language systems. While these works attest to the importance of sustained dialogic practices undertaken by the practitioners of a given testimonio, they also articulate a larger commitment to sparking horizontal dialogue with activists and social justice projects in different locales. These efforts to network and build solidarity—which Medina terms "connected actions" (226)—reinforce the simultaneous local/global commitment of each project. Each work's discursive choices are context specific, reflecting choices that are accounted for in the introductory sections and that create a conceptual framework for the personal narratives.

The representational strategies and organizing principles of feminist activist polyvocal testimonio are guided by a commitment to nonhierarchical modes of activism that allow those who have been historically disempowered to put power to productive use. The collaborative ethos that underpins these collections thus serves as a catalyst for the innovative collective methodologies utilized, which enact a complex politics of difference that models possibilities for coalitional feminist alliance-building. This and the next chapter thus serve to articulate key representational practices that enable these works to *enact* rather than merely "document" their feminist visions. These two chapters seek to account for these telling overlaps and departures in an effort to highlight how these four feminist activist testimonios at once bespeak an overarching feminist methodological pattern while still corresponding with site-specific representational needs.[6]

Co-narration and Multilingualism: Variations on a Theme

As early as Margaret Randall's foundational *Cuban Women Now* (1974) and *Sandino's Daughters: Testimonies of Nicaraguan Women in Struggle* (1985), testimonios have rendered an otherwise "absent polyphony" *present*. While Randall is one of many feminist oral historians to explore alternative representational paradigms, her innovative feminist oral history methods have certainly "traveled" into contemporary feminist activist polyvocal testimonios. Rather than subsuming disparate sets of experiences under one voice meant to represent the many, Randall conducted multiple oral histories with the women involved in these cultural revolutions and positioned their interview responses side-by-side each other within the narrative frame, exposing the seams of testimonio and highlighting the subjective nature of testimony itself.

Randall's formatting decision complicates the reader's relation to her work by extending the dialogic function of testimonio from one of text to reader to the participants themselves. That is, a careful reader does not just encounter a series of individual interviews but is rather able to hear a conversation emerging between interviewees, a direct result of placing differing accounts of specific events in close proximity to each other. By letting the contradictions remain, Randall's technique makes room for the epistemological possibility of coexisting truths. Her narratives resist stasis by representing the fluidity of truth and insisting upon the dynamism of cultures in flux.

For example, in *Sandino's Daughters*, Randall frames the first chapter through an explication of how the Luisa Amanda Espinosa Nicaraguan Women's Association is so named to honor the first woman member of Nicaragua's National Liberation Front to die in combat (1). Giving the reader a subtle but formative directive to "listen while women from the association [re-create] its history" (1), Randall dedicates the second section of the chapter to a series of interviews with Espinosa's family, friends, and comrades in an effort to provide a three-dimensional account of her life and the immediate circumstances that led to her death.

This re-creation of Espinosa's life and death through the narratives of those closest to her illustrates Randall's commitment to producing knowledge that is not only accountable but also *responsive* to her interview subjects. Hearing how the revolutionary figure of Luisa Amanda Espinosa was central to how Nicaraguan women understood themselves as central actors of the revolution, Randall dedicates an entire section to this woman's memory. The chapter serves as a powerful example of collective decision and meaning-making, one that calls attention to the subjective nature of testimony, with individual accounts offering conflicting interpretations and information on Espinosa's life and the circumstances of her death. By letting these contradictions remain, Randall makes room for epistemic counterpoints (Medina 194).

In considering the number of contemporary polyvocal feminist activist texts that have emerged from women's collectives, it is clear that the emphasis on dialogic processes between participants acknowledges the importance of them witnessing themselves and each other. Through the incorporation of multiple voices and subject positions, the collective resonance positions culture as a contested terrain that highlights how the similarities and divergences between individual accounts enable a three-dimensional understanding of sociohistorical conditions in a situated context. Through the heterogeneity of experiential perception, fragmented truth claims subtly emerge; these then need to be pieced together and worked through in order for epistemic wholeness to more thoroughly materialize. The effect is a kaleidoscopic framework that necessarily interrupts homogenous, monolithic representational practices.

Playing with Fire, Walking on Fire, Telling to Live, and *Lionheart Gal* each attest to this, often theorizing their use of a polyvocal structure as a way of resisting static, essentialist representations of "women" and "culture" and as a purposeful strategy in enacting feminist collaborations attentive to a complex politics of difference. For example, in *Lionheart Gal,* Ford-Smith provides an authorial directive for how audiences should interpret the book's multivoiced structure: "The stories can be read individually as accounts of ways in which women come to terms with the difficulties in their personal lives. However, within each story there are different emphases such as work, housing, relations with men and children; so that taken together, they are a composite woman's story, within which there are many layers of experience" (xiii). Reminiscent of the side-by-side style of Randall's oral histories, Ford-Smith attests to the simultaneous individual and collective truth-value of each tale, and encourages readers to engage with the "many layers of experience" the *present* polyphonic style allows for. By listening for the overlaps and divergences between individual accounts, Ford-Smith highlights the effectiveness of thematic and experiential repetition.

Similarly, in the introduction to *Walking on Fire,* editor Beverly Bell contextualizes the significance of the variegated interview responses the text houses by arguing, "The women's diverse responses to their realities call for expansive analyses, challenging monolithic assumptions often made about people in poor and black countries. Through their *istwas* [stories], the *griyos* [storytellers] defy cultural and gender essentialism and implicitly rebuff any attempt to create a paradigm or symbol of 'Haitian woman'" (xvi). Bell's directive helps readers make sense of the coexisting truths within the collection. The members of the Latina Feminist Group articulate how their text's final polyvocal structure reflects the collective storytelling that enabled them to attend to layers of meaning and difference commonly overlooked within the consolidated "Latina" identity descriptor: "*Testimonio* was critical for breaking down essentialist categories since it was through telling life stories and reflecting upon them that we gained nuanced understandings of differences and connections among us. These revelations established respect and deeper understanding for each of us as individuals and as Latinas" (11). Through its dialogic function, telling and listening to individual testimonios allowed members to at once dissect and reinhabit their "Latina" identities through the self-conscious expression of a nuanced understanding of this solidarity-based label. In so doing, they counterbalanced an imposed and/or self-protective understanding of the term: "We self-consciously use 'Latinas' as a coalitional term. We are not homogenizing and leveling our differences into an idealized, unified national/ethnic heritage" (5).

The Sangtin Writers also attend to a complex politics of difference by articulating the polyvocal, collaborative quality of *Playing with Fire*, which resists overly generalized and stereotypical representations: "Even as a 'blended we,' the collective articulates, negotiates, and narrates the complex meanings of heterogeneity, difference, and diversity. We show how seven actors, who might conventionally be lumped together as 'rural poor women of Sitapur,' self-consciously come together to understand their own lives and struggles as interwoven with local structures of class, caste, religion, and gender as well as with broader processes of development and globalization" (141).

This narrative approach also works to more fully explicate what these differences mean by developing a clearer picture of the *relationality between* women within the collective: "As we narrate and interweave seven stories of motherhood and political coming of age, we analyze each woman's struggle with caste, religion, and gender politics in relation to those of six others. New layers of understanding and consciousness unfold as we reevaluate the autobiographers' own past interactions" (142). In this way, *Playing with Fire* enacts Chandra Mohanty's claim that "differences are never just 'differences'" (226). Rather, in moving from positions of critique to reconstruction, the "challenge is to see how differences allow us to explain the connections and border crossings better and more accurately, how specifying difference allows us to theorize universal concerns more fully" (226). Within this formulation, the individual is never eclipsed for the purposes of the collective; it is precisely this tension between the "I" and the "we" that allows for a cross-border coalitional posture. Hence, the multiperspective representational practices serve as meta-framings that allow the texts to literally embody the complex politics of the difference they advocate for.

The polyvocal structure also reinforces Mohanty's suggestion that "common differences" form the basis of meaningful feminist solidarity (225). For the Sangtin Writers, as with the Sistren Theatre Collective and the Latina Feminist Group, the process of generating individual life writings in order to then share and juxtapose them with others within the collective is a way of working through existing social differences and hierarchies in order to develop a more complex understanding of how group solidarity can be achieved, in terms of what issues members are collectively committed to organizing around and how they have personally come to identify these issues as important through the sharing of their experiential knowledge.

Polyvocal structure serves as a powerful symbol of collective meaning-making and alliance-building by encouraging multiple truth claims to emerge without forcing them into a false reconciliation. If Randall's side-by-side structure initially served to expose the seams of collective knowledge production, contemporary polyvocal feminist testimonios continue to theorize and elaborate upon the ways representation can model an active negotiation of social difference. By experimenting with how these methods can be represented in textual form, these works cultivate new ways of imagining and embodying responsive and accountable political postures in coalitional practices.

While these works each employ a polyvocal framework, their utilizations of this underlying structure vary in chosen political purpose and narrative form. Whereas *Walking on Fire*, *Telling to Live*, and *Lionheart Gal* position individual women's stories as stand-alone narratives within the body of the text (continuations of the side-by-side format), *Playing with Fire* opts instead for a "blended but fractured 'we'" (elsewhere articulated as a "braiding" of the collective's voices) to further represent their bond as *sangtins* without glossing over the disparate positionalities and power differentials that exist within the group. While blended in the sense of interlocking narratives, this "chorus" of voices does not remain constant throughout the book. Rather, we are told, "As one of us speaks, the voice of the second or third suddenly blends in to give an entirely new and unique flavor to our music. Our notes blend, disperse in ones or twos or sevens, and regroup" (xxxiv), creating a palimpsest effect.

Beyond the musicality of this metaphor, it highlights the fluid, deliberate shifting of voice(s) throughout the book—at one moment featuring the particular experience of one woman, augmented by an apposite experience of another, then coming back together to produce a collective reading of what these dissonances mean: "While Radha was subjected to scornful meddling for not producing a child after three years of marriage, here was Sandhya, feeling a different kind of pressure: *not* to have one" (59). Such experiential juxtapositions remind us that truth cannot be separated from context. The constant tension maintained between the individual and the collective—the recognition of each woman's story as important enough to stand on its own while simultaneously recognizing the social significance of a chorus of critique—is also visibly marked by the addition of space between individual autobiographers' narratives. These visual breaks serve as a reminder that individual subjectivity is not overwritten by processes of collective meaning-making. These "variations" on similar cultural experiences within feminist activist polyvocal testimonios serve to remind us how social structures enact themselves differently on the bodies of disparately positioned social actors, all the while referring back to the "same economy" (Scott 779). The Sangtin Writers note: "Today we know very well that it is only when we juxtaposed the stories of our personal lives and saw them with new lenses that we were able to arrive at a point where it is becoming possible for us to honestly reevaluate the inequalities pervasive in our work field" (130).

In relation to the role of the reader, the polyvocal structure highlights the epistemological importance of dialogue and facilitates the reader's focused dialogic interaction with the text. The co-narration provides a lens for resisting predetermined, static, impermeable identity categories, replacing them with possibilities of purposeful, cautious, and intentional border crossings. By going beyond the mere incorporation of side-by-side narratives, texts such as *Playing with Fire* structurally reflect the epistemic purpose served by the juxtaposition of experiential knowledge claims. Such texts invite readers to adopt a similar lens when reading their work and by extension to integrate this lens into their daily interpretive practices. In the process, they extend the political reach of testimonio by expanding the ways in which such texts "work" on the reader.

Playing with Fire's particular deployment of polyvocality is not only for poetic effect, or merely concerned with "diversifying" representations of Indian women's lives, but to disrupt dominant paradigms of knowledge production. As members of a collective who have organized around the ways in which NGOs define "poor rural women's issues" without the input of women who occupy these social positions, the *sangtins* are committed to representing themselves as knowledge producers who do not need to rely on outside interpreters: "We want to interrupt the popular practice of representation in the media, NGO reports, and academic analysis, in which the writing voice of the one who is analyzing or reporting as the 'expert' is separated from the voice of the persons who are recounting their lives and opinions" (xxxiv). In addition to using a "fractured we" to better tailor the writing form to suit their immediate needs, the Sangtin Writers include very few direct quotes from the writing journals on which they base their narrative, leaving the reader to distantly encounter third-person accounts of their stories. While all testimonios are mediated to various degrees, this authorial decision performs its own stated theoretical commitment by refusing unmediated access to these accounts and delivering an explicit reminder that *Playing with Fire* does not provide mere experiential "raw material" for a professional or academic elite.

The different situations and contexts in which the other projects emerged rendered this structure less effective for both representational and political reasons. For instance, since Bell's *Walking on Fire* is not the result of a collective but is rather comprised of individual interviews with Haitian feminist activists working in different areas and around a varied set of social issues, the replacement of transcribed interviews into a third-person narrated assemblage could signal an attempt to overwrite the voices of the individual *griyos*, consolidating them for the purpose of Bell's own imposed agenda, or translating their theory-in-the-vernacular to more "acceptable" academic prose. Similarly, while *Telling to Live* boasts a collaboratively generated introduction, the Latina Feminist Group's commitment to deconstructing the extreme glossing of difference the pan-Latina term enacts upon feminist social actors with widely different ethnic, national, religious, class, and sexual histories makes it undesirable for them to speak from a mediated third-person narrative perspective. As stated by Luz del Alba Acevedo, "*Nudos de poder* (nodes of power) could be loosened and untied through a process of collaboration and polyphonic negotiation of difference" (Latina Feminist Group 261).

Rather than "resolve" these representational struggles by submerging differences beneath a "fragmented we," members of the collective wanted to have final say on the framing of their particular stories. Furthermore, given the group's relative privilege and knowledge of feminist theory as US Latina academics, a central part of the exercise was to undergo the labor of enacting the same methods on themselves that they have enacted through their research: "Many of us, in one way or another, are professional *testimoniadoras* [producers of testimonios] . . . [yet many of us] had not yet experienced being on both sides of the process, sharing and generating our own *testimonios* with each other as Latina scholars" (2). Group members thus wrote their own individual testimonio accounts, recognizing both the political importance of this act (to highlight the diversity of "Latinas") and their own relative social privilege (as literate, lettered Latinas). The varied voices, perspectives, and structural forms housed within *Telling to Live* textually testify to the diversity of perspectives, experiences, and skill sets espoused by US Latina academics.

Beyond the incorporation of multiple narrative accounts, polyvocality is evident in other formal aspects as well. For instance, *Telling to Live*, *Walking on Fire*, and *Lionheart Gal* all include visual components. *Lionheart Gal* incorporates artwork inspired by Caribbean and Jamaican folklore and themes from the collection's life stories, some of which were later turned into templates for the silk-screening projects Sistren undertook to generate income for its theater projects.[7] The cover image, inspired by a scene from the story "Veteran by Veteran," is the most intricately detailed and incorporates images of Erzulie (Yoruba goddess of sensuality and love), Yemaya (Yoruba mother and goddess of the sea), Obatala (androgynous god/dess of purity, truth, peace, and wisdom), and Ni (guerilla warrior priestess and queen of the Maroons).[8] Thus, polyvocality within *Lionheart Gal* is also achieved by an explicit visual evocation of how the struggles of Sistren's members deeply resound with the intergenerational histories and legacies of diasporic black women.

Lionheart Gal also includes a posed photograph of the collective, a decision mirrored by *Telling to Live*'s incorporation of candid and posed photos of the Latina Feminist Group from their foundational 1995 conference in Baca, Colorado. *Walking on Fire* uses photography differently, providing snapshots of individual interviewees throughout the collection, named and positioned beside their narrative accounts. This element visually signals how these truth claims are put forth as embodied knowledge, literally rooted in lessons learned from women's daily lives, whether individually or collectively expressed. By writing the body back into the text, these texts work against the abstraction the written word can produce. As stated in *Telling to Live*, "As we give testimony, our bodies awaken, revealing our *llagas* (wounds) and our joys. Our stories celebrate the awakening of our bodies as we also acknowledge the cost exacted because of our gender, race, class, and sexuality" (263). The inclusion of photographs in *Walking on Fire* seems especially important, since although the interview process was fairly collaborative in its employment of participant-focused feminist methodologies, it is still not the product of a collective, which means the *griyos'* fingerprints are less present than in the other projects. By including photographs, Bell ameliorates any associated representational lack.

Polyvocality is also expressed by an incorporation of structurally variant narrative forms. For example, *Telling to Live* includes poetry, essays, diary writing, and experimental prose. In the "Resistance as Expression" section of *Walking on Fire*, Bell includes the *istwas* of different cultural workers: a poet, a singer, a visual artist, and a dancer. Bell emphasizes their articulations of what these forms of creative expression mean to resistance struggles by integrating their song lyrics, poems, and visual art. While the medium of dance does not translate as easily to a written mode, the text nevertheless includes a linguistically fluid description of dance from dancer Florencia Pierre: "This dance is a language. It's a means, a tool, to allow you to speak, to recount your suffering, to recount your pain, your joy, to recount the happiness of your heart. It is dance that does everything, everything, everything, and is everything for me" (89).[9]

Poet and *griyo* Alina "Tibebe" Cajuste also reinforces the epistemological significance of Bell's decision to include these varied linguistic modalities as integral forms of knowledge production: "I am a person who doesn't know how to read, who doesn't know how to write. But I'm intelligent, my spirit works. . . . That's how I come to think—always in terms of poetry. That's what makes my brain work, what makes me live, too" (76, 81). Bell's incorporation of Cajuste's poetry reinforces how social knowledge can be housed within multiple forms of expression, and thus puts forth a vision of polyvocality that moves beyond the incorporation of multiple voices and perspectives to one that extends its relevance to the language and modes of expression housed within by having the *griyos* speak through and about the mediums of their choice.

Rather than subsuming disparate experiences under a collective "I" that represses social difference in an effort to maintain a united front, polyvocal testimonios illustrate how social truths speak louder and more fully when contradictions are encouraged to resound. Thus, this hybrid writing form has an underlying methodology that is capable of nurturing an array of political projects that maintain a commitment to working through difference. By tweaking and adapting this writing form to suit their needs, practitioners utilize multiperspective and multimedia representational practices that embody their espoused political and theoretical commitments.

Multilingualism in Feminist Polyvocal Activist Testimonio: Linguistic Subjectivities of Resistance

Beyond the incorporation of multiple voices and perspectives, mediums, and narrative forms, contemporary feminist activist testimonios extend the relevance of polyvocality through careful consideration of the language systems employed to assert knowledge claims. If language is a fundamental way in which we enact our subjectivity in social culture, it cannot be denied that language is a central constituent of our cultural identity. As articulated by *Lionheart Gal*, "Language is a political issue central to all power relations. It expresses the soul of a people" (Sistren Theatre Collective xxix). Polyvocal feminist testimonios therefore actively displace a utilitarian understanding of language by giving careful attention to how language describes and reflects the corporeally absent self in written representational forms. *Lionheart Gal*, *Playing with Fire*, *Telling to Live*, and *Walking on Fire* subscribe to an intimate and living notion of language, as illustrated through their self-conscious straddling of language systems and linguistic registers.

As texts that seek to interrupt elitist practices of knowledge production, these testimonios are strategic in their language usage, with an eye turned toward their respective audiences and how to best realize their immediate goals. While all of these texts employ standard English to various degrees, they arrive at and employ this linguistic choice in different ways. They "bend" its usage to suit their needs while qualifying how and why English became the central language to communicate the social knowledge each project puts forth. For instance, as director and founder of the Center for Economic Justice in Albuquerque, New Mexico, Beverly Bell translates her interviews, conducted in Haitian Creole, into English in an effort to reach US reading audiences. Bell qualifies this decision with the claim that "the book is not written in the Haitians' language. Even if it were, most Haitian women do not read. Even if they did, most would not have the money to buy the book nor the time to read it" (xvi). Bell seizes the opportunity to succinctly summarize the vast material discrepancies that exist between Haiti and the US and to denaturalize her use of English by reframing it from a paradigm of assumed inevitability to a political choice that is circumstance-bound.

The other texts make similar tactical language decisions. Honor Ford-Smith's encoding of Sistren's stories into a written translation of Jamaican Creole at once serves to undermine a cultural elitism that has designated Creole a "lesser" language while simultaneously testifying to the continued presence of the British colonial legacy in contemporary life. As a collective that does not uniformly identify Spanish or English as its primary language, the Latina Feminist Group decided to incorporate both languages, with individual *testimoniadoras* choosing how much or how little Spanish to include in their narrative accounts. Finally, *Playing with Fire* accounts for its English usage in terms of circumstance and as a multiply translated work. While individual autobiographers originally expressed themselves in Awadhi, a local dialect of Uttar Pradesh, the Sangtin Writers made the decision to publish their book, *Sangtin Yatra*, in Hindi to reach a broader audience of Indian activists and NGO employees. *Sangtin Yatra* was translated into English as a way to counteract the disciplinary measures NSY took to reprimand the Sangtin Writers for writing critically of the organization (154).

These four texts further adapt these language systems to resonate with the historical and local circumstances through which they emerged, and therefore attend to intra- as well as international language bias. The four texts address the politics of their language usage by discussing their negotiations to varying degrees in their introductions. In the case of *Lionheart Gal*, Ford-Smith articulates why and how she chose to transcribe the narratives in written Jamaican Creole: "The whole collection reflects the gamut of language used in Jamaican society and its relationship to class. In the main we hope *Lionheart Gal* makes a case for prose writing in Patwah or creole as the academics call it. Patwah/creole/dialect—the very confusion about what to call it reflects the national insecurity about the language issue" (Sistren Theatre Collective xxviii). Ford-Smith discusses at length the political intent of representing the narratives through a written translation of the oral language the women of Sistren use in their daily lives: "We all know that Jamaican people reflect all the time in their heads or in conversations in Patwah, and we also know that reflection is part of the process of gaining control over one's own life. So, why are certain kinds of written language still dominated totally by English? . . . Not to nurture such a language is to retard the imagination and power of the people who created it" (xxix).

Ford-Smith replicates the particular language patterns of individual narrators, so the language varies between narrative accounts, with distinctions falling along class lines. For instance, while Ford-Smith conducted oral interviews with many of the members, she states how these did not work as well with the middle-class members, who expressed themselves in standard English, and who were more accustomed to expressing themselves in written forms. Though she has been critiqued for what has been viewed as maintaining a rigid class distinction within her work through this editorial choice (Cooper 90), attempting to erase these class distinctions by having middle-class narrators narrate in a voice not their own would have been just as problematic as translating the oral Creole accounts into standard English.[10]

Lionheart Gal also draws heavily on Jamaican and Caribbean folkloric traditions. As Carolyn Cooper argues: "The language of narration is Jamaican, employing proverb, earthy metaphors and folk-tale structures, particularly repetition and apparent digression. In addition, the rural setting of many of the stories reinforces the sense of a 'folk' perspective" (89). Ford-Smith frames her introduction to the collection by evoking the images of Nanny of the Maroons (Ni), a historical figure credited with leading slave rebellions and whose legacy has since taken on mythic proportions (Sistren Theatre Collective xiii). The language of folklore is therefore central to the book's methodology, encoded within an oral language that pays respect to the "legacy of tale-telling which has always preserved the history of Caribbean women" (xv). This framing is strongly paralleled in the introductory section of *Walking on Fire*, "The Women of Millet Mountain." Bell, recounting an early memory of her introduction to Haitian women's oral storytelling practices, recounts a telling of the tale of Anacaona, an "Indian queen" who bravely fought against the Spanish invaders and who was killed by their hand (1). Anacaona's legacy serves to historically testify to the courage of Haitian women. Argues *griyo* Josie, "From Anacaona we were born. When you take our history . . . there were women there standing strong, right next to men. But they're rarely told about in history . . . unless a woman does the telling" (2).

Each text draws upon culturally specific storytelling practices, including the use of locationally distinct metaphors and paradigms. For example, *Playing with Fire* uses the metaphor of "monsoon clouds" to address the weight of the tears the women experienced when sharing their stories with each other (Sangtin Writers 9). Later, the *sangtins* frame inadequate attempts made by development initiatives to address rural poverty in India by using proverb: "The resources made available to the rural poor can be likened to a cumin seed in the mouth of a camel: they are too small to have an impact" (129). In *Walking on Fire*, Bell uses the metaphor of "*peze souse*" to epitomize the conditions of poor Haitian women: "Popular snacks in Haiti are *peze souse*, squeeze and suck, frozen pops . . . The *istwas* in this chapter are told by women being consumed like a *peze souse*" (24). In *Lionheart Gal*'s "Rock Stone a River Bottom No Know Sun Hot," the narrator illustrates her point by recounting a saying her mother used to repeat: "'Member seh man a green lizard,' she used to say. 'Man is a ting weh change. Di instant when dem see one next woman, dem no waan bodder deal wid yuh, especially when dem see yuh tight pon yuh money.' Yuh see, she was disappointed by a man and dat cause her fi go tru a whole heap" (Sistren Theatre Collective 45). Meant to teach her daughter to be wary of relationships with men, her mother's encoding of men as "green lizards" illustrates the pedagogical creativity of the folk tradition, while the daughter's decoding (marked by "Yuh see") highlights how the faculties of the imagination are also used to interpret social truths.

Walking on Fire, while written mainly in standard English, incorporates several phrases and expressions through a written version of Haitian Creole. It also includes interview responses that directly address the importance of using the Creole to communicate with poor Haitians who do not have access to Standard French, as in Lelenne Gilles's "I'll Die with the Words on My Lips" (Bell 68). Bell is careful to frame the interviewees as "*griyos*," a Creole word for storytellers of history, "the repositories and transmitters of wisdom and knowledge" (xv). As she articulates, the "best description of these narratives is the Creole word *istwa*, meaning both story and history. Borrowing on the tradition of the venerated storyteller, which stretches back to Africa and extends across Haiti, those who give their *istwa* here are termed *griyo* . . . In this predominantly oral culture, the *griyo* guard the word and determine how the word is spoken. The women in *Walking on Fire* are far younger than traditional *griyo* elders, and to my knowledge none holds this honor in her own family or village. Yet in this book, they are the keepers and recounters of history, truth, and wisdom" (xv). By providing a preliminary framing that roots the stories in their historical and cultural context, Bell alters the way in which readers come to engage with the work.

Of the four texts, *Telling to Live* is the only one *not* to include an extended glossary for phrases and vocabulary falling outside of standard English. This too is a contextual choice. As a US-based text, the work's mixture of English and Spanish is a political act in a cultural climate in which Spanish is framed as a linguistic invader of an English-only American identity. So too is the Latina Feminist Group's decision to assert knowledge claims through both languages an enactment of the linguistic borderlands, and a linguistic embodiment of hybridized knowledges and cultural identities. Indeed, more so than Hindi, Haitian Creole, and Jamaican Creole, Spanish occupies an increasingly dominant position in US culture, and the non-inclusion of a Spanish glossary indirectly comments on the need for non-Spanish speakers to overcome linguistic and cultural monolingualism and to interact with the Latina Feminist Group's reflections on their own terms and in their own language(s).

By representing social knowledge claims in their own voices—linguistically, idiomatically—these *griyos, sangtins, testimoniadoras,* and Sistren members model forms of resistant linguistic subjectivity, a linguistic praxis that democratizes knowledge production. Lest we question the ability of theory-in-the-vernacular to successfully reach the "halls of power," the fallout of *Playing with Fire*'s language choices proves that one need not only operate in globally dominant language systems to strike institutional fear. As the *sangtins* recount, it was not their English translation that led NSY to take up disciplinary efforts against the eight *sangtins* who at the time worked for the NGO that served as the object of their critiques. Rather, it was precisely their adoption of local languages—specifically Awadhi and Hindi—and their locational and discursive proximity to the institutional practices they critiqued that led to NSY's panic: "Because *Sangtin Yatra* launched the collective's critique in a form that refused to isolate the voices of the nine authors or to highlight the 'expert' voices of a research or a higher-level NGO official, and because the critique was circulated and disseminated in the political and discursive spaces of the 'vernacular' where grassroots NGO actors operated, it became dangerous" (Sangtin Writers 141). The *griyos* in *Walking on Fire* provide a similar analysis regarding the function of the radio station Radio Cacique under the Duvalier regime in the 1980s, a self-defined "station of struggle" that delivered the news in Haitian Creole in an attempt to reach poor populations who were illiterate, did not speak French, or both (Bell 68).

As these examples illustrate, the ability of language to reinforce or destabilize dominant structures of power is context specific, and testimonios must therefore carefully consider questions of audience when asserting knowledge claims. The multilingual and multiperspective practices espoused by polyvocal activist feminist testimonio also allow for the possibility of connecting with multiple audiences. By alternating between language systems and registers, culturally specific and far-reaching idioms, these polyvocal framings allow for specific analyses to simultaneously reach the ears of disparate reading audiences in different registers. Indeed, *Playing with Fire* states that its original Hindi publication symbolizes that "those ideas were being produced, first and foremost, for the group's own communities, friends, and close allies rather than for dissemination to the activists from above" (Sangtin Writers xxxvi).

In contrast to the long-held assumption that the primary function of testimonio is to reach the ears of a first world audience in order to cultivate support, contemporary polyvocal feminist testimonios utilize co-narration and multilingualism to connect with other social justice projects and to embody their theoretical and methodological processes in paradigms capable of furthering egalitarian feminist organizing initiatives.

CHAPTER 5

Resisting Representational Stasis
Dialogic Collaborations in Flux

> Our purpose in describing our process of coming together and
> collaborating over seven years is to illustrate how we came to
> theorize feminist *latinidades* through *testimonio*. While our writings
> may stand on their own, our collaborative process, which used the
> method of *testimonio*, ultimately was framed by common political
> views about how to create knowledge and theory through our
> experiences. In this way, product and process became inseparable.
>
> —LATINA FEMINIST GROUP, *TELLING TO LIVE*

> The complexities of these processes cannot be captured by a formula,
> nor can this kind of writing ever be contained within rules. For this
> reason, in the following pages you will find that even when a conversa-
> tion on a specific topic begins, its focus moves in multiple directions.
>
> —SANGTIN WRITERS, *PLAYING WITH FIRE*

INSOFAR AS THESE TEXTS INTENTIONALLY ENTER THE TERRAIN OF
knowledge production as a way of writing against static, monolithic representational models, they must somehow account for how their storytelling methodology works to articulate epistemic knowledge in *flux*. In order
to accomplish this, these works overtly frame how they want readers to
understand their critical interventions and contributions, allowing them
to more actively shape their texts for racially and geopolitically diverse
audiences. One of their central framing strategies is the development of
extensive methodology sections as a way to set the stage for the social
knowledge their life narratives put forth.

While texts such as *Rigoberta Menchú* and *Lionheart Gal* establish critical frameworks within their introductions for understanding the underlying political assumptions and trajectories of their projects, more recent texts, such as *Walking on Fire*, *Telling to Live*, and *Playing with Fire*, demonstrate how feminist methodology sections have grown increasingly detailed. By actively highlighting a work's underlying theoretical impetus, such discussions work to "legitimize" their stories as knowledge that should be taken seriously by institutional spheres of knowledge production, including academia and development initiatives. These sections document how the group's collaborative processes of writing and reflection become translated into book form and how the book connects to larger goals.

As evidenced by *Walking on Fire* and the work of Margaret Randall, even when a feminist testimonio is not the result of a collective process, the methodology sections intricately document the extent to which feminist collaborative methods have been employed, in turn challenging the dichotomization of theory and method. By highlighting the collective labors that have produced the finished document and bringing into view the particularities of the practitioners' social worlds, the texts render visible the complex social processes that have brought their texts into existence. Through a discussion of the extraliterary factors that have shaped the finished document, feminist activist testimonios highlight a critical component of their intellectual, political, and representational praxis: a process- rather than product-based approach.

This commitment to process can be traced back to foundational feminist testimonial methods. Oral historian Margaret Randall refers to this self-consciously collective, dialogic mode of telling and listening as a "practice," a way of "telling a story [that] is not product-oriented like the traditional (male-defined) [story] based on 'events' . . . we offer process" ("Reclaiming Voices" 61). As a democratic narrative-based storytelling methodology attentive to nuance and contradiction, the processes that create the space for these life narratives to emerge are just as important as the stories themselves, especially given the pedagogical intent of these works. Through this process-based approach, they offer nuanced engagements with questions of privilege while reminding us that the organization and production of knowledge are as important as the final product.

These detailed methodology sections, which rehearse the collective labors that inform the document, also allow the work to reach different audiences in different registers, while the extraliterary backdrops aid in how these audiences encounter the narratives. For instance, if readers are racially and/or geopolitically privileged, as criticism on traditional testimonio has assumed, these sections verse their readerships in the sociopolitical specificities in which the work seeks to intervene. If readers are racially and/or geopolitically marginalized, or already embedded in social justice efforts, the documentation of a collective's processes can help generate ideas on how to adapt and enact the methods espoused by the collective to suit their own situational needs. The visibility of labor processes also counteracts the likelihood of readers reducing them to transparent, positivist "evidence."

It is ironic that these works, which resist analytical and representational stasis through the penning of dynamic life narratives, boast intricately detailed methodology sections that record anything from specific dates of group meetings, to gender-based economic statistics, to clear statements of a project's intended goals. This trafficking in traditional analytical paradigms (i.e., recognizable "academic speak") serves a Sandovalian purpose. By utilizing familiar paradigms of what constitutes "knowledge," these works gain legitimacy and trust. Such careful documentation and framing is both poignant and practical; should the fluid, multilayered representational practices evidenced by the nuanced storytelling methods raise doubts on whether a given text lacks a central theoretical framework—or whether it is "just" a collection of compelling stories—the methodology section serves to displace these suspicions with an articulation of each project's focused interventions and goals.

Of the four texts, *Playing with Fire* and *Telling to Live* both employ the term "methodology" to refer to their projects. While *Telling to Live* explicitly names testimonio as its methodology of choice (Latina Feminist Group 8), *Playing with Fire* articulates how the *sangtins* chose diary writing as a centerpiece through which to realize their methodology: "Our main goal at the outset was to imagine and mold a methodology that would enable us to reflect and understand our lives and work and give us the strength and perspective to envision our future directions" (Sangtin Writers 8). This responsive and context-aware approach bespeaks an open-ended, explorative methodology—"Let's try this and we'll see where it takes us"—that illustrates a decidedly pedagogical and process- rather than product-oriented approach. Rather than "applying" a one-size-fits-all structure, which invites premature conclusions, these projects adapt their narratives to best suit their individual projects in a way that is both focused ("What do we want to get out of this?") and flexible ("How should we go about achieving this?" "What do we take these responses to mean?").

Before mapping out the specifics of their interventions, practitioners paint a detailed social backdrop for their projects. These conditions of emergence may alternately be located temporally, organizationally, or materially, and help to set the imaginative stage for contextualizing each collection of life stories. For instance, *Playing with Fire*, *Walking on Fire*, and *Lionheart Gal* incorporate brief histories and statistics meant to raise the consciousness of their readership by introducing critical aspects of the cultural landscapes with which they engage.

In the "Status of Haitian Women" section of *Walking on Fire*'s introduction, statistical information is provided on the gendered division of labor, women's roles in factory work, intimate partner violence, state-sponsored violence, and gendered property rights (Bell 18–19). The introduction to *Lionheart Gal* similarly provides a gendered account of employment rates and the division of labor while also providing information on women-headed households and the role of migration (Sistren Theatre Collective xvi). In *Playing with Fire*, the *sangtins* provide statistics on the socioeconomic conditions of Sitapur district while summarizing the area's sociopolitical landscape, with a particular emphasis on the introduction of NGOs to the area in the mid-1990s (Sangtin Writers xxvi). *Lionheart Gal* and *Walking on Fire* perform similar sociohistorical overviews for readers unacquainted with the area's specific context. As a text set in the political landscape of the US academy, *Telling to Live* differently situates itself in genealogical relation to Chicana feminist thought. These elements serve to define testimonio as a "socioliterary" writing form that highlights the social science training of many of its practitioners.

Contextual framings occur on other textual levels as well. Bell and Ford-Smith locate the women's stories within Haitian and Jamaican cultural folkloric traditions. *Playing with Fire* locates the place-based ethos of the *sangtins'* analyses by documenting how this text, a translation of the Hindi book *Sangtin Yatra*, is meant to bring attention to the disciplinary action brought against them for writing critically of NSY (Sangtin Writers xiii). The "place" that *Playing with Fire* occupies is therefore as situational and ideological as it is geopolitical; by cultivating a transnational network of solidarity, it places itself in a larger struggle over knowledge production.

The importance of place is also evidenced on a more literal level in the documentation of the conditions under which the collectives and interviewees met. For instance, in *Walking on Fire*, Bell paints a detailed picture of the material and cultural conditions in which the interviews were carried out:

> Women told their stories in sweltering tin shacks with flies buzzing around our sweat-covered bodies, in dirt yards with goats or chickens, and in an underground organizing center scarred with the broken windows and battered doors of a recent military attack. One woman recounted her story on a rooftop in a raging thunderstorm, another in a vodou temple, a third in a busy coffin-manufacturing workshop. The women and I sat on cement floors or lumpy beds or chairs with no seats. Often it was a strain to hear the women over the noise of children and roosters and car horns. Over and over, meetings took place in the pitch darkness of a *blakaout*, blackout, when whole parts of town—more often than not, the poor parts—lost electricity. (xiv)

If this passage borders on perpetuating a possibly dangerous picture of the desperate material conditions in which Haitian women find themselves, it is a line toed with purpose. The sensorial directives cueing the bustling sounds, extreme heat, and lack of comfortable meeting spaces (whether due to economic, military, or infrastructural concerns) reinforce the devotion and seriousness with which the *griyos* convey their stories. What might seem to be extreme conditions to a socially removed reading audience are instead put forth as the familiar sounds and events of daily life. This descriptive passage thus brings to life a dynamic sociopolitical backdrop that sharpens the significance of the poignant insights delivered by the *griyos* in less-than-ideal material conditions.

Telling to Live also focuses on the significance of the physical space in which the collective met—Baca, Colorado—but shifts its focus to the spiritual and symbolic dimensions of this meeting place:

Baca is literally on the Central Divide, in the middle of the country. Meeting at Baca was fortuitous, a real turning point for us as a group . . . Part of the magic of Baca is that historically it is a site of spiritual meaning, a sacred space for Native Americans where there have never been wars between indigenous peoples. The Sangre de Cristo Mountains are the mythical place of emergence for the Navajo, who were displaced by the violent incursions of Spanish and Anglo settlers. Today Baca is home to a diverse group of spiritual traditions, including a Christian monastery, a Buddhist temple, a Zen meditation center, and a Hindu ashram. For us, Baca became a site that inspired narration. (Latina Feminist Group 13)

Baca's location in the middle of the US is certainly noteworthy given the collective's commitment to bridging regional differences. Given the social intimacies and overlapping histories of indigenous and Latinx groups in what became the US, Baca is also significant in its particular history of settler colonialism and the ways in which historical displacement continues to affect social relations. The multiple spiritual centers currently located in Baca, in tandem with its historic lack of intergroup conflict between Native Americans, mark it a powerful site of successful border crossings and negotiations. If the Latina Feminist Group considers its "sustaining practice of community" as a "gift to other Latinas, particularly young women, to inspire them to create their own expressions of feminist Latina identities," then the border-crossing ethos of Baca seems especially resonant (21).

Once context is established, the methodology sections provide an overview of the prompts and goals that motivate the project/collective. The documentation of the specific prompts that led to each work reinforces the issues they deem most important, and why specific themes remain prominent in the main body of the text. In *Lionheart Gal*, a text concerned with understanding how women are oppressed *as women* in the Jamaican context, Ford-Smith relied on three initial interview prompts: "How did you first become aware of the fact that you were oppressed as a woman? How did that experience affect your life? How have you tried to change it?" (Sistren Theatre Collective xxvii). In reading these three preliminary questions, one is better able to see the skeletal progression of *Lionheart Gal*'s individual narratives: an articulation of one or more childhood events that raised questions for the speaker on the inevitability of her gender restrictions; a description of consequences, emotions, and life choices stemming from these events; and perspective on overcoming or facing these circumstances.

In *Walking on Fire*, Bell used a more open-ended prompt: "Tell me anything you want about your life, about what it's like to be a Haitian woman" (xv). The collection's organization of thematic chapters seeks to account for the wide-ranging responses she received, with "resistance" as the enjoining theme ("Resistance for Political and Economic Change," "Resistance as Expression"). In the case of *Playing with Fire*, initial life writing focused on childhood, adolescence, and sexuality (Sangtin Writers xxix), topics that were used as a way to articulate sites of inherited social difference that influenced tensions between individual members of the collective, and that were exaggerated by the hierarchical structure of the NGO where most were employed. As in the rest of the text, the prompts are not included in the final manuscript so as to direct attention away from the "raw material" of their labors and to focus on *how* and *why* life writing was used within the larger project. This rhetorical choice critiques the hierarchical NGO and dominant research practices in which the testimonies of oppressed subjects are used as raw material to advance agendas that the storytellers are locked out of.

Often, these initial prompts are responsible for facilitating multistage projects. Both *Playing with Fire* and *Telling to Live* highlight their reliance on a series of prompts in which the responses given shaped future directions of the collective, as well as the next set of prompts. For the *testimoniadoras*, the initial prompts that shaped *Telling to Live* operate on a meta-level that bespeaks the group's prior awareness of testimonio as methodology: "How do we bear witness to our own becoming? How do we define who we are? How have we made *testimonio* the core of our work? What are some important turning points of consciousness? What is our relationship to political identities and intellectual work? What is our relationship to building new paradigms or models? What are we transgressing?" (Latina Feminist Group 12). While individual accounts range from thought provoking to stylistically stunning, the collection is marked by a lack of internal consistency that seems symptomatic of this ambitious and ubiquitous question set. The strongest resonances across texts speak to the more concrete and experientially based question subset focused on why and how women within the group came to academia: "Why did we pursue higher education? What did we think we were doing? What was the enticement? What did we get out of it?" (13). Given that one of the collective's goals is to more thoroughly articulate the overlaps and departures between Latinas with distinct ethnic, national, religious, and sexual backgrounds, the unruly range of topics and forms actively writes against the effects of pan-ethnic consolidation.

While the inclusion of thematic prompts works to actively frame the issues that brought the practitioners to collectively pursue the project, they also articulate the text's pedagogical intentions by identifying the specific goals they hope to achieve through this discursive representation of their labors. These framings are as diverse as their social situations. While *Walking on Fire* places importance on diversifying representations of "poor Haitian women," the *sangtins* downplay their concern with representational "accuracy," arguing instead that the "usefulness or effectiveness of *Playing with Fire* . . . [should] be assessed not in terms of whether it accurately or authentically represents the *sangtins* to the readers but on the basis of whether and how it can become a part of the authors' individual and collective agency and serve activism out of which the book evolved" (Sangtin Writers 154). In *Lionheart Gal*, Ford-Smith focuses on the importance of creative expression in women's processes of self-actualization by suggesting that the stories "attest to the fact that when women select their own creative organisational forms, they begin to build a base from which they do transform their lives" (Sistren Theatre Collective xx). Ford-Smith places particular emphasis on Sistren's *collective* creative process; for Sistren, a central function of *Lionheart Gal* is to move beyond gaining "recognition" for the lives of working-class Jamaican women by illustrating the type of knowledge that can be produced when the creative and the political are linked through artistic collaboration.

In the spirit of their process-based approach, the methodology sections do not simply state the project's "hoped-for" goals; they also document the path leading up to the finished document by making visible the accumulated "backstage" labors of their "staged performances." In doing so, they render their story-based methodology intelligible *as* legitimate social knowledge while simultaneously critiquing and transforming the way in which knowledge is generated. This is especially true of testimonios authored as part of a collective that document how and when the collective first emerged; the issues around which they organized; the conditions under which they met; critical dates, events, and stages that shaped the process and form of book writing; internal and external challenges and how they have been addressed; and how the book fits into the collective's larger goals and political platform. Beyond the articulation of the logistical details, the practitioners also detail the labor involved in the processes of the memory and dream work that went into the final document.

Out of the four texts engaged in this chapter, *Playing with Fire* and *Telling to Live* are the most explicit in framing their books in terms of labor and work. A subsection of *Playing with Fire*'s introduction is called "The Labor Process" (Sangtin Writers xxix). In the introduction to *Telling to Live*, the Latina Feminist Group informs the reader that the production of the text "involved an elaborate collaboration and division of labor among eighteen women of diverse Latina backgrounds . . . When we think about the work we have accomplished, we envision not only the product but the human connection between us, the *cariño* (affection), *respeto* (respect), and commitment to each other" (xi). It is not just logistical, but also *emotional* labors that are given weight and rendered visible. *Playing with Fire* similarly attests to the essential role that vulnerability played in strengthening group commitment (xxxvii), reinforcing how tears were shed at almost every group meeting.

Emotional labor is positioned as a critical component of each project, with trust being an overlapping theme. But it is not a naïve trust that is vocalized. Rather, it is a trust emerging from extended dialogue, time spent together, and intellectual and political disagreement. The documentation of intragroup trust emerging from sustained dialogue is clearly evidenced by how the testifiers discursively frame themselves as "*sangtins*," "Sistren," "*testimoniadoras*," and "*griyos*," culturally resonant terms that denote an intragroup commitment to reciprocity, accountability, and solidarity. Collective emotional, intellectual, and political trust thus becomes a necessary ingredient for moving beyond superficial solidarity efforts, crossing social boundaries, and establishing lasting relationships with group members that extend beyond the collective's immediate goals.

Insofar as the methodology sections highlight the multifaceted labor processes that lie outside the purview of self-contained life narratives, this focus on labor also dovetails with another critical component of their collaborative methodologies: dialogic process. As Paulo Freire explains, "Dialogue becomes a horizontal relationship of which mutual trust between the dialoguers is the logical consequence. It would be a contradiction in terms if dialogue—loving, humble, and full of faith—did not produce this climate of mutual trust, which leads dialoguers into ever close partnership in the naming of the world" (91). As Ford-Smith recounts in an afterword penned in 2005, "This commitment to dialogue and to small-scale coalition and collaboration across what is now called difference was the ethical centerpiece of the early work of Sistren, and of this collection . . . It would not have been possible without a commitment to this process over a protracted period of time" (296). The Latina Feminist Group articulates a similar political conviction: "To write and theorize about a range of Latina experiences . . . required being in sustained dialogue with one another. Hence, we were motivated to convene physically in one place and begin this process" (9).

Telling to Live's assertion that "sharing can begin a process of empowerment" reiterates the importance of sustained intragroup dialogue (Latina Feminist Group 1). In *Lionheart Gal* Ford-Smith highlights how the production of the book is one manifestation of the collective's dialogic processes of writing and reflection: "Each finished testimony still remains to be discussed as fully as it deserves within the group. In a sense until this is done, the work process will not be complete" (5). Even when the works are not the result of a collective, individual life narratives highlight how the practitioners are elsewhere involved in collective efforts. As Claudette Phene suggests in *Walking on Fire's* "A Little Light": "When you get into an organization, you change completely. What makes you change? I come to see you, know you, share ideas. That allows a change in both of us" (Bell 115). While a wider readership is invited to read and engage with the knowledge produced by each text, this focus on sustained intragroup dialogue reinforces how the discussions internal to the collective are necessary for the accomplishment of the collective's immediate goals. In this way, feminist testimonios redefine the dialogic function of traditional testimonio by insisting that their primary relationship is with the women who have told their stories through extensive processes of telling/writing and reflecting, often in a collaborative setting; it is only following these labors that an invitation is extended to outside audiences.

These works highlight the importance of dialogue *outside* of their methodology sections as well. By incorporating detailed testaments on the power of dialogics throughout the body of the text, the works convey the power of interpersonal exchange to produce foundational social change while actively highlighting how their dialogic methodologies have meaning beyond the locational specificity of their chosen intervention, shifting the reader's attention to a more careful awareness of the processes and underlying theory that led to the development of the text.

This emphasis on dialogic process does not suggest that the principles of "sharing" and "trust" were arrived at easily. Rather, sharing and trust become markers of the sustained emotional labor the project/collective achieved through hard work. As member of the Latina Feminist Group Luz del Alba Acevedo recounts, "What I experienced was the kind of friendship built through disagreements, critical discussions, and caring constructive arguments directed to enrich rather than diminish and discredit our personal lives and work" (261). A critical enabling factor in these productive interactions is that rather than assuming shared perspectives and experiences, the Latina Feminist Group began with a deconstruction of "Latina," an exercise that encouraged productive critical dialogue between members with different knowledge bases and social perspectives, "an open negotiation of difference" (20).

This marks a critical departure from earlier feminist consciousness-raising initiatives based on a presumption of sameness and social sharedness as "women," enacting a "connected" activist paradigm (Medina 229) in which difference need not be suppressed for solidarity to be achieved. As Chandra Mohanty notes in the foreword to *Playing with Fire*, "The memory work of the Sangtin Writers [embodies] the differences *within* women's collectives—the caste, class, and religious tensions that enable women from distinct backgrounds and lifeways to work, struggle, and imagine a collective space of empowerment for themselves and their sisters . . . the *sangtins* assume no such shared experience: their collectively crafted individual stories are shaped through painful dialogue" (Sangtin Writers xiii). Indeed, as the *sangtins* reflect, "It is extremely difficult for all of us to challenge one another on the question of caste difference to this day" (83). As the *sangtins* make clear, central to these intragroup negotiations of social difference are the varying levels of social power present within the group, whether in terms of geopolitical, class, sexual, linguistic, educational, or religious privilege, to name a few. Dialogue, rather than represented as an uninhibited exchange of ideas, is reconceived as a fraught, fought-for space that creates the grounds of epistemic friction that enable border crossings to occur.

This representational choice to enact a commitment to dialogue is also evidenced by the inclusion and exclusion of certain social voices, as each project handles class and geopolitical privilege differently. As noted, *Lionheart Gal* maintains a linguistic stratification that renders visible the class separation between the majority of working-class members and the two middle-class members of Sistren by narrating the respective accounts in Jamaican Creole and standard English. The narratives of the Latina Feminist Group bespeak material differences (specifically that of graduate student members versus full professors, concerning family backgrounds and professional trajectories), and yet the members of the group still choose to highlight their converging social positions as Latinas working within the US academy. *Playing with Fire*, in its observance of the extreme power and experiential differences between the field workers and the middle-class *sangtins* (one a US professor, the other a one-time regional NGO coordinator), while collectively organized as the "Sangtin Writers," chose to incorporate only the life stories of the seven field workers, not the narratives of the middle-class *sangtins*; the group decided that such inclusion would take attention away from the social struggles experienced by the majority.

In *Walking on Fire*, Bell states her commitment to focusing on the life stories of poor and peasant Haitian women, but does still incorporate a select few middle-class voices, whose actions, she suggests, have signified a sustained political commitment to stand and struggle alongside those most marginalized. Bell's incorporation of these voices performs an alternate pedagogical function, as the middle-class narrators explicitly name their socially privileged backgrounds and articulate a defining moment in which they actively chose to align themselves with the political struggles of underclass Haitians. Given that Bell marketed this book to a US readership, these narratives of social privilege assume a meta-instructional quality on how readers can adapt a similar stance of political solidarity by recognizing their epistemic responsibility.[1] Indeed, the notion of "privilege" is frequently rewritten as "responsibility." As articulated by *griyo* Lise-Marie Dejean: "For me, power is a service. When I'm in power, I'm in a position that lets me serve the most people possible . . . I don't conceive of power as a privilege. You yourself may be at the table, but you're at the service of the people, you see. You're educating people to let them participate in power" (216). This participatory framework is echoed by the middle-class narrators throughout *Walking on Fire*. Says *griyo* Myrto Celestin Saurel, "Our partners in power must make a special effort to listen to those who do not shout" (227).

Acknowledging these responsibilities and intragroup social hierarchies, but not becoming paralyzed by them, marks the increasingly self-reflexive methodologies of contemporary polyvocal activist feminist testimonio and confronts the possibilities and foreclosures of differently positioned women working in coalitional alliance. Each text's polyvocal framework reminds us that the naming of social difference in the context of social justice organizing works not so much to identify difference as difference as to identify potential border crossings, social possibilities, and coalitional convergences. As the Latina Feminist Group reflects, whatever social differences exist between members of the collective, their project was nevertheless "framed by common political views about how to create knowledge and theory through our experiences" (8). These epistemological convergences align them in a shared political vision and temporarily and situationally override individual social differences even while they do not overcome them.

Each text's commitment to dialogue reminds readers that while the particularities of their project are context specific, their underlying methods are not. Beyond the documentation of a collective's immediate intragroup dialogue, then, the importance of dialogic process is emphasized as an integral component of social justice movements. In "Minister of the Status and Rights of Women," Lise-Marie Dejean recounts how she came to be appointed minister by President Aristide. Specifically, Dejean remembers two demonstrations that occurred while she served in that position: "While I was minister, there were two big demonstrations against the ministry. Some people couldn't understand why that pleased me. But we don't have the solution for everything; it's normal that people question us . . . That demonstration gave me more strength to put pressure on" (Bell 161). Dejean's recognition that protests encourage political dialogue is evident in her suggestion that "if you want decentralized power, you must begin by sitting with people and listening to them. This let[s] us sharpen our programs to be in touch with the women and respond to their needs" (160). Dejean's commitment to participatory democracy is clearly expressed in this statement and reinforces the broader political importance of dialogic interaction in social justice efforts.

Insofar as the discursive representations of their labors bespeak a textual praxis, their detailed accounts of the labor processes and sustained dialogues undertaken throughout the production of the text perform a pedagogical function in reminding audiences that their theory and methods are intertwined. While process and dialogue form two quintessential tropes in contemporary polyvocal feminist testimonios, these works also employ more direct ways of interpellating the reader; these are closely explored in the next section.

Interpellating the Reader and the Power of Direct Address

The polyvocal strategy of feminist activist testimonio structurally "deliberates" on the epistemological possibility of coexisting truths. It insists on contradiction and utilizes this textual framework to signal its commitment to working through social difference and bridging epistemic worlds. While these works make effective horizontal connections with other transnational feminist activists, this section turns attention to the rhetorical strategies that also make them connect with racially and geopolitically privileged readerships. As Kimberly Nance asserts, polyvocal feminist activist testimonio is a prime example of the "deliberative" strand of this writing form, "a literature of people who do not expect soon to be able to control official versions, and who are insistent and candid in acknowledging errors, contradiction, and dissent within their own ranks" (36). These moments of dissent and ambivalence are channeled to affect the interpretive practices of the reading audience by paradoxically increasing the level of trust they have in truth claims put forth by the text, precisely by calling attention to the limits of their knowledge claims.

If the overall polyvocal framework signals the large-scale evidence of these deliberative methodologies, they can also be found at seemingly unnoteworthy moments. For instance, in *Telling to Live*'s "Silence Begins at Home," Patricia Zavella opens her narrative with an attempt to re-create her maternal lineage. Rather than presenting herself as one hundred percent clear on the genealogical picture she paints, she interrupts herself with, "I think. From my attempts to piece together my grandmother's story, I learned that she was one of fourteen children, with two sets of twins . . . Grandma does not want to tell any more about her history" (Latina Feminist Group 43, 44). This moment of narrative ambivalence, while calling attention to the limits of her own knowledge and the less-than-objective nature of historical memory, paradoxically marks the rest of what she says as more honest and trustworthy; if she is willing to call attention to that which she does not know, so the reader reasons, she must be confident in the social information that she *does* present. This narrative digression performs an informal discussion between friends, more of a real-time discussion rather than closed text. These moments of contradiction, dissent, and confusion are purposeful. If "deliberating" on the imperfect processes and collective tensions that mark their organizing initiatives serves a pedagogical function in encouraging their readers to think more sharply about ways of working through social difference, then so do these small-scale narrative maneuvers encourage readers to deliberate on their own epistemic truths.

As Nance argues, the project of deliberative testimonio actively encourages readers to call into question the assumed stability of their worldview and to more fully realize the messy webs of entanglement between themselves and the lives at the center of the text: "The future orientation of deliberative testimonio requires a hybrid and much more sophisticated rhetorical strategy, one that will persuade readers to think critically about the world at the same time that it confronts them with a personal obligation to combat injustice" (38). In order to accomplish this, deliberative testimonios must groom their readers to make them feel comfortable enough to have their worldviews challenged. As Nance argues, the "rhetorical strategy is to get readers to accept a certain definition of themselves so that they will then feel obligated to live up to it" (59). As such, feminist activist polyvocal testimonios must actively *construct* their readers if they are to successfully redirect their defensive disengagements and interpellate them as allies to their cause. By *antici-pating* and *directing* their responses toward empathetic readings of their works, they create and direct their readers-turned-allies by interpellating the reader on two main levels. First, these works extend the peda-gogical function of their methodology sections by incorporating instructional passages that model alternative modes of engagement and train the reader to read and see differently. Second, individual life narratives house a range of rhetorical devices that subtly—and sometimes explicitly—direct the reader's interpretive processes, most notably accomplished through modes of direct address.

To varying degrees, these rhetorical devices utilize pathos—a focused deployment of emotion—in order to gain full access to the reader's ana-lytical and emotional worlds. In *Lionheart Gal*, Ford-Smith recounts how the importance of the collection's story-based approach as a paradigm necessarily engages the imaginative capabilities of its readership, which in turn "evokes both thought and feeling" (Sistren Theatre Collective xvi), leading readers to "reason" with both head and heart.

In fact, the very language of "head and heart" is utilized by the Sangtin Writers to great effect. In one of the collection's distinctive interpretive codas, the *sangtins* state: "Along with the sharpening of our analytical abilities, we wish to open the doors of others' hearts in such a way that we all can find enough space to fight our battles against everyday social, physical, and emotional exploitation, so that the voices that have been suffocating for years can find the desired notes to sing and scream" (67). Beyond the aesthetic force of this statement, the phrase "emotional exploitation" serves as a powerful reminder that oppression is multidimensional—that knowing the "facts" of a social situation does not constitute *understanding* it. The *sangtins* state how their "only wish is to find the strength to end the restlessness caused by the half-shut boxes that are still hiding in [their] chests," where the imagery of "half-shut boxes" serves as both invitation and challenge to their readership, an opportunity to decolonize their own world views and "clean house." Readers must open their own "half-shut boxes" to fully experience the emotional power and social truths the *sangtins'* stories convey, and to more fully understand the multidimensionality of epistemic truths.

Lest readers surmise that this utilization of pathos is a thinly veiled attempt to "win readers over," the *sangtins* assure them that it is the collective's simultaneous analytic and emotional labor that has marked the liberatory possibilities of their journey: "Whenever we have confronted this reality, we have acutely realized how difficult it has been to release ourselves from the values and fears that were instilled in us in the name of religion and purity. But our collective struggles with these messy questions have also loosened many knots in our heads and hearts" (89). The image of knotted heads and hearts is one that "travels" fairly easily to signify the confusion and consequent emotional hardness that social circumstances can lead to and is made all the more effective because it is immediately followed by the statement that "attempts are being made to fill our children's brains with the same communal hatred and fears that were once stuffed into our brains" (89). The image of forceful inundation—of being the unknowing and unwilling participant of social prejudice—especially when framed as a perpetual, intergenerational, and unceasing action, reiterates that if it is the "brain" that is responsible for perpetuating such social inequity; clearly, then, the "head and heart" are needed to heal from and confront such oppression.

But if the emotional dimensions of reader responses are actively cultivated, they are also eased into. The analytical frameworks utilized by the methodology sections serve to put the reader at ease by communicating that the pathos-based life stories each collection houses are nonetheless authored by people of "sense." This balance between the objective and subjective makes it more possible for the life narratives to be interpreted as social knowledge rather than as "raw material."

For example, in *Walking on Fire*, Beverly Bell devotes much time to providing working definitions of seemingly basic but foundational terms used within the text, such as "resistance," "power," and "solidarity." These directives cue readers to temporarily suspend their own understandings of these terms in order to engage with how these terms work in the lives of the collection's *griyos*. Bell's discussion of "resistance" proves to be the most detailed and powerful. While the shorthand definition offered is "the negotiation of power by the weaker against the strong" (5), she soon follows this up by suggesting how the "standard criteria are far too narrow to encapsulate the breadth of Haitian resistance" (5). Further: "The definition of resistance is expanded to include any act that keeps the margins of power from being further encroached upon, even where the protagonist cannot expand those margins. Given the forces arrayed against a Haitian woman, simply to *kenbe la*, hold the line—even without making any advance—is a victory. If she does no more than maintain her resources and rights—in the face of attempts by other people, institutions, or systems to deny her them—then she practices resistance" (5).

Here Bell succinctly contests and redirects standard understandings of large-scale resistance efforts and replaces them with an alternate yet equally as powerful understanding of resistance in this specific context. Given the extremity of Haiti's poverty and illiteracy rates, Bell asserts that survival itself can be a "purposeful act of defiance" (5). In so doing, Bell directs the reader to engage with the narratives with a more nuanced eye, attuned to the reality that in this context "resistance is often subtle or imperceptible. It bubbles beneath the surface, outside obvious public domains. Even where the women appear to be quiescent or the margins of maneuverability to be completely constrained, they might be engaged in multilayered negotiations of power" (6). Bell is doing more than providing her working definition of "resistance." She is giving the reader a crash course in understanding resistance efforts as seen from below and penning her own epistemology of resistance. By rejecting textbook definitions, she provides a realist perspective on the scale of the daily tactical maneuvers employed by Haitian women to fight against further denial of agency. Indeed, Bell's discussion of resistance could easily translate to a nuanced understanding of what agency looks like in restrictive conditions.[2]

Bell moves beyond the incorporation of detailed definitions to connect these concepts to actual circumstances as lived by the *griyos* whose voices are heard within the book. In a subsection entitled "Daily Acts of Resistance" in the book's first chapter, "Resistance in Survival," Bell explicitly states how "detecting the prevalence of dissent among Haitian women necessitates radically changing one's perceptions of what resistance is and where to look for it" (25). Immediately following this claim, Bell gives her initial impression of *griyo* Roselie Jean-Juste:

> Her hand crippled by a beating from her husband, her face and
> carriage showing the strain of life on the run from him, at first

glance Roselie seems broken. On the contrary. When she came to our meeting to give her narrative, Roselie had just left a human rights advocate from whom she was seeking help. She also was engaged in complex self-protection strategies, including sleeping at a different house each night. And she was vehement about having her full story, including her husband's name, told in this book so as to publicize the man's brutality and pressure him to stop. (25)

Bell's interpretive framing of Roselie's situation assumes a "take this woman, here's how you might read her situation, here's what's really going on" approach and performs a literal rereading that encourages readers to revisit their own initial assumptions and biases and to engage the collection's *istwas* with a "widened gaze" (25) that makes it possible to broaden one's epistemic lens.

It is not that Bell attempts to "assign" agency to situations where it does not exist. Rather, a stated goal of the collection is to "demonstrate that there is no *absolute* line between power and powerlessness. How women challenge their constraints, or amass strength and resources *within* those constraints is the focus" (8). Without downplaying the complexity of the social context or the dire material conditions in which the women find themselves, Bell nevertheless aims at highlighting the determination and social consciousness of the women within these conditions. *Lionheart Gal*'s depiction of the social landscape of working-class black Jamaican women performs a similar function. The narratives are certainly not attuned to bourgeois notions of what defines feminist consciousness; rather, they provide richly detailed accounts of the social circumstances that working-class Jamaican women face.

In the introduction, Ford-Smith provides the formative directive that "these tales demand to be decoded" since the process of decoding "creates a situation in which the awareness of social contradictions is sharpened" (Sistren Theatre Collective xvi). Ford-Smith uses the example of Nanny of the Maroons to suggest how the folktale about her "bouncing bullets off her bottom" signifies on two simultaneous levels: it documents an event that might have happened, and it conveys a more far-reaching symbolism about the strength of Jamaican women (xvi). As such, Ford-Smith directs the reader to understand how "these stories are invaluable in the effort to change the effect of oppressive forces on [their] lives" (xvi).

Ford-Smith then enacts a series of critical decodings in which she walks readers through individual narrative accounts and discusses their thematic importance. In so doing, she reiterates how these accounts, which document situations of unemployment, intimate partner violence, and teen pregnancy, are always about more than the literal plot; these microsocial events simultaneously correspond to larger macrosocial forces of gender inequity, globalization, migration, and the education system. The very narrative structure of Ford-Smith's walk-through illustrates this point as she fluidly interweaves social analysis with discussions of how the macrosocial is evidenced within specific narrative accounts, in turn modeling a process of decoding multiple registers of meaning-making.

In contrast to how *Lionheart Gal* provides an initial interpretive framework and then sends readers off on their own, *Playing with Fire* continues to provide collectively generated interpretations throughout the collection.[3] *Playing with Fire* does not provide these analytical walkthroughs within its methodology sections, choosing instead to intermittently perform these processes of decoding for its readers within the main body of the text. This is accomplished through interpretive codas that serve to reflect on what and how individual narratives mean when juxtaposed with each other. For instance, the chapter "From the Streets of Babul to the Wetness of *Aanchal*" is concerned with the themes of adolescence, marriage, and motherhood and consists of interlocking snippets of each woman's narrative. Once all of the seven voices have spoken, a comparative analysis provides an overarching interpretation of the collective stories as achieved through the *sangtins'* dialogic processes: "The families of Garima, Sandhya, Shikha, and Pallavi were economically more secure and resourceful than were Radha's and Chaandni's parents. For this reason, the sorrows that fell into the laps of these four women involved fewer pains of livelihood and hunger and more aches of middle-class respectability and caste-based social status" (48). Through these interpretive codas the *sangtins* take control of how their stories will be received, interrupting the reader's consumption of their stories with evidence of how the collective has already thoroughly processed these accounts for themselves.

But if these examples illustrate how feminist activist polyvocal testimonios guide reader interpretation through overtly pedagogical methods of direct address, they do not account for the subtle, often imperceptible, ways they do so within the narrative frame. One of the most powerful ways this is accomplished is through a more traditional usage of direct address, in which the narrative voice speaks directly to readers, addressing them as trusted recipients of their testimonies. This narrative device aims to make readers feel visible—and thus accountable—to the social information they are receiving. No longer anonymous, readers are called into being within these moments of address.

If the editors of these collections break with the self-enclosed world of the narrative frame in order to pedagogically instruct readers of the social function of these tales, so do the narrators. For instance, in "Chaleron's Lesson" in *Walking on Fire*, Gracita Osias discusses the social power of literacy and documents her role in peasant literacy initiatives. Within her *istwa* she reinforces the social power of literacy by recounting how the combination of illiteracy and falsified legal documents led her family to lose their own land (Bell 85). Before initiating this personal tale, however, the *griyo* forthrightly states the purpose of the account to the reader: "Okay, this is a short story of my family history. I tell you this story to show you the importance of knowing how to read and write" (85). Through this instance of direct address, Osias claims for herself a moment of purposeful storytelling that demonstrates a larger social truth. By breaking with the self-sealed narrative frame, Osias piques the interest of the reader and reinforces her cognizance of speaking *to* an audience. She claims power over what readers should take from her family account.

While this offhand, informal phrasing might seem to denote the narrative's apparent artlessness, it in fact marks quite the opposite. By incorporating a dialogic, oral framing into the text, Osias and Bell frame the reader as a friend, trusted with this privileged personal information. The narrators in *Lionheart Gal* utilize similar methods. Often, the oral quality of address serves to "soften the blow" of incisive social critique. For instance in "Red Ibo," the narrator delivers a critical reading of the social dynamics of her childhood school: "Come to think of it, a lot of it had to do with race issues, like the time with this white Scottish math and science teacher who everyone—even the white girls—hated because she was prejudiced not only against everything black but against everything Jamaican. Why she came here to teach I'll never know. Maybe she just wanted some sun . . . Anyway, this middle class black girl Heather asked her a question in class" (Sistren Theatre Collective 224–25). The narrator's employment of ambivalent, indecisive phrases—"come to think of it," "maybe," "anyway"—reframe the content of her critique of Jamaica's racialized class system into a series of unrefined, or in-process, reflections.

In "Get Up, Shake Your Bodies," Alerte Belance extends the function of purposeful storytelling by directly articulating how she hopes her story will affect the reader: "I would like people who are reading this to put Haiti in their consciences. It deserves to have the rule of law and democracy, so that the children of Haiti can speak, the children of Haiti can work, the children of Haiti can go to school and know how to read" (233). Belance's purpose of contributing to the collection is voiced as a series of legitimate concerns: a stable government, employment opportunities, an educational system available to all. Belance's particular focus on "the children" is also not accidental; if the failed attempts of adult Haitian leaders to bring prosperity to their nation do not affect the minds of uncommitted readers, then surely the innocents are still worthy of a better future. This reassurance of innocence is another recurring trope of deliberative testimonio (Nance 75).

Belance extends this utilization of pathos a few paragraphs down:

> That's why, activists of conscience, I would like you to help me shoulder this burden. Even though my body isn't intact, I still carry this burden on my back. God let me live so I could lay this burden at the feet of activists and concerned citizens. Come help me and the others so we can see our way free of the biggest country that has put its foot on our neck and is squeezing us. That's why I give you this message—see if you can help carry the burden on Haiti's back . . . Those who would like to help us get out from under this situation, look at me, a victim still standing on my own two feet. You who are not victims, you should lend a hand. Because many hands make the burden light. (233)

This passage is laden with strategic rhetorical maneuvers, and it is not incidental that Belance's narrative is the very last of the collection, coming even after Bell's own closing remarks. From hailing the readers as "activists of conscience" and "concerned citizens" to the evocation of the Christian god, to referring to herself as a victim, to closing with the adage that "many hands make the burden light," this passage is brimming with a focused utilization of pathos. Even the phrase "that's why I give you this message" evidences a prophetic quality that makes it hard to turn away from Belance's demands without feeling that you are letting her, and the children of Haiti, down.

The utilization of rhetorical questions, another narrative form of direct address, is also a key component of deliberative testimonio. For instance, in *Playing with Fire* the *sangtins* often interrupt the narrative by posing several questions to the reader: "What are we trying to tell you, our readers, by engaging in this exercise of writing? Are these stories important simply because they were articulated as a result of a collective process?" (Sangtin Writers 61). These might indeed be central questions that the collective has grappled with, but their inclusion in the text marks them as a purposeful rhetorical device that forces the reader to grapple with these very same questions. In so doing, the theoretical, interpretive, and ethical questions the collective has confronted throughout the process become dialogically extended to the reader. The above questions, while addressed from the position of the authors—"What are we trying to achieve?" "What is significant about our stories?"—in turn raise questions for the reader as recipient of their efforts: "Why am I reading these?" "What am I taking from these stories?"

The other collections similarly employ direct address in the form of questions posed to the reader. For instance, *Lionheart Gal*'s "Veteran by Veteran," where the narrative voice provides an extended analysis of the Jamaican working-class landscape, ends with: "Yuh see how it go? After yuh get nice lickle house and a live up and plenty people all plant up dem garden, dem start up dem war. Is like politicians no waan working class people fi live good for when dem have dem political differences is always inna di working class area dem fight it out" (Sistren Theatre Collective 170). The offhand informal question "Yuh see how it go?" again positions the reader as privileged friend, capable of understanding and empathizing with the social critique that immediately follows.

Lionheart Gal's "Red Ibo" takes rhetorical questions a step further: "You see how subtly class assumptions crept into the content of my own rebellion? I didn't analyse it that way then" (Sistren Theatre Collective 225). By directly addressing readers and asking if they are maintaining a critical eye through the statement, "I didn't analyze it that way then," the narrator reinforces how this critical eye is refined through sustained practice. In *Telling to Live*'s "You Speak Spanish Because You Are Jewish?," Rina Benmayor's decision to frame her entire narrative with a question mark provides a dual function (Latina Feminist Group 55). While this rhetorical framing piques reader interest through its evocation of seemingly incongruent language and ethnicity, Benmayor cleverly utilizes the device to claim the space to answer the suspicions she has always experienced regarding the complexity of her identity as a Sephardic Jew.

In breaking with the internal logic of the narrative frame, the practitioners at once call attention to its artifice and grab the emotional and ethical attention of their readers. Direct address is used as a way of calling attention to how they maintain a level of interpretive control over how their works are received by choosing what to share with readers for the accomplishment of their goals. This trope of withholding information is widely used within the testimonio tradition, most memorably evidenced by Menchú's insistence that she chose to keep parts of her Indian identity a "secret." In *Playing with Fire*, this selective "withholding" is alternately evidenced by the translations of the *sangtins*' journal entries into a rewritten third-person narrative account, a mediated textual form that reminds the reader that they do not have direct access to the collective's internal discussions. Similarly, in *Walking on Fire*, Bell frames the narratives with the assertion that "this collection represents only a fraction of the strategies employed on a daily basis. Others have been omitted, at the hushed warning of the book's collaborators so as to remain effective" (7).

These tropes reinforce Nance's point about the construction of the reader as intimate friend and potential ally, but these passages hint at selective withholdings that keep the reader at a safe distance and frame practitioners as politically savvy agents capable of proactively shaping their terms of engagement. As Nance suggests, "The practice of testimonial speakers should be of as much interest to social science researchers as to analysts of testimonio. Such resemblances confirm what a recognition of empirical expertise would suggest—deliberative testimonio's speakers seem to know what they are doing" (94).

"Collective Journeys of Creation": Testimonio as Solidarity

If the combined deployments of polyvocality, extended process-based methodology sections, and modes of direct address provide an overarching interpretive road map that offers readers an epistemic bridge, each collection's articulations of their immediate and far-reaching modes of intervention make explicit their use of testimonio as a methodological intervention to further transnational feminist organizing efforts.

Whereas traditional understandings of testimonio have operated within a top-down model of power relations, feminist activist polyvocal testimonios claim for themselves a much more dynamic understanding of power relations that invite their readers to join them in their journey toward epistemic justice. In *Walking on Fire*, Bell articulates a bidirectional picture of such solidarity: "Solidarity . . . contributes to a mutual conversion. It has a boomerang effect: In collaborating with Haitians as they fight detrimental US policies and influence in Haiti, Americans can also shift power within the United States. Through working for more just foreign policy toward Haiti, we are also building democracy and accountability at home" (232). This statement opens the possibility of readers becoming more aware of global interdependencies and serves to challenge readers to consider their own inherited benefits; but she does not stop there. She continues, "Less acknowledged, but vividly real, is what Haitians have to offer us. Haitian women—and more generally, the Haitian people—can teach and inspire us with new concepts and models for our own struggles for fully participatory democracy and the enrichment of humanity" (232).

More than a simplistic "they can offer us things too," Bell reinforces the multiple audiences *for* and the simultaneous global/local resonance *of* feminist testimonio projects. The *griyos* deliver their stories not just to highlight their particular social problems, but also to highlight how they are creating solutions through informal daily negotiations as well as through formal social justice efforts. Their stories and ideas hold out the possibility of "sparking" ideas and inspiring other organizers situated in different contexts. Indeed, while the Sangtin Writers' *Sangtin Yatra* was meant to primarily benefit and spark passion in more localized networks of activists, the translation served to mobilize a broader network with activists not literate in Hindi (xxiii).

At the very least, these works maintain a hopeful view of the emerging epistemic possibilities transnational feminist solidarity efforts enable. In "A Stubborn Hope," *griyo* Kesta Occident poses the question, "How can we help build these bridges of solidarity all over the world? How are we going to pull ourselves together to create that alternative?" (Bell 228). Answering her own question, she suggests that "a collective international conscience is developing more than before. Our labor unions are meeting with labor unions from other countries. Haitian peasants are meeting with Latin American peasants . . . What a beacon of hope!" Within their pages hierarchies are creatively reexplored and reworked so that all members of the project are respected for their particular skills and knowledge sets. Through their dialogic methodologies, practitioners are invited to be both teachers and learners, listeners and tellers.

Despite the diverse forms and functions of these polyvocal feminist texts, Honor Ford-Smith aptly states the shared ethos that connects these works: "The women who speak in these stories are not unique . . . Their lives here show that women are actively creating solutions, that they are not passively awaiting outside agitators to 'stir them up' into action" (Sistren Theatre Collective xxx). More than just "reaching" socially privileged audiences, these works actively claim story-based models of memory and dream work as important modes of critical praxis that give way to epistemic expansion. They employ testimonio as a methodology for organizing and present themselves as a form of connected activism that cultivates both horizontal and vertical relationships. In so doing, these texts offer themselves in the spirit of coalitional alliance, with the hope that their contributions will spark in others the desire to add to a conceptual and story-based mapping of existing social conditions in all of their gendered dimensions.

PART III

Testifying to the Politics of the Imagined

CHAPTER 6

"Sometimes My Geographies Get Jumbled"

The Temporal and Spatial Disruptions of Living Memory

> Literature should not be charged with the awesome burden of
> chastising readers into guilt and burdensome recollections. Neither
> should literature completely neglect the testimonial voice of the
> times.
>
> —SAÚL SOSNOWSKI, "OF MEMORY'S LITERARY SITES"

IN *HUMANISM AND DEMOCRATIC CRITICISM*, EDWARD SAID SUGGESTS
that while the arts and humanities have no obligation to solve the
world's problems, they nevertheless comprise a critical component of
social justice projects for the critical perspectives and imaginative
visions they provide (53). Feminist literary testimonios seem to understand themselves in a parallel fashion. If activist testimonios utilize the
writing form to stage political interventions, literary testimonios perform more epistemological reflections that come to bear on pressing
social issues, including the uses of historical memory, the social function of writing, and the ability of language to convey traumatic circumstance. These literary deployments collectively capitalize on the
increasing cultural currency and recognition of testimonio by applying
a testimonial narrative framework to works that do not otherwise conform to traditional conceptions of what constitutes testimonio.

Chapters 6 and 7 are centrally concerned with how and why actual historical events become translated into the world of fiction, and what

opportunities this affords. While some directly draw upon oral histories and interviews to produce an imaginative text, others either loosely interpret what little exists in historical archives or create stories within a testimonial framework that imagine how else life could be. The effect is more exploratory and deliberative than functionary. While most do not utilize a co-narrational framework that mirrors those in activist deployments, they do employ other polyvocal tactics—through experimentation with narrative point of view and fragmented narrative practices—or find other ways of making the absent polyphony present. While not as pointed in considering how their words resonate with specific audiences, these works nevertheless offer epistemic possibilities for diverse readerships, regardless of their racial or national locations. Such practices open conceptual doors to reassess how historical events have been conceived and to prompt readers to consider new ways of being in the world through modeling alternate modes of epistemic dialogue.

Through narrative disruptions and poetic reflections on the subject of memory, literary testimonios work to mirror the disorienting effects of how the past continues to haunt and overshadow the present, and to dramatize the feelings of isolation and misrecognition that often accompany these experiences. These reflections on the living past continue a critique of recent quandaries on the relevance of testimonio when it lives beyond the immediate circumstances of its intervention by highlighting how these traces of personal and national trauma are always bubbling under the surface. Through poetic language, the writers of literary testimonio shift readers to move from "knowing" about specific historical circumstances to "understanding" their continued effects on the present; in so doing, they take testimonio to new cognitive places, opening up new epistemic possibilities for this writing project.

Testimonios have become more widely recognized as legitimate texts since the days of the Menchú controversy, and racially and geopolitically privileged readers are now better positioned to recognize the ethical component that accompanies this writing form. Such readers are thereby encouraged to engage with these texts in terms of a reciprocal social pact rooted in epistemic responsibility rather than as a unidirectional form of entertainment. Recent feminist literary testimonios build upon this cultural legibility. Jamaica Kincaid's *A Small Place* and Nawal el Saadawi's

Woman at Point Zero both utilize a testimonial frame to immediately alter their readers' terms of engagement with their thematic explorations but otherwise do not conform to the structure of traditional testimonio.

Following Beverley's logic, the texts I work with here signify the genre's depoliticization, but if we understand testimonios instead as an expansive resistant ethos rather than as a predefined genre, these structurally and thematically experimental feminist literary works are evidence of the writing project's continued political relevance and its ability to lend itself to a variety of social justice projects. Chapters 6 and 7 specifically explore such work undertaken by feminist literary testimonios through the representational examples of Nora Strejilevich's *A Single, Numberless Death*, Alicia Kozameh's *Steps under Water*, Shani Mootoo's *Cereus Blooms at Night*, and to a lesser degree, Alicia Partnoy's *The Little School*. Within these works, three dominant themes emerge: the ethical representation of trauma in aesthetic works, the temporal disruptions that trauma can cause, and alternate models of relationality that emerge out of traumatic circumstances. The effect is a penetratingly "transformative but not shattering lucidity" (Medina 220) regarding the instances of trauma the texts convey.[1]

Originally published in Spanish as *Una sola muerte numerosa* in 1997 and translated into English in 2002, Nora Strejilevich's *A Single, Numberless Death* is an intertextual exercise in collective memory work in which the author utilizes the narrative to counter official Argentine legal reparation proceedings that define the Dirty War as an occasion of national trauma confined to the past. Rather than recounting events that occurred during the Dirty War, Strejilevich frames the book to primarily reflect on the psychological aftermath as explored through the daily lives of Argentines and to illustrate how the nation's unsettling past continues to haunt its present. Strejilevich writes from her relatively privileged class background in Argentina, a precarious position heightened by her imprisonment and subsequent travel across national borders.

While the poetic wording and format call attention to the literariness of the narrative, Strejilevich's language has a tension-ridden tone and sense of immediacy that sets the terms for how readers approach the text. Strejilevich follows the narrative with a brief glossary of terms and groups that she cites throughout the narrative, including CONADEP

(National Commission on Disappeared Persons) and Madres de Plaza de Mayo, in addition to a list of sources she consulted in drafting the narrative, including the Center for Legal and Social Studies, the Association of Former Detained-Disappeared, and CONADEP (176). In addition to externally framing her narrative with documentary-based and archival materials, Strejilevich continuously disrupts a strictly literary flow by including fragments of these materials within the narrative body. She juxtaposes legally documented testimony from Nunca Más (the Argentine equivalent of the South African truth commissions), quotations from former military officials, and official statements made by CONADEP and other organizations formed to document stories of the disappeared, all in addition to quotes taken from interviews Strejilevich conducted, as well as her personal letters and poems. As a result, Strejilevich's narrative confounds any simple categorization, weaving a complex narrative out of myriad parts. Polyvocality is achieved through these fragmentary threads and incongruent discourses and epistemes.

Alicia Kozameh's testimonio *Steps under Water*, also about the Argentine Dirty War, seems more literary in scope in that it does not include appendixes and historical documentation. Less concerned with confronting large-scale national amnesia, Kozameh crafts carefully framed meta-narratives that are preoccupied with the relationship between writing and trauma and the role of art and literature in social justice projects. The narrative is specifically organized around the perspective of the relatively privileged narrator, Sara, and her gradual reincorporation into civil society through her reflections on the challenges she confronts in adjusting to daily life outside of prison.

Kozameh's narrative maintains a fundamentally polyvocal component throughout, with each chapter taking on a slightly different structural form. Whereas the opening and closing chapters, both entitled "A Way Back," are rooted in Sara's internal cognitive processes of coming to terms with her release and the contradictions of such "freedom," the intermediary chapters include situational-based dialogue, epistolary exchange and diary writing, a multivoiced chapter documenting a complicated love triangle as narrated from the perspectives of all those involved, and even an extended response to the question, "Sara, what does a jacket mean to you?" (which also serves as the chapter title). Through the course of these diverse narrational practices and perspectives, we glean not only an intimate perspective on the struggles faced by the formerly imprisoned when picking up the pieces of their lives, but also an intimate look at the tender yet powerful bonds between *compañeras*—relationships that while forged through situational circumstance, continue to thrive beyond prison walls.

Shani Mootoo's *Cereus Blooms at Night*, set in Trinidad, employs more recognizable uses of testimonio in its self-conscious evocation of testimonio in the fictional realm. Following a widespread trend in Caribbean literature, Mootoo's renaming of the recognizable island of Trinidad to the made-up island of Lantanacamara provides her with more creative license for penning her epistemologically resistant narrative. The text is not rigidly confined by the actual geopolitical site and history of Trinidad, but it nonetheless remains historically grounded and geographically framed by references to Canada, Africa, and India. The "Shivering Northern Wetlands" (the fictionalized colonial power of England) serves as a persistent backdrop to the intergenerational accounts of the two main characters, Mala and Tyler. This authorial decision can be seen as a purposeful disidentification (Muñoz) that recognizes the continued effects of colonialism in people's daily lives while refusing to remain within its terms. *Cereus Blooms at Night* dramatizes the long-lasting effects of childhood sexual abuse as experienced by the elderly protagonist, Mala Ramchandin, against the backdrop of colonial legacies that haunts the text. As the narrative unfolds, we come to know of Mala's frequent molestation by her father and how she willingly became the target of her father's sexual abuse in order to protect her younger sister, Asha, a figure who continues to pervade her consciousness as an old woman despite years of separation.

Mala's story is filtered through the narrative perspective of Tyler, a racially ambiguous, genderqueer nurse whose own personal growth is catalyzed through his relationship with her.[2] The social juxtaposition of Mala and Tyler in this mediated narration calls attention to how reliant a story is on the socially situated perspective of the teller. Simultaneously, it optimistically suggests the ability of disparate social subjects to cultivate epistemic bridges that allow them to see the world beyond their own narrow perspectives. Moreover, the narrative framework is rooted in an ethos of interdependence and reciprocity in which Tyler holds himself epistemically responsible to Mala, insofar as Mala's story could not be told without Tyler's help, and Tyler only begins to grow when he opens himself up to Mala. This framing provides an alternative approach to co-narrational practice while suggesting that people are epistemically co-creators of their social worlds. With the particularities of Tyler's and Mala's individual stories placed in tension with the backdrop of colonialism, Mootoo's narrative works to craft "an oppositional community consciousness to resist the rigid mores and violent rationalities of empire, heteronormativity, and sexual domination," in which ethical interpersonal relations are key to epistemic expansion (May, "Trauma in Paradise" 114).

In such texts, the imaginary element allows more creative license in how the writers choose to write about their chosen social issues. For instance, the foreword to *A Single, Numberless Death*, whose textual makeup is marked by its intertextual inclusion of interview, legal material, diary writing, and journalism, suggests that the "text is both fictional and documentary" (Strejilevich x). It is fictional in its use of individual accounts to paint a picture of a national landscape and in its use of governmental and legal documentation. *Steps under Water* similarly pushes the boundaries of history and fiction; its cover, for example, identifies it as "a novel," and Kozameh subsequently counterbalances this categorization by suggesting that the "substance of the story, of every episode, is real" (xvi). Following publication of the novel *Steps under Water*, she was threatened by members of the Buenos Aires police (xvii).

While works steeped in actual historical events such as *Steps under Water* and *A Single, Numberless Death* work to challenge the documentary-based impetus of testimonio through their extended engagement with the psychological and historical aftermath of Argentina's Dirty War, works rooted in historical landscapes that focus on imagined accounts, such as *Cereus Blooms at Night*, call attention to where else testimonio is traveling; the focus moves toward more epistemically just futures rather than epistemically just tellings of the past while trusting the power of the imaginary to comment on relevant social issues.

While these texts employ widely varied representational practices, they nevertheless illustrate how the activity of creative memory work functions as a trope within literary testimonio, becoming a meta-discourse on the importance of representational efforts contesting dominant social narratives. The deliberations on the role of art in social justice projects within the narrative frames of *Steps under Water* and *A Single, Numberless Death* confront and contest discourses that narrowly assess the pedagogical success of the writing project in terms of quantitative outcome. *Cereus Blooms at Night* illustrates the possibility of another, more ethical, mode of relationality through the witness-testifier paradigm, both between Mala and Taylor and between the reader and the text. Collectively, these works raise epistemic questions on alternative kinship and relationship formations and the possibility of positive social interdependence.

Writing Trauma, Disrupting Temporality

In Alicia Partnoy's testimonio *The Little School*, the narrator berates herself for reciting poetry before explaining the "rules" of survival to a new arrival: "Instead of reciting poems I should have explained to the new prisoners . . . I should have told them that at the Little School we are beaten whenever our blindfolds are loose" (106). Similarly, Kozameh's narrator continually trivializes the "little lies" she constructs in order to keep herself and the other women prisoners going. At one point, she questions the value of trying to record her experience at all: "What I'm doing just isn't working, trying to describe a moment of that magnitude. Almost absurd. Possible, but absurd. And let this be a sterile clarification: I believe in the word. Fervently . . . there's no recourse other than words that are heard, read. Images or no images, always the word" (143). Despite Kozameh's "fervent" belief in the power of language and narrative, this passage reflects how she seems to falter in her belief in her own writing project.

With Partnoy publishing *The Little School* in 1986, and Kozameh publishing *Steps under Water* in 1987, the nearness of the loss and despair resulting from the national trauma inflicted by the dictatorship almost necessitates such skepticism. Compelled by the need to *tell* their stories, both authors remain unsure of what to expect as a result of their accounts being published. The role of art in confronting oppressive social structures remains a constant trope in literary testimonio. The mere existence of these texts suggests that the authors felt compelled to represent the experiences of themselves and their fellow political prisoners. In contrast, Strejilevich's *A Single, Numberless Death*, published over a decade later, in 1997, has a decidedly more confident and accomplished tone. Claiming the process of "interpretation as a counterpoint to silence" (152), Strejilevich's account has the benefit of seeing the publication of *Nunca más* and witnessing the enactment of significant legal reparations.

Strejilevich's narrative pointedly critiques the insufficiency of such government-sanctioned programs to address the profound traumatic effects the dictatorship had on the country, and yet her ability to witness these changes renews her faith in testimonio and more generally, the ability of the masses to collectively respond to injustice. Strejilevich recounts the initial suspicion former political prisoners faced in documenting their experiences. "We came out of nowhere asking weird questions about a remote past that none of them can recall" (126). She also notes with irony how, after having her testimony recorded in *Nunca más*, her story was accepted and legitimated by a governmental official: "Giddy from the impact of abruptly finding such a fortuitous witness to corroborate my existence, I leave the office . . . Will my steps be audible as I exit?" (118).

The narrative delivers harsh critique of the amount of time, energy, and pain the government caused those like herself, who carried the burden of proving their existence, and her account clearly finds more hope in an invitation to speak at a ceremony that seeks to memorialize the atrocities that occurred at the "Athletic Club"—a name given to the five largest concentration camps during the dictatorship—than in legal reparations (173). Suggesting that "it's the birthday of our second skin, almost two decades old, and we celebrate it here, at the ruins of the Athletic Club," the ceremony literalizes testimonio's goal of bearing witness, of insisting on presence in the face of so much absence. Telling the crowd, "Compañeros / *We've come here today / to tell stories / because they never could / vanquish our memories*" (169), she ends her narrative with a call to collective memory work, "a chorus of voices resisting armed monologues that turned so much life into a single, numberless death" (171). Insisting that "no ceremonies [can] help [to] close those wounds," she claims that such wounds stay open forever: "Let mine remain wide open. Death and its turns. I build no monuments for you, but I carry you in my body, in my cells, in my feet" (144). The act of remembering becomes memorialized as an essential form of resistance that offers the possibility of a more profound sense of historical understanding, even if it cannot offer personal healing.

While feminist literary testimonios favor the act of memory work over documenting specific instances of what may become fetishized trauma, they do at times seek to give expression to the abject as a way to epistemically reflect on the very difficulty of such expression. As suggested by Elaine Scarry in *The Body in Pain*, "Whatever pain achieves, it achieves part through its unsharability, and it ensures this unsharability through its resistance to language" (4). Because of this, much "is at stake in the attempt to invent linguistic structures that will reach and accommodate this area of experience normally so inaccessible to language" (6). Given the inexpressibility of pain, figurative language is frequently utilized in the narration of experiences of torture to develop alternative representations for conveying such intensity of emotion and physical abjection, and to avoid a mere fetishization of pain. Thus, the silences and absences become just as important as what is present.

One way that Strejilevich's narrative attempts such representation is by focusing on the bodily sensations that accompanied the electric shocks she endured while imprisoned:

> The voice is accompanied by a strange percussion that jolts my skin. It's not blows but rather something that brushes past without stinging or burning or shaking or hurting or drilling but still burns, drills, stings, hurts, shakes. It kills. That humming, that agony, the precarious fraction of a second that precedes the shocks, the loathing for that sharp tip that explodes on contact with my skin, vibrating and hurting and cutting and piercing and destroying brain, teeth, gums, ears, breasts, eyelids, ovaries, nails, the soles of the feet. My head, my ears, my vagina, my scalp, the pores of my skin give off a burnt smell. (23)

While intensely painful to read, Strejilevich's text enacts a form of fragmented narration to call attention to the excess of pain that escapes representation in language. Her reliance on a series of disjointed clauses joined together by a never-ending stream of commas, "and's," and "or's" conveys excessiveness through the excessiveness of the sentence itself. Her extensive listing of inner and outer body parts conveys the totalizing effects of the shocks. Still, the fragmented narration of the scene resists a sensationalized reading. She does not provide a lucid narration of the tortured body for readers to passively consume. It is only through the gaps, through active reading, that the reader is able to fully recognize the appalling image of this body in pain.

Strejilevich also destabilizes an otherwise familiar visit to the dentist as a way of calling attention to the long-term psychic effects of torture: "Finally the doctor invades my intimate spaces with his clamps, picks, and expert glances . . . My mute body, spectator if its own agony, has no strength to react. The current of pain that penetrates to the roots of my gums at least diverts my thoughts away from the surgeon's face . . . The good thing is that one gets used to suffering, so I summon my courage. I'm prepared to pay in a lump sum, all four molars in one sitting. Just then the tormentor takes pity on me" (101).

Strejilevich relies upon vivid language to transform this everyday scene into a site of torture. The dentist "invades" her "intimate spaces" with instruments of torture that consist of "clamps, picks, and expert glances." Her body is rendered "mute," a "spectator" to "its own agony." Rendered completely passive, the narrator can only accept the pain, and is ultimately at the hands of her "tormentor" until he "takes pity" on her. By utilizing the everyday scene of the dentist's office, Strejilevich calls attention to how the psychic effects of torture endure, so that at any moment one can experience a psychological relapse. By using an image and experience widely shared by her readers, Strejilevich connects the seemingly distant experiences of the political prisoners with something we can relate to, or at least previously thought we could.

Traditional accounts of torture create a narrative framework for understanding the torturers as mythically other-than-human; Strejilevich instead reminds us that it is their unrelenting normalness that defines their monstrosity. The above passage is the closest we come to a "torture scene" as normalized and naturalized in a North American sense, and even then, the importance of the scene is in its attempt to bear witness to the pain of another, not of oneself. As articulated by Alicia Kozameh, the narrative approach is more akin to "saying 'blood' without saying the word."[3] As such, it effectively resists a simplified reading that renders it easily consumable.

One way the authors resist sensationalized accounts of physical torture is by focusing on the mundane monotony of their prison experiences, providing details that illustrate an alternative account of violence, one embedded in the psychical effects of their detainment. As Strejilevich's narrator tells us: "The mind gradually shrinks, and your world becomes limited to when they open the door, when they close it, what you eat today, what you'll eat tomorrow, when you're punished, and when you're not. Those were the things that mattered to me. When your life gets so small, you forget where you are, who you are. You're grateful for any friendly gesture, for a plate of decent food; you're happy to be outdoors for a bit. Thinking becomes pointless" (60).

It is precisely this smallness of life that the mundane reiterates—humans stripped to bare existence (Agamben). As Kaminsky argues in relation to Partnoy's *The Little School*, the "tight focus on discrete objects that in other circumstances would be unremarkable (plastic flower, matchbox, tooth, jacket), the investment of emotional and aesthetic energy in unlikely places, is dictated by the constraints of the circumstances" (58). Such constraints lead to passages focused on clothing, food, and bodily functions. In such constrained atmospheres, mundane details gain symbolic proportions: "More than nourishment, soup is a timepiece for me. It marks my nights and my dawns until I lose track and dwell in unrelieved twilight" (Strejilevich 44). By using the presence of the soup to maintain her orientation in time, Strejilevich's narrator resists succumbing to a passive existence.

Such passages safeguard against a simplistic fetishization of suffering in which discussions of torture are replaced by figuratively explored meditations on the inexpressibility of abjection, and actively claiming creatively shaped memory work as a way of countering the quantitative, functionary expectations frequently placed on testimonio. Temporal disruption is another distinguishing trope that feminist literary testimonios utilize. By calling attention to how traumatic circumstance gives way to psychological effects that extend well after the immediate social situation has been resolved, these texts help readers gain an understanding of how such trauma is experienced, moving us beyond a factual recognition of its existence. They accomplish this in part by experimenting with structural fragmentation and temporal disruption.

A countercurrent to memorializing the act of remembering is confronting the terror of memory and the threat of its undoing a subject's ability to act in the present. This tension between the need to remember and the need to forget calls attention not only to the difficult "work" of "memory work" and "counternarrative," but also to the courage it takes to remember when such an act always carries with it the ability to reenact individual, familial, and national trauma. This paradox is at the heart of all three narratives. For instance, in *Steps under Water*, Sara's friend constantly tells her, "Wouldn't it be better to try to forget a little?" And: "It's best not to stir things up" (Kozameh 131, 133). Yet she also suggests, "The day when we can sit down and have a talk will be a happy one, even though all the catching up is bound to get us down" (132). Similarly, in *A Single, Numberless Death*, the narrator begins by telling us, "I succeed thanks to a technique that obliterates memory . . . The strategy is to remember nothing" (Strejilevich 35). Yet the narrator soon arrives at a point where she needs to remember: "Right then I seal a pact with Nora-to-Come: to remember. I store away these images in the pocket of my memory so I can reach for them whenever necessary" (41).

Saúl Sosnowski asserts that in contrast to more traditional Latin American testimonios, in *Steps under Water* "neither the core of authoritarianism nor the ideological tenets that led to the left's call to arms are evident . . . It engages the aftermath, daily survival after defeat as victory is sought in the very act of staying alive" (xiii). The framing chapters of the novel are aptly titled "A Way Back," dramatizing the ways in which the past continually threatens to invade the present for those who have undergone traumatic situations: "Everything is at once firm and slippery, it's there and then it vanishes" (1). As the book opens, the narrator, Sara (although the narration shuttles between first- and third-person), struggles to reconcile the strangeness of being released from prison with the ordinariness of being back on her parents' patio. The strange and the ordinary become entangled, with "familiar" memories of the space taking on new, troubling meanings. Intimate memories and preferences become overdetermined. Walking becomes a measured activity. Cats, formerly an object of affection, become something to fear: "Going years without seeing animals is not something to take lightly. But she should try to remember how much she liked cats" (6). Kozameh's depiction of Sara's seemingly bizarre, irrational reactions to "ordinary" life re-creates the sense of isolation and misrecognition that many imprisoned Argentines experienced when reintegrating into society, an isolation that becomes further marked by the distance she feels from her own parents: "For my father a cat is a cat. To me it is a gesture of mock reverence that freedom makes at me today" (7).

Throughout the text, such feelings of isolation and emotional distance become normalized; paranoia and disorientation are positioned as likely reactions to the mundane for political prisoners who were the targets of sanctioned state terror. Indeed, it is the perspectives of those on the outside, those unable to intimately understand the disorienting feeling of "normalcy," that become suspect. A recurring trope in Kozameh's novel is the jacket of her boyfriend, Hugo, at the time of her imprisonment. Upon being released, Sara suggests that she is being intentionally followed and tormented by a military official wearing Hugo's jacket. The repeated image of this man wearing the jacket throughout the narrative marks it a site of extreme distress for her, and yet, as Sara recounts, her parents either don't believe her or don't understand the significance it holds for her: "That guy. The same one. But they wouldn't understand that either . . . The guy didn't even bother looking over at me, but he left wearing the jacket, just so I'd see him. And my parents don't believe that, they don't understand what it means. They don't want to recognize that vulnerability is a daily fact. And that it's not easy to neutralize it. Defend against it" (3).

It is precisely the vulnerability of unwitting victims that is dramatized in literary testimonio, leading readers to recognize the more individuated forms of distress experienced by those directly affected and to build an awareness of the psychological imprints such imposed circumstances leave on their daily lives, long after the official "end" of a historical event. By giving readers glimpses of what this reality feels like, such narratives work to build empathetic bridges that have the capacity to lead to increased epistemic knowledge on the part of readers on how trauma continually haunts the edges of the present:

> I feel like I'm sitting in a movie audience. Each little action, each word, isn't coming from me. I'm not the protagonist. I sit in a coffee shop and from the window I observe all the people walking, running to catch the bus, missing it, I see them talking to others, waving their hands around, I don't know, I see them living. I guess that's what they're doing. But it's like I'm so far removed from that. I'm in the middle of all

that movement, but emotionally I just don't take part . . . Ever since I was released, I feel like a prisoner more than ever. (54)

The emotional deadening expressed in this passage gains its force through metaphor and simile. The passage invites us to imagine what it might feel like to not understand oneself as protagonist of one's own life, but rather as passive observer to life happening around one. "Freedom" is not positioned as the inevitable consequence of release from prison. Rather, the release, especially when others remain imprisoned, only adds to a sense of isolation and trauma. Through such potent illustrations, feminist literary testimonios beg for a reconsideration of what testimonio as a writing project can and should accomplish, and work toward decolonizing readers' consciousness more than taking aim at specific material conditions.

Similar to how Kozameh's opening and closing chapters represent Sara's disrupted consciousness, Strejilevich's *A Single, Numberless Death* structurally mimics the flooding of repressed memories that a seemingly mundane life event can trigger. In the second section of the book, the narrator revisits the Navy Mechanics School, the site of a well-known detention camp during the coup. As the narrator suggests, "After thousands were killed there, the land around the Navy School of Mechanics was turned into a sports field. There's no limit to national plastic surgery . . . Today the plan is to interview the students from private schools who are playing ball on these very fields: all-purpose lots that twenty years ago housed torture chambers" (104). Strejilevich actively disrupts the present by interweaving this main narrative thread with interviews and legal statements that testify to the torture that took place on the grounds. This interplay of past and present reminds us of the psychological distress that accompanies such an act of historical confrontation, and how challenging and brave Strejilevich's actions are. As her narrator suggests, "I'm standing at the scene of the events, where life curdles into clumps of horror" (110).

From this statement forward the narrative becomes more sprawling and difficult to temporally navigate, furthering a demand for the audience's active reading. Strejilevich soon moves into a reflection on the limits of legal reparations, then into specific memories of traveling to Israel, Spain, and Canada, and the challenges in communicating her legal and national status: "According to a new decree passed in the early nineties by the party then in office, former political prisoners can claim a certain amount of money for each day spent behind bars. That's fine for the ones who were given due process. But those of us in legal limbo, neither officially incarcerated nor held by legitimately recognized military forces, logically don't appear in any records. We, therefore, do not exist, and our existence is precisely what we're trying to prove" (113). Within Strejilevich's narrative, existence as a national citizen itself becomes formulated as a privilege, one taken for granted by those who have not jumped through bureaucratic hoops to receive legal recognition. The feelings of nonpersonhood that she recalls in her process to regain her legal identity begin to spill into the narrative present, in which she dramatizes the feelings of anxiety she experiences when speaking to the officers at the school, which in turn triggers a sense of re-living the interrogations she endured as a political prisoner.

Whereas *Steps under Water* and *A Single, Numberless Death* dramatize the psychological effects of macro-level state-induced trauma on former prisoners, *Cereus Blooms at Night* focuses on the micro-level, dramatizing the long-lasting effects of child sexual abuse as experienced by the elderly Mala Ramchandin. The narrator, Tyler, helps us to understand how the molestation ultimately led to Mala's predilection for nonverbal communication. It is only toward the end of the novel that Mootoo directly dramatizes her divided consciousness and the psychological continuity she experiences between past memories and the present.

Within this multilayered narrative account, we learn that Otoh Mohanty, the son of the former childhood friend and one-time lover of Mala, Ambrose Mohanty, has taken an interest in Mala. On one occasion, Otoh decides to dress up in his father's clothes and bring a gramophone to Mala's house, like his father said he used to do. As Otoh presents himself to his father before heading to Mala's, Ambrose reassuringly tells him that "by appearing in front of me like this you have given me the gift of remembering" (145). For Mala, however, whose consciousness already hovers between past and present as her mind continuously replays her childhood trauma, the effect is much more disruptive. Otoh's visit coincides with the blooming of the cereus plant, an event that Mala ritually acknowledges, and that also reminds her of her mother leaving—the very event that marked the advent of her father's abuse. As Otoh approaches dressed in Ambrose's clothing, with gramophone in hand, Mala is busy replaying memories of "Pohpoh," her chosen name for her childhood self, wishing she could protect her: "Mala wished that she could go back in time and be a friend to this Pohpoh. She would storm into the house and, with one flick of her wrist, banish the father into a pit of pain and suffering from which there would be no escape" (142). Mala's revisitation of such memories reflects her wish that someone could have protected her from her father's sexual abuse in the same way she protected her own sister, Asha.

The expression of her divided consciousness, while relatively subdued in this passage, soon sets into effect a series of events that reinforce her temporal disorientation, and she experiences a simultaneity of past and present. Thinking that Otoh is Ambrose, Mala is eager to show him that her father can no longer hurt them. Taking Otoh by the hand, Mala walks him down into the basement, and into a locked room where the decomposing body of her father rests. Otoh immediately reacts, but given Mala's disorientation, she does not understand why he flees. And yet, the narration informs the readers, "as soon as Otoh bolted out of her yard, Mala had sensed that trouble would follow. She wrung her hands in desperation and sadness, wondering if what she thought was a visit from her beloved Ambrose was simply a memory, as vivid as her daydreams about Pohpoh's adventures" (172).

Mootoo's narrative becomes increasingly fragmented within the next several pages, with page breaks spaced between Mala's mental fluctuation between past and present, and with her shifting consciousness further reflected through the alternate usage of the referents "Mala" and "Pohpoh." Her memories become a site of refuge as her present is disrupted, with police asking questions and people stepping onto her property for the first time in years: "A man's voice called out . . . She did not answer. She thought harder of Pohpoh. She ignored the sounds of her fence being torn down" (173). At once a way to resist the disruption of the present and a symptom of her traumatic past, memory serves Mala as a source of comfort: "Mala remembered. She heard the voices of the police. She reconfigured what they said to match her story of how she saved Pohpoh that day . . . Mala bit the inside of her lip and willed herself to think. She squeezed her eyes tightly and ignored the people trampling, destroying her yard. She put all her efforts into protecting Pohpoh" (175).

Unable to understand the inner workings of Mala's mind, the police can only witness Mala's troubled psyche in a decontextualized way: "When he signaled that she was to accompany them he saw her look off to her side and nod, as though in agreement with some imaginary person" (181).

By dramatizing how trauma affects consciousness on such a deep-rooted level, feminist literary testimonios ask us to revisit the notion of memory as confined to the past, and to consider the concept of living memory. While these works explore how memory can serve a redemptive function—an understanding of self, a refusal to forget historical injustice—they also confront how it can threaten to take over one's present. As Strejilevich suggests, "Sometimes my geographies get jumbled. . . . Memories flood over me, and I'm reliving, reliving, reliving everything" (101, 82). As feminist literary testimonios simultaneously explore how active, intentional memory work can safeguard against temporal and spatial disorientation, so too do they call attention to the creative means through which survivors of trauma resist the isolating and dehumanizing conditions of their oppression. More than merely "documenting" a myriad of small-scale resistance measures, these works highlight how such moments cultivate essential interpersonal means of resistance that allow survivors of trauma to maintain a sense of dignity, imagination, and even humor, in otherwise bare life (Agamben) conditions.

CHAPTER 7

Cultivating Community through Creative Communication

> It was obvious that I was going to start talking . . . That's what
> I wished someone would do for me when I was inside. That's why
> I never stopped wanting to talk.
>
> —NORA STREJILEVICH, *A SINGLE, NUMBERLESS DEATH*

IF TESTIMONIO ATTESTS TO THE IMPORTANCE OF TALKING, OR
testifying, to the atrocities that the writer has seen as an essential mode
of resistance, then within its pages it also positions readers to acknowledge the numerous daily, seemingly mundane acts of resistance that
often go unseen, reflecting on the resilience of the human spirit and
how it is that people continue to cultivate dignity, connection, and community in repressive circumstances. Similar to how Beverly Bell's *Walking on Fire* devotes much time articulating a more nuanced understanding
of "resistance" for readerships removed from the material and sociopolitical conditions in which the *griyos* are entrenched, literary testimonios often utilize metaphor to convey the symbolic importance of
people's ways of coping and to dramatize poignant instances of claiming
agency in trying circumstances.

For instance, in Partnoy's *The Little School* the narrator transforms
individual constipation into an act of collective resistance:

> "I've discovered the cure for constipation," I told Maria Elena one
> morning . . .
> "Really?"

"Yeah, just pretend that Chiche's face is inside the latrine and shitting becomes a pleasure." . . .

We all managed to see Chiche's face. (29)

Reclaiming an act of humiliation in which the guards watched the prisoners relieve themselves, this act of resistance gives renewed meaning to a normal bodily function that enables the prisoners to individually and collectively assert their subjectivity. Similarly, in a particularly tense scene in *A Single, Numberless Death*, a woman is forced to relieve herself while a military official holds a gun to her head:

A warm and liberating river flows between her legs, and she no longer knows, or cares, if the warrior is aiming at her, or if the musical tinkle will arouse his instincts, or if he'll let go of the trigger to grab hold of his penis in the heat of battle. She's no longer there with him, she's alone with her body in a corner of her house, with her waterfall of words, which will be flushed down labyrinths of pipes and start on their journey south, moving unimpeded under barrios, under streets, toward the river; and from there spreading to every shore. (Strejilevich 52)

In claiming ownership of her body, the woman refuses to succumb to the terror the military man seeks to impose on her, and rather imagines her private act of urination as a means of resistance, one that extends her body beyond the confines of her present situation. As both examples suggest, it is precisely when the prisoners are positioned as most abject that they utilize their bodies as a safe space from which to engage in collective forms of resistance. Nor are these just symbolic narrative strategies: "*When you're surrounded by terror you just don't realize it: you go to bed with terror, you live with terror; it somehow gets incorporated into your routine*" (54). In a constant state of terror, making meaning out of the mundane becomes the only way to survive.

In Argentine prison testimonios, especially, there is a repeated insistence on the prisoners' recognition of the necessity of collectivity. One of the most profoundly ritualized scenes that articulate creative communications between prisoners as constituting communal resistance is found in the section titled "Bread" in *The Little School*. Describing her need to pass on her portion of bread to the other prisoners, the narrator explains, "Bread is also a means of communicating, a way of telling the person next to me: 'I'm here. I care for you. I want to share the only possession I have'" (84). Partnoy's detailed description of the narrator dividing up her portion of bread into twenty-five bread balls to share with the others insists on the necessity of the collective: "To be given some bread is to receive a comforting hug" (85). Sharing bread is a way of communicating without utilizing the mode of speech, for which they would be punished. The narrator's act becomes adopted by the other prisoners, and as such, effectively challenges the authority of the guards; by communicating in a way that is unreadable, and in fact unknowable, to their captors, the prisoners destabilize the mode of individual isolation the guards seek to impose upon them.

Kozameh's narrative includes a similar scene in which she and the other women prisoners are compelled to perform the ritual of New Year's Eve dinner, despite their individual physical and psychic unwillingness to do so. Referring to how the dinner was thwarted the previous year after one of the women lost control of her emotions, and describing the chaos that later ensued between the women and the guards, Kozameh depicts what Sara experiences as she faces the dinner:

I sweat. My armpits are drenched. I feel faint, blood pressure dropping, words coming to me, over and over again . . . I don't feel good . . . My ears go cold. My neck. Andrea and Griselda are late in joining the others. They talk, almost whispering, as if there were no other moments in their lives. Just now, when it's imperative that we mingle. My brow is dripping wet. I hope I get over this before somebody notices. Better not have any embarrassing moments on this December 31, at dinnertime. Grist for the piss-eye-chologists. Plenty of them. This isn't going away. And some of them even enjoy the approval of the majorities here. This crap, make it go away. Go away. (125)

After watching the physical manifestations of internal struggle that some of the other prisoners experience, Sara ultimately overcomes her temporary inability to join the women already at the table by reminding herself that "it's imperative that we mingle." New Year's Eve dinner has come to occupy a naturalized, normalized place in culture, one that is expected to remain unaffected by the less-than-ordinary conditions in which the women prisoners find themselves. Hence, Sara and the other prisoners are compelled to repeat the ritual in order to remain recognizably "human" and to avoid becoming fodder for the psychologists. Thus, there is nothing "voluntary" about partaking in the dinner, and in fact, something inherently selfish about not joining in. They dread the enforced dinner, but they realize that *not* coming together for it threatens to undo their ability to survive; by coming together they make themselves accountable to each other, and it is precisely this accountability that keeps them going.

The strong communicative bonds between the prisoners in these narratives do more than reinforce their individual will to survive. Their collective identification can also threaten to undo their subjectivity. For instance, in one particularly painful scene, Strejilevich's narrator conveys in present tense the horror of hearing her brother being tortured: "His moans rip me apart, tear me into countless shreds . . . No, don't pierce me with that scream! Don't let them kill you! My voice breaks as it fleetingly joins yours. Then there is silence. I no longer hear you. I no longer feel myself" (30). The slippage between the "I" and the "you" in this scene is telling. The narrator conveys a sense of physical pain and suffering by bearing witness to the sounds of her brother being tortured, followed by a profound silence that marks his absence. As the narrator more directly suggests further on in the narrative, the loss of her brother profoundly undoes her own claims to subjectivity: "By definition a younger sister's life demands an older brother. I'm left without my basic premise" (119).

Beyond exploring the relationality of human existence, these passages convey the difficulty of survival when we come to define our own subjectivity in terms of our relationship to a collective.[1] Whereas a paradigm of individualism marks a break between self and other, the move to the collective means that the loss of each individual becomes intimately felt as a loss of self. These passages specifically reference the loss of kinship ties; Kozameh's narrator, Sara, similarly articulates the difficulty of functioning as an individual unit after coming to identify so closely with her *compañeras*: "Do you want to know what I feel right now? I want to go back to prison. I miss my friends. I feel guilty. They should be free, all of them. And sometimes I don't think I deserve this freedom I have" (49). For Sara, as for all of the narrators in these works, "freedom" becomes circumscribed in an interrelational paradigm; until all are free, none are free.

Mootoo's *Cereus Blooms at Night* is slightly less pessimistic in its interpretation of interdependence, offering one of the most marked examples of the benefits of creative communication by putting forth alternative forms of affiliation and collectivity (Hong 76). The relationship at the heart of the novel between the young(ish) gender queer nurse Tyler and the elderly, isolated Mala Ramchandin is central to this vision. Both in narrative structure and in the alternative forms of communication developed between these two characters, Mootoo asserts a vision in which the disparate positionalities of Tyler and Mala become the foundation of their "shared queerness" (Mootoo 48). Tyler and Mala's shared racialized colonial subjectivities and nonnormative sexualities—specifically Tyler's queer sexuality and gender performance and Mala's position as incest survivor—reinforce a sense of solidarity that simultaneously refuses to elide difference or privilege alterity. Rather, through labor-ridden and self-reflexive posturing, Tyler and Mala carefully develop a relationship that depends on an understanding of self in relation to other.

Mootoo structurally achieves this effect by establishing immediate temporal and spatial connections between Tyler (the narrator) and Mala at the beginning of the novel, with both causing a commotion upon their almost simultaneous arrival at the almshouse. With Tyler's alternative masculine performance and "questionable" sexuality causing an initial stir among his fellow female nurses, the anomaly of his person is temporarily overshadowed by the excitement of Mala's arrival and the rumors of incest, murder, and insanity that precede—and in a very real way, overdetermine—her. The characters' temporal and spatial connection is maintained throughout the novel. For instance, soon after Tyler has been assigned to Mala, he goes to find food for her only to discover that the "other residents had already been fed and the nurses were finishing their meals in the dining room" (13). Tyler responds to the nurses' disregard for their nourishment by bringing back a cup of soup for Mala as well as for himself, telling his still unresponsive patient, "I thought we could eat together" (15).

One of the most significant ways in which Tyler and Mala come to know each other is through their nonverbal, or extralinguistic, modes of communication. As Vivian May argues, since language is intimately bound with colonial and imperial projects of domination ("Trauma in Paradise" 125), their seeming abandonment of it suggests a mutual embrace of listening differently (127). This is certainly not to romanticize the sexual violations that led to Mala's reluctance to speak, but rather that even in the face of such trauma, new opportunities and alternative paradigms can emerge. It is precisely through this "listening differently," a fully sensory, embodied listening, that Mala comes to gain trust through Tyler's touch, while Tyler comes to understand Mala through the "words in her eyes" (21). Donna McCormack, in *Queer Postcolonial Narratives and the Ethics of Witnessing*, argues that their relationship is premised on a "multisensory witnessing" that queers modes of belonging by "decoloniz-ing epistemologies of the body, the family home and the nation" (40). Mala's refusal to use the colonizer's language can also be considered an example of Muñoz's disidentification.

In his early encounters with Mala, Tyler tells us how "my actions spoke more eloquently than any words" (17), and he continuously strives to make sure his actions can communicate with Mala the way he wants them to. Almost immediately upon meeting Mala, the importance of touch becomes central to his relationship with her: "The urge to touch overcame me . . . I rested my palm gently on her silver hair . . . This one touch turned her from the incarnation of fearful tales into a living human being, an elderly person such as those I had dedicated my life to serving. I needed to know the woman who lay hidden by the white sheet" (11). In this passage, it is the intimacy of touch that reverses the economies of fear that seek to isolate Mala from a definition of the human. Indeed, Mootoo's ability to construct such a delicate and profoundly ethical scene is only matched by the "one touch" that enables Tyler to recognize Mala's humanity. When Mala awakes, Tyler remains focused not only on her, but also on the ways in which she reads his movements: "I began to talk to her, to tell her where she was and who I was, but on hearing my voice she began a deep, fearful moaning. It did not take me long to realize that my movements, no matter how slight, terrified her. I sat still on a chair by her bed, and for an hour she watched as I tried to remain still . . . Still I did not move" (13). And later: "I became actually conscious of my movements and subtleties of my tone, which may have been all that communicated with her" (16).

This embodied form of listening leads Tyler to render himself vul-nerable to Mala's gaze. Tyler depends upon his "intuition" (itself an alternative epistemology to nursing as a form of medical expertise), which tells him that "the woman on the bed was going to prove herself to be neither crazy nor failing in health, and that she would fare better given more freedom" (20). At first it seems that he is speaking in reference to his recognition of her actions, but he blurs the lines by telling us, "Perhaps my intuition was nothing more than recalcitrant yearning, for I did fancy that she and I shared a common reception from the rest of the world" (20). Tyler's self is once again brought to bear on Mala's person; he admits that his perception of her is continually in tension with his own sense of self.

Importantly, it is through Tyler's narrative filtering that Mala's actions are described. We watch her grow increasingly trusting and responsive through his eyes, and see her communicate by what he sees in her eyes: "I tried to decipher the words in her eyes. I did not see fear in them but a pleading. I took that pleading to mean she hoped I would be true to my word" (21). Later, however, he tells us, "I watched her eyes, which I had come to believe were what she used for communicating. Then one evening, perched on the edge of the grounds, we were taking in the yellow sunset and the purpling of the distant valley—well, I was taking it in; I did not know what she was up to in her mind—when a pair of parrots flapped across the sky, squawking leisurely. She made no movement but I distinctly heard a perfect imitation of the parrots' calls. I dropped to my knees at her side" (23).

This vivid scene marks a significant turning point in their relationship. In tune with Mala's use of vision to communicate, and yet still separated by her lack of speech, Tyler literally falls to his knees when she trusts him enough to verbalize her reactions to the beautiful night. As a result of her sexual abuse, rather than "cultivating domination," Mala "crafts an embodied, nonhierarchical relation between plant, animal, land, and human, an alternative economy of being in which the pecking order between human, animal, and plant life has been abandoned" (May, "Trauma in Paradise" 123–24). Before allowing Tyler into this world, she has to know that he knows how to "listen differently." The rest of the people at the almshouse "lost interest in this new resident . . . she was uncommunicative and seemed to live in a world that did not include them" (23). In this nonreceptive environment, Mala continually watches Tyler for clues. Indeed, after his initial reaction to her parrot sounds, she responds by imitating a cricket: "I looked into her face, my jaw dropped in admiration and disbelief. She looked directly and proudly back, for the first time a hint of a smile lighting her face . . . Days passed with her calling out, only loud enough for me to hear . . . I would catch her watching me though the side of her eyes, as she did bird, cricket, and frog calls as though to entertain me" (24).

It is when Mala steals a women's nursing uniform for Tyler that we realize how she has been actively reading Tyler as well. He is waiting for her to make "real" communication, but he is forced to reconsider when she tells him, "You. You want to wear it" (76). Tyler realizes that Mala has been observing him: "I felt she had been watching me and seeing the same things that everyone saw. But she had stolen a dress for me. No one had ever done anything like that before. She knows what I am, was all I could think. She knows my nature" (76). Mala does not dwell on the uniform; rather, she immediately goes about constructing sculptures out of furniture, her nightly routine. Tyler is initially disappointed by her lack of attention, but then he realizes that her unconcern is a sign of generosity: "The reason Miss Ramchandin paid me no attention was that, to her mind, the outfit was not something to either congratulate or scorn—it simply was. She was not one to manacle nature, and I sensed that she was permitting mine its freedom" (77). As Tyler reflects on the meaning of Mala's actions, he tells us, "It had been a day and an evening to treasure. I had never felt so extremely ordinary, and I quite loved it" (78).

The privilege to be ordinary is what Mala and Tyler come to expect from, and respect most, about each other's willingness to engage in creative communication. As Tyler comes to realize, this may not be something utterly unique to their relationship, but it is only through Mala that he is able to reflect on and past relationships, which become legible only through an ability to see, listen, and read differently. Through this epistemic opening, he is able to comb through past experiences with new eyes. Whether in his developing relationship with Otoh or his closeness with his grandmother, Nana, his relationship with Mala is important: "Miss Ramchandin and I, too, had a camaraderie: we had found our own ways and fortified ourselves against the rest of the world" (48).

This sense of camaraderie, of "fortifying ourselves against the rest of the world," is a current that runs through all of these works, and it especially manifests itself in each author's experimentations with polyvocality. Insofar as creative modes of communication allow for inter-personal relations to prosper in sites of profound isolation and through gestures and silences, each author extends this symbolic emphasis by putting forth visions of positive, self-conscious interdependence as that which can destabilize unequal structures of power and potentially pro-pel us toward more egalitarian models of relationality that can enable new modes of subjectivity and political consciousness.

Toward an Epistemology of Polyvocality

Polyvocal narrative structures are an important element in feminist literary testimonios, reinforcing the ways in which multiple perspec-tives work to strengthen the epistemological relevance of the fragmented stories told within their pages. This narrative framing promotes a rela-tional account of human community in which the boundaries between self and other become overlapping and mutually constituting. While *A Single, Numberless Death*, *Steps Under Water*, and *The Little School* utilize testimonio to highlight the complex power dynamics of the imagined community of a nation, *Cereus Blooms at Night* turns attention to a var-ied racialized and ethnic national landscape as a result of colonization. In *Steps under Water* and *A Single, Numberless Death*, this is accomplished through their structural intercutting of interviews, diaries, and official documents alongside of, and entangled with, personal literary narratives, all of which bring attention to the processes of dialogic exchange that enabled the books to be written. In *Cereus Blooms at Night*, the narrative perspective shifts between multiple speakers, with each contributing dif-ferent anecdotal snippets and personal knowledge of the complicated family history that contributes to Mala Ramchandin's "queerness," and that reinforces the epistemic importance of a community of knowers working together to arrive at a more complete truth.

In *Steps under Water* and *A Single, Numberless Death*, one of the central ways the epistemological strength of a polyvocal approach to historical memory is taken up is through different characters' and authors' reflec-tions on the topic of "freedom." Within the fragmented narration in *A Single, Numberless Death*, Strejilevich juxtaposes several different responses to "freedom." For instance, one of her interviewees expresses shock at how quickly she adjusted to being outside of prison: "*I got used* to being free in no time. *Whenever I thought of being released I imagined it would be kind of weird, that I'd stumble on the sidewalk, feel totally disoriented. But no, it wasn't that way at all. I went out and felt great joy in simply walking down the street*" (81).

Another interviewee provides an account of the sensual dimension of her release, "*My first day out of jail I got up at dawn and stepped outside very early to see my first sunrise in nine years. I took a walk, wet my feet on the dew-covered grass, meandered along the train tracks, whatever—simply to experience that thing called freedom. That night, I remember, I went out for an ice cream. The lights made my head spin*" (80). While this account documents a sense of being overwhelmed ("the lights made my head spin"), it also conveys a sense of appreciation and delight in what the world has to offer. In contrast, Strejilevich's own account conveys a much deeper, more threatening sense of disorientation at reentering civic society: "My head is spinning, I don't have any documents and not a single penny. I tell the waiter I was mugged and ask him for change. I run to the bus stop clutching the coins in my hand. I'm fleeing, unused to being free" (80). Strejilevich's perspective self-consciously focuses on the material challenges of reintegration, especially in terms of finances and documents, and how one's physical "release" does not equate to an easy cognitive transition. Similarly, in *Steps under Water*, the stream-of-consciousness narrative style of the opening and closing chapters dramatizes the surrealism the narrator, Sara, experiences: "Everything else that came along seemed to me to be a lie. How could all those living trees be real, those cornfields, those shadows? There was only one truth and that was jail, the state of confinement" (Kozameh 145).

But the most exciting use of a polyvocal framework manifests when it is taken *beyond* its function of voicing multiple narrative reflections on a single theme. In feminist literary testimonios, multiperspective narrational practices become utilized to explore alternative kinship and relationship formations that move readers to think differently about questions of difference and interdependence. In providing reflection on the epistemic possibilities available to us when we recognize diversity of social location as an epistemic resource rather than as a hurdle to interconnection, these works articulate how a self-conscious acknowledgment of our multiple webs of entanglement with others—whether chosen or imposed—can move us toward relational modes of consciousness that can be utilized to confront these very same barriers, whether on structural or personal levels. This is what Strejilevich means when she speaks of needing to talk to people from the "same place" in order to better know and understand the historical gravity of her own story. By seeking out her own self-defined community of knowers, she does not reduce her conception of "same place" to social homogeneity, but rather frames it in terms of interpretive congruence. By connecting with others who maintain a shared conception of the world in response to their own experiences as political prisoners during the Dirty War, whether as family and friends to those imprisoned or disappeared or as activists who have politically dedicated themselves to seeking retribution for those affected, Strejilevich enables an interpretive process that allows for a more objective, three-dimensional understanding of her own social situation and articulates a complex politics of and commitment to bridging epistemic worlds.

While historical circumstance might determine how we come to know each other, literary feminist testimonios put forward a cautious hope that the relationships forged in the midst of imposed, oppressive social situations can nevertheless *have meaning in excess of the conditions themselves*. Indeed, in the face of structural injustice, and as these narratives differently suggest, sometimes interpersonal connection is all we have, as we see through the unlikely friendships of Mala and Tyler. Such representations strongly resonate with M. Jacqui Alexander's assertion in *Pedagogies of Crossing* that the process of becoming "more fully human" is intimately linked to "the urgent task of configuring new ways of being and knowing and to plot the different metaphysics that are needed to move away from living alterity premised in difference to living intersubjectivity premised in relationality and solidarity" (17, 8).[2]

This is why the polyvocal structure is so important in all feminist testimonio, as it insists upon such dialogic understanding. For Strejilevich this is primarily accomplished through her narrative framework, as evidenced in her transparent acknowledgment of the diverse resources, discourses, and perspectives needed to create a more historical, less subjective account of her experience as an Argentine political prisoner and in her search for meaning in the aftermath of her imprisonment. While Kozameh also structurally plays with dialogic exchange, her grappling with the epistemic possibilities of alternative forms of kinship and interdependence forged through situational circumstance is in her exploration of the bonds formed between *compañeras* that give way to lifelong friendships upon their release. Mootoo's tale is propelled just as much by the interconnections she forms between Tyler and Mala as by the work's sprawling web of characters and plot development. Even through the central trope of the cereus plant, described as a "network of spiny, three-sided stems and fleshy leaves" (130), we hear the theoretical echoes of Deleuze and Guattari's notion of the rhizome. With multiple entry and exit points between characters and subplots, interconnected traumas and tribulations, the cereus plant becomes representative of epistemic expansion and possibility.

In fact, the overlapping and interconnected stories serve to foreground how *all* interpersonal webs of entanglement, like the cereus plants itself, have their moments of beauty and decay: "With the force of a broken fire hydrant, the cereus blossoms spewed heavy perfume in the air . . . The scent of the cereus with its two edges—one a vanilla-like sweetness, the other a curdling—so permeated the air that she could taste it on her tongue as though she were lapping it from a bowl" (152). Similar to the two fragrant edges of the cereus plant, in Mootoo's narrative world, interpersonal interdependencies are not innately good or bad, they simply *are*. It is Mala's trial and the disruption of her quiet life that bring Tyler and Otoh together; it is Mala's mother's decision to escape a life of unhappiness to be free to be with her lover, Lavinia, that leads to Mala's sexual abuse at the hands of her father; it is the brief period of happiness and consensual sexual pleasure with Ambrose that leads to Mala's retreat from sanity; it is Mr. Hector's tender memory of his sexually persecuted brother that enables him to develop a "kinship forged out of situational circumstance" with Tyler (74); it is through their mutual ostracization that Mala and Tyler develop a beautiful relationship that allows them both to "bloom" in otherwise inhospitable circumstances. Indeed, as Otoh is voicing his guilt for the role he played in Mala's ending up in the almshouse, Tyler narrates: "I reminded him that if it weren't for his intervention, as unfortunate as it may have seemed in the moment, she and I, *and* he and I, would likely not have met" (123).

While Mala is considered beyond the rational, and so is dismissed by those in the ironically named "Paradise," Lantanacamara, it is through her character and the relationship she cultivates with the natural world that Mootoo positions us to recognize fundamental lessons about how it is only the principles of interdependence and social difference that remain constant in a life filled with epistemic multiplicity and parallel social worlds. While both of these realities maintain the dual edge of beauty and decay, as symbolically represented by the cereus plant, Mootoo's narrative suggests that it is only when we accept and stop actively working against these principles and place our own social wounds alongside of those experienced by others that we allow them to serve as resources rather than divisions.

This is beautifully summarized in a scene between Mr. Hector, the gardener, and Tyler, when Mr. Hector offers Tyler a flower to give to Mala. Tyler says, "I don't really know how to explain, but Miss Ramchandin might not react well to it. I think it is a very generous thing, that you want to give it to her. It's very touching, actually. No one here has really been kind to her . . . I am beginning to understand some things about her and I think that she does not like things in nature to be hurt. To her, the flower and the plant would be both suffering because they were separated from each other." (69) This truth is, of course, observed by Tyler when Mala steals the women's nurse's uniform for him, and is refreshingly unphased by him wearing it: "She knows what I am, was all I could think. She knows my nature" (75). By opening herself up to the "nature" of others rather than forcing upon them her own expectations, Mootoo develops Mala's character to position readers to reconsider their own modes of relationality. Mala's character prompts us to work toward modes of epistemic interconnectedness that recognize difference and interdependencies as epistemic resources that can help us to more fully reveal ourselves to each other, and that don't necessitate separating the flower from the plant, or blossom from decay. Once we come to accept the inherent imperfections of all human relationships, we can begin to imagine how alternative kinship systems might just be what can take us beyond relations of domination.

Cereus Blooms at Night most intimately explores this theme through the unlikely yet deeply transformational relationship established between Tyler and Mala Ramchandin. The spatial and temporal proximity between the two is established immediately and structurally woven into the narrative framework insofar as Tyler, as narrator, becomes conveyer of Mala's story as well as his own. As Tyler suggests, he is hardly able to tell his own story without simultaneously knowing it *through*

Mala's (3, 105). The intersubjective relationality and epistemic bridging of their stories is established on the first page of the novel, when Tyler explains, "My own intention, as the relater of this story, is not to bring notice to myself or my own plight. However, I cannot escape myself, and being a narrator who also existed on the periphery of the events, I am bound to be present . . . Forgive the lapses, for there are some, and read them with the understanding that to have erased them would have been to do the same to myself" (3).

Tyler's deliberative assertion adeptly calls into question any notion of a neutral, or "objective," narrative account, thereby disrupting hegemonic accounts of history that naturalize the teller and threaten to render silent nonnormative and marginalized voices such as his own. This vision of human interdependence, in which we know ourselves in and through our relationality to others, thus assumes a prominent role in Mootoo's novel, as modeled through Tyler's attempt to make transparent his own traces on Mala's story, in which he holds himself accountable to her.

Tyler's second instance of narrative posturing is when he speaks to an imagined Asha: "Thanks to your sister, my own life has finally—and not too late I might add—begun to bloom" (105). As such, Tyler continues to narrate an epistemically expansive vision in which he weaves together a "single garment out of myriad parts" (105), a delicate task that on the one hand resists romanticizing a shared identification with Mala, and on the other continues to highlight how the disparate social positionings Tyler and Mala inhabit do not keep them from relating to, and through, each other.

Despite his affinity with Mala, however, Tyler is not immune to the scandalous rumors that abound. Even as we understand him to share a deep empathy with her, he tells us, "Sometimes, I have to admit, I thought of the stories I had heard. I would edge myself out of Miss Ramchandin's sight whenever I tried to imagine her in the roles they had cast her in" (24). Despite their affinity, Tyler is not immune to this outwardly imposed social knowledge and must un-know much of what he takes for granted in order to enter into a truly epistemically just relationship with Mala. This unlearning takes many forms, beginning with their first meeting:

For such a tiny spectre of a being, the new resident breathed deeply and loudly in her drugged sleep. I squatted at the side of the canvas stretcher, peering at her. I expected her facial skin to be grey but it was ochre, like richly fired clay. . . . I rested my palm gently on her silver hair. I expected it to be coarse and wiry, qualities that would have fit the rumours. But her hair, though oily from lack of care, was soft and silken . . . She did not have the sweet yet sour smell I had come to expect whenever close to an old person. Instead, an aroma resembling rich vegetable compost escaped from under the sheet. (11)

From their first encounter, Mala challenges the many assumptions Tyler has about her. He does not expect that such a physically delicate person would be able to breathe that deeply. Nor does he expect her skin to be so vibrant, her hair so soft, her smell so robust. Soon after, he is also forced to reconsider the weight of her person: "Having judged only by her frail looks, I was surprised at her weight, forgetting for a moment the density of bone" (12). This constant reevaluation and reconsideration of all that Tyler thinks he knows becomes a profound commentary on the process of decolonizing interpersonal relations. He is suddenly estranged from what his expertise as nurse has taught him, and his encounter with Mala fundamentally disrupts his will to know; it is his gradual willingness to un-know, or perhaps to know differently, that marks his relationship with Mala.

The threat of overidentification is also present in the novel's opening pages. Tyler continually reveals how his admiration for Mala runs the risk of romanticizing and patronizing her. Just after he and Mala share their highly ritualistic meal of bread and soup, he tells us, "Filled with a sense of success, I pulled the sheet up around her neck and quietly left . . . I imagined further successes, immeasurable feats that I might accomplish with my great understanding and magnanimity. Finally, nausea at my own ballooning sense of self wore me down and I slept" (17). Mootoo's pairing of Tyler's tendency toward self-aggrandizement with a wry sense of humor that probingly interrogates his motives and their implications adds a refreshing layer of believability to his character.

Even when Tyler does risk eschewing their differences, Mootoo insists that he hold himself accountable: "The temptation is strong, I will admit, to be the romantic victim. There is in me a performer dying for the part, but I must be strict with myself and stay with my intention to relate Mala Ramchandin's story" (15). Tyler's indulgences mark him as imperfect, and thus fundamentally human. As such, we do not fault him when he does not immediately undo Mala's restraints. Rather, we applaud his courage when he does and as he holds himself accountable for not doing so sooner: "I sat by her head, slipped my arm under her back and pulled her into my arms. I held her against my chest, rocking her until the first streaks of morning light broke through the pitch black sky" (21).

While *Cereus Blooms at Night* allows Mootoo to thematically explore relational possibilities to poetic depths, Kozameh's exploration of the bonds formed between *compañeras* provides a parallel consideration of how imposed social circumstance need not serve as an impediment to interconnection; rather, such circumstances can enable opportunities to meaningfully work across social difference and open up new relational potential. For instance, when Sara is first imprisoned, Kozameh takes the opportunity to have another inmate, Adriana, comment on how the class system does not simply disappear in these altered circumstances: "And those two that won't come over here, see them? They're prostitutes. They never fit in anywhere. They feel that the regulars like us are high class. We really make them sick. I can imagine what you must be feeling facing all of us. All the political ones are professional and students, from rich families. Or almost all of them right?" (25).

Through Adriana's summary of how the class system is maintained within prison walls, readers are positioned to resist an overly utopic notion of the solidarity formed between *compañeras*. In a chapter entitled "Sara, Elsa, Marco, and the Dance of Great Sadness," Kozameh counters this in a realistic, heartbreaking scenario that insists on the strength of such relations forged through situational circumstance. In striking parallel to how the "shared queerness" between Mala and Tyler allows them to negotiate their social differences and to join forces against the unwelcoming almshouse atmosphere they both face, this chapter highlights how the bonds established between Sara and Elsa, as a result of their shared prison experience, allow them to work beyond a heteronormative relational paradigm when they find themselves on "the outside."

Through several different narrative "versions," Kozameh paints a portrait of a love triangle in which the hetero marriage of Elsa and Marco is disrupted by Marco's relationship with Sara, *compañera* of Elsa. As Kozameh moves between "Christina's Version," "Sara and Marco's Version," to

"Elsa and Marco's Version, That Same Night," to "Sara and Elsa's Version, in the Train That Will Take Sara Far Away," readers become privy to contradictions that former political prisoners experience as they reenter their preexisting personal relationships and lives. Sara's budding relationship with Marco highlights her personal floundering to regain some sense of human connection, and yet this very relationship threatens to undo her friendship with Elsa. Such an act certainly challenges a utopic notion of solidarity established between *compañeras*, in its embodied betrayal of such trust.

Rather than reinforce the worn narrative of women's bonds severed through heteronormative relations, Sara and Elsa's narrative takes a detour. Whereas it is usually the male who is positioned as having the upper hand in such romantic situations, Marco instead vocalizes his feelings of exclusion from Elsa's life: "Prison changed you, Elsa. You don't love me anymore . . . Your friends and your son hold a privileged place in your life" (68). As the "versions" progress, Elsa grows cognizant of how Marco's relationship with Sara is a misdirected attempt at regaining her own affection and attentions. Whereas the aftermath of state-sponsored terror might lead some readers to anticipate a contraction of human relationships of those affected, this moment highlights quite the opposite: an expansion. Rather than simply purging Sara from their relationship to regain their footing as a couple, they come to express a shared concern for Sara's well-being. In "Elsa and Marco's Version, In Their Car Parked Near the Command Post at the II Army Corps," they ask: "What are we doing here, together, looking out for Sara, so afraid of what might be happening behind those walls, desperate to see her come out, walk, move like any human being on the street, fretting over the possibility that she might not appear, that she might never emerge from that fortress of horror?" (69). Even in such a difficult moment in their relationship—a difficulty induced by Sara herself—Marco and Elsa find themselves thinking beyond themselves, of experiencing an overwhelming concern for Sara. It is through this sense of expansion that they come to a reorganization of the relationships between them: "What are the two of us doing, inside our car, our arms around each other? What are we doing? Maybe we're already in a position to give ourselves a unique and enviable response: we watch over Sara" (70).

Whereas many narratives would end here, with hetero-romantic love triumphing over women's friendship, Kozameh writes beyond this ending. In the final, understated scene of the chapter, Sara and Elsa are talking just before Sara's departure:

"What a mess . . ."

"Sara, listen, that was just a very tiny part of all this horror. And, if you think about it, my being away all those years. You being so beautiful, intelligent and sophisticated, crazy and ballsy . . . Me getting out of prison and completely dedicated to getting Lucas back again. How could Marco not fall in love with you? And you, with Hugo in jail, love-starved, like anyone else, you get your freedom and are alone, how could you not be tempted by someone like Marco? Warm, protective, a good person. He's very weak now, after all these years. I have to take care of him . . . And you know what? You were right: you and I know a lot about life . . . We know so much . . . . Sara, all of us have been very strong, but we've suffered a lot. We're still suffering. And I love you." (70–71)

While profound simplicity and truth resound within the entirety of this passage, it is the final two phrases that most highlight the sense of expansion. It is only in thinking beyond themselves that Elsa and Sara can attest to the strength of the bonds formed between the *compañeras* due to situational circumstance: "We're still suffering. And I love you." Given the scale of horror both have witnessed, the personal indiscretions they speak of pale in comparison. It is not that they do not matter—as readers we have witnessed all three characters on the verge of their own undoing—rather, it is that Sara and Elsa have gleaned enough perspective to know that their bond extends beyond this situation; their relationship runs deeper than such a betrayal can cut. Though they might not even have been friends, or so closely connected without their shared experience as political prisoners, the imposed conditions of their friendship mean less than the relational connections they have been able to create. It is no accident that Kozameh closes the chapter with their narrational perspectives. Here the women are configured as the strong ones, the knowers ("You're right. We know so much."); Marco, the would-be dominant figure in another tale, is so "very weak," in need of Elsa's caretaking.

It important to note that none of the relationships explored within these texts fall outside of a web of complex power relations, nor do these texts sidestep the power asymmetries involved in their diverse characters exploring questions of nation, race, sexuality, class, or gender. Rather, by acknowledging, and often dramatizing, their entrenchment in such structural inequities, these literary testimonios deal with highly contentious social issues to highlight how meaningful connection and community can also exist outside of socially imposed scripts.

The decision of feminist literary testimonios to focus on interpersonal connections more than structural inequalities is a conscious choice worthy of more consideration than simply romanticizing "small-scale resistance." Such works seek to highlight the *experience* of memory, and to actively explore how the various ways we remember and tell might enable us to create new epistemological possibilities out of well-worn social narratives, including those of oppression and resistance.

Beyond the mere "survival" of imaginative capabilities in the face of state-sponsored terror and personal trauma, these works highlight a more profound truth: how repressive conditions both *enable* and *necessitate* the imagination to flourish. While oppressive social conditions necessarily interrupt and infiltrate the ways in which social actors experience their present, it is precisely by accepting and working through hardships that we come to imagine different ways of being in the world. These other ways of being in the world become inseparable from the work of imagining epistemic bridges that give way to kaleidoscopic consciousness without seeking simple or transparent resolutions.

The epistemological value of such relationships, even when explored in an imagined, literary way, opens new doors for conceptions of subjectivity, history, and knowledge production, allowing the polyvocal frameworks established by these works to move beyond narrative strategy and to open the hearts and minds of their readers. At their most ambitious, they work to develop an epistemology of polyvocality that insists on the epistemic value of communities of meaning, and that enables us to appreciate the ways in which diversity of perspectives, social locations, and experiences are assets in expansive and equitable social realities. Even while engaging with the underbelly of human relations, feminist literary testimonios put forth their truths as cautious, deliberate, and hard-won symbols of hope.

PART IV

Storytelling the Archive

CHAPTER 8

Retransmissions

Reaching across Languages, Genres, and Readerships with Danticat's Multilingual "Fake-lore"

> Translating—retranslating—that story form the original English in which I had written it had been a surreal experience. It was as if the voice in which I write, the voice in which people speak Creole that comes out English on paper, had been released and finally I was writing for people like my Tante Illyana, people who did not read, not because they did not have enough time or because they had too many other gadgets or distractions, but because they had never learned how.
>
> —EDWIDGE DANTICAT, *CREATE DANGEROUSLY*

> Create dangerously, for people who read dangerously . . . Coming from where I come from, with the history I have—having spent the first twelve years of my life under both dictatorships of Papa Doc and his son, Jean-Claude—this is what I've always seen as the unifying principle among all writers . . . . boldly embracing the public and private terrors that would silence us, then bravely moving forward even when it feels as though we are chasing or being chased by ghosts.
>
> —EDWIDGE DANTICAT, *CREATE DANGEROUSLY*

STORYTELLER EDWIDGE DANTICAT HAS BUILT A CAREER ON producing historically grounded fictions that testify to the lives and cultural vitality of Haitians and Haitian Americans in the face of colonial legacies and neocolonial conditions, particularly the intergenerational lives of women. Danticat's 1995 short story cycle *Krik? Krak!* received wide acclaim in the United States, including a National Book Award nomination, and was seen as a strong follow-up to her debut novel, *Breath, Eyes, Memory*, which itself earned a spot in Oprah's Book Club. Since then, she has received the MacArthur Genius Award, and her books have consistently found themselves on the *New York Times* bestseller list, a compelling marker that Danticat and her work have been accepted by a US mainstream readership. In 2010, Danticat was also approached by several mainstream media sources to weigh in on the disastrous consequences of Haiti's earthquake, and she has become increasingly outspoken on US immigration policies.[1] Danticat's work spans the genres of novel, short story, memoir, young adult literature, children's literature, magazine articles, and nonfiction testimonies. She has readily made herself available for news interviews, author interviews, literary panels, and educational lecturing.

Combined, Danticat's public persona and literary presence highlight the significance she places on cultural representations. She is a politically engaged black Haitian American author who understands representational politics as occupying a central terrain in social struggle. The multiple hats she wears as a public figure—storyteller, journalist, cultural critic—highlight her increasing strides to gain access to the imagination of mainstream (white, middle-class) American readers. Chapters 8 and 9 perform a series of close readings of Danticat's work to highlight the subtle and explicit evocations of testimonio within her corpus of historically grounded literature. These discussions stretch the concept of polyvocality to consider the multivocal techniques Danticat employs to reach multiple audiences in multiple genres and (epistemic, linguistic) registers. By claiming a space in the US publishing market and news media, Danticat enables an opening for the life experiences of Haitians and Haitian Americans—particularly women—to reach a readership that has been comfortably able to ignore the imperialist historical relations between the United States and Haiti and the marginalization of Haitian Americans within US borders. Danticat's ability to maneuver these various genres and forums highlights her investment in representation as a highly political and epistemic act; the complexities of her self-conscious labors are as present in her discussions of her work as in her literary representations themselves.

While not ignoring the tokenizing interpretive practices embedded in a mainstream US readership, these two chapters focus on the ways that Danticat *anticipates* such modes of neocolonial, consumptive reading practices by utilizing language and representational techniques that resist such readings from the outset. I close the book with this engagement of Danticat's corpus as a way of weaving together several of the book's threads and to offer a deep dive into the multiple works and worlds of a single author.

While Danticat explicitly offsets dominant national and secular western epistemes through her thematic engagements with immigration and diaspora, Haitian folklore and Vodou epistemology, it remains less immediately obvious how she is able to accomplish this through her employment of English, a dominant US and global language. Chapters 8 and 9 highlight how this linguistic choice enables her to gain access to a readership that writing in French or Creole would not allow her. This choice accounts for Danticat as a historically situated subject, showing how her linguistic "choices" are highly entwined with the reality of her having lived in the US from the age of twelve.[2] While French and Creole served as her primary languages in Haiti, her entrance into the US—and particularly its education system—significantly restricted these languages to the private sphere in exchanges with family and friends.[3] If it is true that language shapes thought, then the multilingual strategies that resonate within Danticat's use of English speak to processes of socialization she underwent upon moving to the US and the psychical effects she experienced. Indeed, Danticat "creolizes" English through both her phrasings and her explicit maneuvering between (national) language systems.[4] Through such actions, Danticat blurs distinctions between "western" and "nonwestern" epistemes by creating linkages between and across nations and audiences, and embodying the hyphenated social position of the author herself.

Born in Haiti, Danticat became Haitian American at age twelve when her parents, already living in Brooklyn, sent for her. Danticat's diasporic identity has proven confounding and controversial to disparate audiences. To some, it is Danticat's residence within the US—despite her living in places with a decidedly Haitian presence, including Brooklyn and Miami—that determines the way in which her fiction should be categorized. Mainstream US anglo audiences are often quick to claim her work as squarely within "American" literature, even as some continue to position her in the "ethnic" sector, a positioning Danticat works hard to challenge (Capshaw Smith 195). Alternately, Haitians living in Haiti are sometimes suspicious of her physical proximity to the metropole, and thus in some cases, reluctant to claim her as their own.[5] In *The Butterfly's Way*, a collection of Haitian American writings edited by Danticat, she discusses how calling someone a "dyaspora" serves as a distancing mechanism meant to challenge knowledge claims from someone considered not-quite-Haitian-enough: "When expressing an opposing political point of view in discussion with friends and family members living in Haiti . . . [they] knew that they could easily silence me by saying, 'What do you know? You're a 'Dyaspora'" (xiv).

Danticat's biography attests to her ability to straddle multiple worlds as well as her motivation to using her creative writing as a way to actively engage in cross-border cultural work by speaking to and across multiple audiences. Danticat's own personal border crossings problematize the oversimplified notions of "authenticity" and "origins" that normative geographical literary categories demand. Rather, Danticat actively works against such cultural ownership by drawing upon her autobiographical experiences as a diasporic subject to render intelligible her both/and approach to language and culture: "When I say 'my country' to some Haitians, they think I mean the United States. When I say 'my country' to some Americans, they think of Haiti.' My country, I felt, both as an immigrant and as an artist, was something that was then being called the tenth department. Haiti had nine geographic departments and the tenth was the floating homeland, the ideological one, which joined all Haitians living outside of Haiti" (*Create Dangerously* 49). In discussing how she and other Haitian Americans inhabit a "between-worlds space." Danticat invokes the words of influential Haitian political journalist Jean Dominique, who once reassuringly told her, "The Dyaspora are people with their feet planted in both worlds . . . There's no need to be ashamed of that. There are more than a million of you. You all are not alone" (*Create Dangerously* 51).

Danticat has also claimed her hybrid, diasporic perspective as an epistemological resource in terms of how this cultural in-betweenness benefits her writing: "It's easier to see us as something foreign. But that's great for a writer as you can't be a complete insider . . . And maybe to write, it's right that we are not seen as producers of national culture. I don't think immigration is tragic for a writer. Suddenly you find yourself inside and outside a culture. It adds some nuance, some depth. Of course you lose some direct line to your culture, but distance can also give you another kind of eye with which to examine things" (Candelario 82).

While this quotation to some degree resonates with Salman Rushdie's uncritical celebration of the migrant in *Imaginary Homelands*, Danticat's understanding of her position seems more in line with Gloria Anzaldúa's notion of *la frontera*/the borderland and Medina's notion of kaleidoscopic consciousness. Rather than professing this between-worlds space as a valorized and privileged position, she frames it as a marginalized position that simultaneously lends itself to productive and creative effects.[6] Statements such as this make it difficult for her readerships to claim her as a writer working in the service of any one national project.

Danticat's decision to write in English remains a controversial choice. There are those who consider this choice a marker of her valuing the "American" over the "Haitian" part of her hyphenated identity. No doubt, the language in which one chooses to write and therefore make knowledge claims is never a neutral decision, especially when one is writing in the dominant language of English, a tongue closely connected to ongoing histories of conquest and oppression. But Danticat is quite aware of the linguistic "choices" she makes, and has addressed how writing in English is both necessity and compromise. Referring to English as her "stepmother tongue," she suggests:

> You have a mother tongue and then an adopted language that you take
> on because your family circumstances have changed, sometimes not by
> your own choice. But I don't think of it as something ugly. I've always
> thought my relationship to language is precarious because in the
> first part of my life, I was balancing languages. As I was growing up,
> we spoke Creole at home, but when you go out, you speak French in
> the office, at the bank . . . French is the socially valid and accepted
> language, but then the people who speak Creole are not validated and
> in some way are being told their voice isn't heard. So I've always felt this
> dichotomy in language anyway. (Shea 387–88)

Speaking to how language is always circumscribed and determined by sociocultural conditions, Danticat highlights the simultaneous "foreignness" and intimacy involved in her relationship to English. At once the "step" that comes to stand in for her "mother" tongues (French, Creole), the distance/intimacy Danticat implies in the above quotation becomes embodied in her very usage of the term "stepmother"—an often tenuous yet intimate relationship that becomes supplemental to the relationship with the mother. Never replacing it and yet forevermore complicating and in many ways enriching it, the relationship with the stepmother (tongue) paradoxically allows a critical distance and perspective on an originary relationship with the mother. If we understand language as laden with epistemic value, Danticat's ability to cross between languages allows her to effectively traffic between epistemes, understanding the ability of each to contribute to her kaleidoscopic narrations and offering the potential for further intimacy with each.

Equally important, in this passage Danticat displaces romanticized and gendered configurations of her "mother" tongue(s), highlighting how her originary tongues were never simple, or for that matter, singular or reflective of a supposed linguistic authenticity and origin. Rather, identifying French and Creole as "co-mothers" competing for recognition, Danticat articulates how her relationship with English, though uneasy, nevertheless provides a vehicle to connect the oral and the written, the vernacular and the formal, in a way that her childhood languages did not: "I wrote in a language I didn't speak regularly and spoke a language I couldn't write. When I came here [US] and learned English, it was the first time I could write and speak the same language" (Lyons 189).

This bridging of the oral (Creole) and the written (French) through the vehicle of English is central to Danticat's ability to bring seemingly disparate voices and worldviews into conversation; by linking spheres, peoples, and geopolitical sites through the medium of language, Danticat attests to the importance of a living language that is able to cut across and through social registers while implicitly commenting on the limiting effects of these imposed borders. Her embrace of English, while displacing a romanticized view of her native languages, does not constitute a "break" with her connections to French and Creole. If anything her acquisition of English has furthered her appreciation of them, suggesting that the advantage of growing up in a bilingual country is that it raises your consciousness of the uses to which language can be put (Lyons 189).

Danticat's multilayered relation to language is further evidenced in her referral to all translations of her work as "retranslations." In addition to shuttling between language systems in her mind and on the page, Danticat says, "I always think of the translation as a retranslation because I am transferring an image in my head onto a page. Add to this the fact that my native language is not the one I am writing in and you also have another kind of translation" (Candelario 84). These layers of translation (modal, linguistic, experiential, epistemic) resonate with Gayatri Spivak's concept of ethical translation, which is attentive to the amount of "fraying" between the original and shadow ("Translation" 180). While Spivak suggests that "risky fraying" always underpins this act of translation, similar to Danticat, she understands this "risk" as worth taking when in line with an ethical commitment (187). But while Spivak suggests the *idea*, she does not offer a *how* (Tissot 37). Danticat, along with her contemporary feminist polyvocal testimonial co-travelers, puts her cultural translations forth as one possible way forward. By keeping these questions in her central line of vision, Danticat attempts to negotiate linguistic representations that best serve her own agenda rather than that of the metropole.

Through these statements Danticat importantly reinforces how *any* language decision is imbued with political consequences and how perhaps more important than the specific language in which one writes is the *intentionality* that motivates the choice and the context from which it emerges—something she seeks to make transparent. In interviews, Danticat speaks openly and deliberately about the various ways in which she uses language, most probably to complicate and problematize people's own assumptions about the unidirectionality of dominant languages: "People sometimes say to me, 'Why do you write in English?' It's the circumstances of my life that led to this. If you grew up in the United States and ended up in Mexico and wrote in Spanish, is your doing that saying you are rejecting something else? It's not to say that if you write in English, you don't think Creole or French should be written in" (Shea 388). Danticat's points complicate the assumption that every immigrant has the skill set and opportunity to write in their originary tongue(s) as well as adopted languages, and highlights how this expectation fails to see that "choosing" which language to write in is not always an option.

By "written in," Danticat refers not only to her inclusion of French and Creole phrases, but also a *shadowing*, or echoing, of these languages *within* the English itself. Speaking to her language concerns when writing *Breath, Eyes, Memory*, Danticat suggests that there are "three languages in play—implied—in the novel: sometimes characters speak Spanish, sometimes in Creole, but it's all in English" (Shea 388). Similarly, Marie-José N'Zengou-Tayo suggests that this approach allows Haitian sentiments to be cloaked in English "attire" (136). Further, N'Zengou-Tayo describes the "implicit presence of Creole underneath the English sentences" as manifesting itself "when the English sentence is *twisted* by the Haitian turn of phrase given to it" (136, my emphasis).[7]

The ways in which Danticat utilizes American English to register Haitian sentiments, epistemes, and phrasings—whether we call it cloaking, shadowing, echoing, or twisting—emphasize how language is a social and political tool. Specifically in terms of the Haitian American subset of the US audience and more generally in reference to the various immigrant groups within US borders, Danticat's English usage can be read as a bridging mechanism to bring together geographically and linguistically fragmented "minority" groups who do not find themselves represented in US print media but whose various experiences might affectively resonate with the questions of identity and displacement Danticat's fiction explores. Danticat's English usage can also be read as a way of bridging the geographic and linguistic borders of the Caribbean islands, another community to which Danticat belongs.

The potentialities of the epistemic connections that can be made through Danticat's English usage seem for her to outweigh the negative forms of appropriation and (mis)recognition that might result when disparate audiences encounter her work. At times, Danticat proactively addresses the politics of her language choices through the brief usage of direct address. For instance, in the postscript to her young adult first-person fiction *Behind the Mountains*, she states, "What might seem odd is that even though the primary language of Haiti is Creole, this diary is written in English. However I would like you to imagine that Celiane wrote these words in her native tongue and that I am merely her translator" (166). Through this succinct authorial direction, Danticat informs her young readers that Haiti's national language is not in fact English, while instructing them to hear the echoes of Creole within Celiane's words.

Ifeona Fulani similarly understands Danticat's usage of English as an epistemic strategy that allows her to gain access to mainstream US publishing markets while creating positive representations of Caribbean cultures and opening up the market for other Caribbean women's voices, thereby destabilizing extreme asymmetrical relations of power.[8] Concerned with the "practice of 'unhearing' by influential individuals in the U.S. publishing industry" (64), Fulani articulates strategies for combatting the publishing industry's suppression of Caribbean women's writings. Central to Fulani's discussion is the story "Anancy and the Sky God," an Ashanti tale in which a spider (Anancy) tries to get back all of the stories of the world that the Sky God has claimed for his own enjoyment.[9] For Fulani, Danticat's writing is an example of literary "anancyism," which she describes as

> a model of subtle and perspicacious strategizing . . . Anancy displays characteristics in common with the ex-isled figure . . . capable both of dwelling inside society, all the better to view and access objectively . . . Anancy is the signifyin(g) spider who, in the continuous spinning of his web, tests the limits of language in a perpetual "discourse of trickery." In this manifestation Anancy is a potent emblem for the Caribbean writer at large in the United States. A writer in this outsider/insider position is as liminal a figure as Anancy, necessitating quick-wittedness and perspicacity . . . and persistence in plying her trade— weaving her web of stories. (69)

Reminiscent of Danticat's own description of how her diasporic identity marks her as an insider/outsider, and identifying the US publishing industry as a cultural colonizer, Fulani recognizes subtle language manipulations and negotiations as central strategies for "outsmarting" these contemporary "sky gods," suggesting that "with an ease that invokes Anancy," Danticat "inhabits at least three literary identities: to those who would mainstream her, she is American; she is Haitian American to the multiculturalists; and to the Haitian- and Caribbean-based audience, she is simply Haitian" (75).

To be sure, Danticat's multilingual narrative strategies enable her to simultaneously inhabit these various writerly identities and allegiances. The question of whether any single audience is Danticat's "proper" one is confounded by Danticat's claiming of the "tenth department" and her concept of diaspora as a floating homeland. By hybridizing her linguistic choices and straddling several language systems, Danticat carves out a representational fluidity that is fearless and expansive, and capable of representing *linguistically* the *epistemic* complexities that her diasporic positioning enables her to see.

Oraliture, Kitchen Poets, and Women's Cultural Transmission in Danticat's "Fake-lore"

In *Caribbean Discourse* Edouard Glissant suggests that it is "an oralizing of the written" that most directly points to a Caribbean aesthetics (244). The term "oraliture" is itself a recent Haitian neologism that refers to an insistence on remaining within "the realm of the "oral" (188).[10] Orality is present not only in the occasional Creole turn of phrases that "twist" Danticat's English sentences, but also in her conception of herself as a cultural worker. When asked in interviews to describe the way she sees herself as an artist, Danticat repeatedly responds by insisting that she is a "storyteller," or one who tells stories (Capshaw Smith 197). "Storyteller" is subtly yet significantly distinct from "writer," a term that privileges the written. Indeed, the oral residue of "storyteller" enhances the significance of the title of her short story collection, *Krik? Krak!* and its culturally rooted allegiance to an active form of storytelling session that suggests both a willing and accountable teller and a listener/audience.

Danticat first introduces this form of storytelling in the opening story of the collection, "Children of the Sea." Recounting the sea voyage of political Haitian refugees in the early nineties, the narrator of the story writes: "We spent most of yesterday telling stories. Someone says, Krik? You answer, Krak! And they say, I have many stories I could tell you, and then they go on and tell these stories to you, but mostly to themselves" (14). Given the dire circumstances of the situation and the narrator's assertion that these stories are told "mostly to [the tellers] themselves" (14), storytelling is configured as a mode of survival, a way to ensure one's existence and to save one's life—a truth that closely resounds with the *griyo/istwa* paradigm articulated by the Haitian storytellers in Bell's *Walking on Fire*.

This understanding of "storytelling as survival" echoes the claim made by women-of-color feminists that to tell one's story is to radically resist cultural silencing as well as a fundamental tenet of the testimonio ethos.[11] Within Danticat's corpus, bearing witness to the speakers' stories is framed as an ethical act accomplished through active listening, one that pays credence to the complex personhood of the speaker in the face of dehumanizing conditions. It is no accident readers are introduced to the collection through a culturally resonant call/response framework. Denise Shaw understands Haitian women's rich oral tradition as a central tool employed by Danticat in all of her works (2). Danticat's tactical decision to anticipatorily frame the collection around the concept of "Krik? Krak!" speaks to the terms through which she hopes her stories will be read and engaged. Based on this understanding of writer and reader, storyteller and witness, Danticat offers a collection that attests to the vitality and richness of Haitian culture in the face of colonial, political, and economic struggle, accomplished through her exploration of the cultural, epistemological, and historical circumstances that circumscribe the life stories of her characters.

Beyond this, most often it is the women in her stories who undertake the cultural and political work of storytelling. By linking together the lives of several individual women across temporal, geographic, class, generational, and epistemic borders, Danticat enables readers to imagine a multilayered landscape of the lives of past and present Haitian women, while connecting them through themes of kinship (not necessarily related to bloodlines), interdependence, and reciprocity. This is performed in *Krik? Krak!* through the collection's variegated panorama of socially located characters, which anticipates and contests neocolonial impulses to "know" Haitian culture through a homogenizing lens. Simultaneously, her attention to cultural tensions and biases resists a superficial romanticization of community. As Danticat reminds us through her narratives, and echoing the vision of *Cereus Blooms at Night*, it is precisely because of the ugly, encompassing gendered dimensions of colonial, economic, and class violence that such a community of women is forged.

If the opening story of *Krik? Krak!* offers insight on the epistemological importance of storytelling in Haitian culture generally, the ethical,
spiritual, and gendered elements present in this form of oral, embodied
storytelling are most powerfully articulated in the collection's epilogue,
entitled "Women Like Us." In remembrance of and in dedication to all of
the narrator's kinswomen, whom she refers to as "kitchen poets," the narrator reflects on how she has only come to writing through their stories:[12]

> Kitchen poets, you call them . . . These women, they ask for your voice
> so that they could tell your mother in your place that yes, women
> like you do speak, even if they speak in a tongue that is hard to
> understand. Even if it's patois, dialect, Creole . . . Most of the women
> in your life had their heads down . . . sometimes, they were talking to
> faces across the ages, faces like yours and mine. You thought that if you
> didn't tell the stories, the sky would fall on your head . . . You have
> never been able to escape the pounding of a thousand other hearts that
> have outlived you by thousands of years. Over the years when you have
> needed us, you have always cried, "Krik?" and we have answered
> "Krak!" and it has shown us that you have not forgotten us . . . [your
> mother] would ask you to name each braid after those nine hundred
> and ninety-nine women who were boiling in your blood, and since you
> had written them down and memorized them, the names would come
> rolling off your tongue. (222–24)

This multifaceted and poetic epilogue can be understood as Danticat's
own personal manifesto on what propels her to write, and how she considers her writing to be in the service of her kinswomen—an exercise in
historical collective meaning-making. By rooting herself and her work in
the lives of ordinary Haitian women, of those whose social knowledge is
intimately connected to the domestic sphere, Danticat's encoding of them
as "kitchen poets" imbues them with a level of critical agency and dignity that is reminiscent of Aurora Levins Morales's suggestion that testimonio is capable of "making theory out of the stuff in our pockets, out
of the stories, incidents, dreams, frustrations that were never acceptable
anywhere else" (Latina Feminist Group 32). Her theoretical reflections are
deliberately counterbalanced and heavily interwoven with the embodied
domestic and ritualistic imagery of cooking and hair braiding.

The figure of the kitchen poet more broadly resonates with US women-of-color feminists' reclamation of "kitchen table theorizing," an americanized framing of testimonio, and of valuing knowledge in the vernacular, claiming the domestic an important site of collective meaning-making even if and when it is not recognized in academic realms as knowledge "proper." While the narrative voice articulates her mother's disappointment in her writing habit, this extended reflection highlights how writing for her is a way *in* rather than *out*, a way of connecting herself with the community of women who came before her and paying tribute to their legacy. In this way we can understand the voice that comes through her writings as a lending to those women who have been historically silenced not only by masculinist and imperial histories but also by other Haitian women ("They ask for your voice so that they could tell your mother in your place that yes, women like you do speak, even if they speak in a tongue that is hard to understand"). Danticat's impetus to write is not defined by a need to "give women a voice," or even a "speaking with." Rather, the need to storytell is framed as being in service to something bigger than herself: "These women, they ask for your voice"—in which cultural representation is offered as a mode of accountability that honors the lives of ordinary Haitian women and the unique knowledge and perspectives their social locations afford.

And yet, this passage proposes that while these women may be poor in material, "real" ways, their inner worlds and epistemes enable them to exist outside of these material concerns. Beyond the confines of imposed poverty, gendered social scripts, and even beyond the material world, they operate in epistemes that connect them to a collective unconscious that necessarily disrupts the temporality of chronological time measurements and exists outside of a colonial framework. In this way, Danticat extends the reach of the reflections of Strejilevich, Kozameh, and Mootoo on the notion of a "living past." The possibility of a collective unconscious disrupts the binaries of past/present, individual/collective at a fundamental level, and allows for an expansive understanding of the epistemic relevance of interpretive communities and the possibilities of collective meaning-making. If the archive is something understood as within you ("those nine hundred and ninety-nine women who were boiling in your blood"), or as handed down through the oral stories that accompany cooking and hair braiding—rather than something located outside of you in the form of written historical record—one's sense of social responsibility must also shift from an autonomous to collective, or connected, accountability.

This is why Danticat positions her writing in horizontal relationship with the traditional ritualized cultural transmissions of cooking, braiding, and oral tale-telling, and as a skill that best enables her to listen to stories, tell stories, and name the voices of the women who came before her. Here writing is configured as an ethical communal and political act, as she pens the oral knowledge of her kinswomen into a formal narration that literally writes their lives back into history. Through the chaotic, cacophonous phrase "You have never been able to escape the pounding of a thousand other hearts that have outlived you by thousands of years," she illustrates how these women's stories will not leave her alone; that they must be told for her to understand her own.

This relationality is marked by a shift in narrative voice that decenters the initial first-person "I" of the narrator to the third person "you" as her kinswomen speak through her and her writing—a fluid, mutual exchange between the dead and the living laden with tremendous responsibility; it is hard, it is a struggle. There is no escaping "the pounding of a thousand other hearts," of these women's life stories "boiling" in her blood, except to write them, since to write their stories is also to write herself and to know herself through them, testifying to the meaning of their lives through their ability to give meaning to her own memory work. The decidedly collective testimonial quality in this passage reinforces the ethical component in the hearing and telling of Danticat's stories. Through "hearing" the ancestral voices, Danticat suggests that she must change the way she listens, a subtle directive to readers themselves, who must interrogate and alter their own worldviews to account for the truths of the women for whom she writes. Elements of testimonio are repeated throughout Danticat's corpus as a way of producing "a narrative space [that] allows readers to participate as witnesses to collective and individual atrocities that have shaped the imagination of Haitian writers" (Shaw 12). Shaw's claim closely resonates with Fulani's point that Danticat uses writing strategies by which she "gain[s] access to the imagination of the non-Haitian, non-Caribbean reader, and enter[s] the American imagination" (77).

Danticat also takes creative license within the testimonial sphere and takes imaginative liberties in writing this gendered archive by referring to many of her women-focused folkloric evocations as "fake-lore," "self-created folklore . . . hybrid and *métisse* warm-weather daffodils" (*Create Dangerously* 68). And it is no wonder; Danticat's work specifically focuses on the lives of Haitian and Haitian American women whose life stories continue to be silenced through masculinist renderings of Haitian and Caribbean histories. If anything is sacred in Danticat's work, it is the communities of women that remain the centerpieces of her stories. By testifying to the beauty, strength, and existence of their lives and beliefs, Danticat positions her women characters in close proximity to the asymmetrical power relations (within and outside Haiti's borders) that often serve to discount and erase their experiences.

By magnifying the communities of Haitian women who have been marginalized, she is able to highlight how these are at once a source of support and healing and internally marked by generational, class, regional, and epistemic struggle; the disparate social positionings and belief systems of individual women characters at times collide and compete for recognition and validity. These distinct voices and perspectives straddle ideologic and epistemic divides, enabling a polyphonic quality that Danticat masterfully utilizes to bring different voices into productive proximity through polyvocal narrative strategies.

Polyvocal Narration as Collective Meaning-Making in *Krik? Krak!*

One of Danticat's consistent thematics is the continuing influence of French colonialism in the daily lives of Haitian citizens, as well as the ways in which US-Haitian relations affect Haitian politics and the marginalized status of Haitian American immigrants within US borders. In addition to her highly effective uses of sympathy and affect are the multilayered and intricately explored snapshots of her Haitian and Haitian American characters and the sociohistorical relations that circumscribe their lives. Her ability to hold the tensions arising between individual and larger structural relations in such close proximity is what gives such power to her work. The complex, debilitating, and ongoing effects of these (neo)colonial relationships are often dramatized in the crevices of her characters' personal lives, including through their relationships to language.

Krik? Krak! is a short story collection that ambitiously spans an array of temporal, historical, geographical, and sociocultural positionings complete with varied narrative styles. It opens with a heart-wrenching epistolary exchange that documents the unsent letters written between two young lovers who become separated as a result of the US-assisted coup that removed Aristide from power in the early 1990s and ends with the story of a Brooklyn-based Haitian American family whose members continue to struggle with often conflicting cultural viewpoints despite having lived in the US for a number of years.[13] *Krik? Krak!* delicately balances these forms of extreme geographical and epistemological displacement with stories "rooted" in the rural Haitian village of Ville Rose, a physical space that serves to connect the lives and stories of the generations of women that permeate Danticat's text.[14]

But if Ville Rose serves as a focal point around which to develop the interrelated and intergenerational stories within her collection, the constancy of this space is offset by Danticat's temporal disruptions. Refusing a teleological model of history, Danticat instead weaves in and out of historically marked but otherwise unspecified time periods in which the reader is forced to rely upon his or her own knowledge of Haitian history and *listen* for the interconnections between stories to reconfigure a chronological mapping of events and voices. For example, in "Between the Pool and the Gardenias," the fifth story in the collection, we discover that the narrator is the granddaughter of Défilé, a character in the collection's second story ("Nineteen Thirty-Seven") and the goddaughter of Lili, the mother in "A Wall of Fire Rising," the third story in the collection.[15] For the characters within the text, the interrelations with one's kinswomen becomes a means of marking the passage of time as chronological units.[16]

Time for Danticat is never just in the here and now, but always in profound resonance with the echoes of history, turning attention to cultural and historical crosscurrents and interdependencies. One pointed example of this is in "The Children of the Sea" when the exiled narrator makes repeated references to the Middle Passage and his African ancestors: "I feel like we are sailing for Africa. Maybe we will go to Guinin, to live with the spirits, to be with everyone who has come and has died before us" (14); "Do you want to know how people go to the bathroom on the boat? Probably the same way they did on those slave ships years ago" (15).[17] Similarly, in "The Wall of Fire Rising," Danticat highlights the parallels between Haiti under French colonial rule and the neocolonial economic relations that continue to impoverish Haiti and its people. When Guy's seven-year-old son is cast as Dutty Boukman (a symbol of revolution and Haitian independence) in the school play, Guy becomes affected by the power of the speech: "[He] felt as though for a moment they had been given the rare pleasure of hearing the voice of one of the forefathers of Haitian independence in the forced baritone of their only child" (57). At the same time, the language utilized in the speech makes it "obvious that this was a speech written by a European man, who gave to the slave revolutionary Boukman the kind of European phrasing that might have sent the real Boukman turning in his grave" (56).

Throughout the story, the power of the speech haunts Guy and reminds him of his inability to attain regular, profitable work. It is when he is finally granted a day's work at the local sugar mill that Guy is able to express outrage and despair toward his living situation: "'I was born in the shadow of that sugar mill,' Guy said. 'Probably the first thing my mother gave me to drink as a baby was some sweet water tea from the pulp of the sugarcane. If anyone deserves to work there, I should.'" Instead, Guy remains "number seventy-eight on the permanent hire list" (66), a reality that influences his suicide. Danticat ends the story by explicitly linking Guy's fate with that of the enslaved in the Haitian Revolution as Guy's son recites the line from Boukman's speech: "*We shall all let out one piercing cry that we may either live freely or we should die*" (80).

In addition to the collection's commentary on Haiti's history of slavery and French colonialism, it documents the entanglements of US and Haitian histories. Danticat has elsewhere spoken of her particular investment in speaking to intertwined histories: "I want the readers, both Haitian and American kids of other backgrounds, to understand that there have been times before when Haitian and American history have intersected. A lot of kids don't know that. I hope to change the way the reader defines Haiti as well as the way he or she defines America, to let them know that indeed Haitian-Americans have earned themselves a place here. We've not only taken from this country, but we've given a lot of ourselves as well" (Capshaw Smith 203).

For Danticat, it is important for her readers not only to gain a more historically grounded understanding of Haiti and its challenges, but to also reenvision the position of Haitian Americans within the US cultural imagination. To this effect, the closing stories of the collection, "New York Day Women" and "Caroline's Wedding," comment on the marginalized positioning of many Haitian American immigrant families.

In "New York Day Women" the reader is positioned to hear the narrator's thoughts as she secretly follows her mother around the streets, describing her disorientation as she watches her perform the role of caretaker while also "peering into Chanel and Tiffany's," which mark the affluent neighborhood in which she works (145). Bewildered, all the narrator can offer is, "My mother never shops outside of Brooklyn" (145). And yet, here her mother is, walking around with a child in her care and meeting up with "a group of women who are taking other people's children on an afternoon outing," a spectacle the narrator humorously likens to a "Third World Parent-Teacher Association meeting" (152). We learn that the narrator's father is a taxi driver (a parallel to Danticat's own father). In "Caroline's Wedding" we learn that Caroline's Bahamian fiancé is a janitor (182), and that both the narrator and Caroline are ESL teachers of Haitian students (182).

With all of these characters working within different aspects of the service sector, Danticat highlights the ways in which Haitian Americans—and Caribbean immigrants more broadly—are folded in to the US economy by working low-wage, no-benefit positions that offer little possibility for the upward mobility heralded by the American dream. As a character offhandedly remarks in "Caroline's Wedding," "In New York, women give their eight hours to the white man . . . No one has time to be cradling no other man" (166). This sentiment perhaps more than any other signifies what Danticat means when she speaks to her desire for the American readership to recognize how Haitian Americans have not just "taken from this country, but we've given a lot of ourselves as well" (Capshaw Smith 203). The personal and economic sacrifices involved in the lives of recent American immigrants gain affective currency through Danticat's nuanced, humorous, and understated portrayal of her character's daily lives.

A US presence in Haiti permates Danticat's texts as well. For instance, in "Nineteen Thirty-Seven," when the narrator visits her mother in prison she comments that "the yellow prison building was like a fort, as large and strong as in the days when it was used by the American marines who had built it. The Americans taught us how to build prisons" (35). Specifically citing the 1915 US occupation as evidence of where US and Haitian histories have previously intersected, Danticat utilizes the physical presence of the prison building to figuratively comment on the continued effects (structural, physical, and epistemological) of US military interventions on the Haitian people. The internalized colonial mind-set the police learn from the US military teaches them "how to hold human beings trapped in cages," addressing the devastating psychic effects of the US presence. In connecting the effects of the US occupation to "women like Manman" who have been "accused" of practicing Vodou, Danticat addresses the violent suppression of spiritual practices of Haitian women that fall outside of US intelligible belief systems.

But Danticat also addresses US-Haitian intersections through personal relationships. In "The Missing Peace," set at the collapse of the Duvalier regime, the narrator is a young teenage girl living in Ville Rose with her grandmother, who rents rooms out to boarders. The narrator— whose name shifts from "Lamort" (death) to Marie Magdalène within the story—tells us how many of their boarders were "French and American journalists who wanted to take pictures of the churchyard where you could see dead bodies" (106). Here, Danticat takes aim at the fascination with representing the "bare life" conditions (Agamben) in Haiti by highlighting how forms of epistemic violence that are perpetuated through the media spectacle have outlasted the physical occupations of France and the United States. And yet she complicates the story by blurring US-Haitian borders through an exploration of their messiness in the personal lives of her characters.

The story centers on the exchanges between Marie Magdalène and a Haitian American boarder, Emilie. Emilie is visiting Haiti to find her mother, a journalist under the Duvalier regime who has gone missing. While Marie Magdalène is at first intimidated by Emilie's American accent and attire, it is Emilie who becomes dependent upon the formally illiterate narrator for her knowledge of the coup and where the bodies have been taken. As they converse in Creole, Emilie tells Marie, "At your age, you already have a wide reputation. I have a journalist friend who has stayed in this house. He told me you are the only person who would take me to the yard" (115). The respect they develop for each other throughout their encounter is enhanced through their situation as motherless daughters. In the tense circumstances in which they encounter each other, Danticat offers their forged friendship as an instance of human connection in the midst of dehumanizing conditions and in spite of national borders. Furthermore, Danticat counters the narrative of domestic Haitians as dependent upon their more privileged Haitian American relations for economic survival by having Marie Magdalène save Emilie's life after a confrontation with area soldiers.

As the above examples illustrate, *Krik? Krak!* represents Haitians and Haitian Americans in different cultural and personal moments and positionings, and in so doing challenges notions of "identity" and "culture" as sets of fixed and pre-given attributes. Rather, culture is presented as a site of creative resistance and struggle marked by violent occupations and governments arising from inter- and intranational conflicts as often as it is explored through epistemological differences between characters. One central way in which Danticat addresses such cultural negotiations is through her characters' differing relations to Vodou—a Haitian religion marked by violent cultural struggle and compromised synthesis in the convergence of Catholic and West African belief systems under the colonial plantation system. Vodou is a constant presence in *Krik? Krak!*, at times referenced implicitly, assuming the reader's familiarity with Vodou rites and beliefs, and at other times overtly discussed. Tellingly, Vodou is discussed without explanation in reference to the characters who practice it, suggesting Danticat's dedication to decentering western epistemes and centralizing the voices of differently positioned Haitian women.[18]

For instance, in "Between the Pool and the Gardenias" the narrator, a young servant, finds a dead infant whom she names Rose: "At first I was afraid to touch her . . . She might have been some kind of *wanga*, a charm sent to trap me. My enemies were many and crafty. The girls who slept with my husband while I was still grieving over my miscarriages. They might have sent that vision of loveliness to blind me so that I would never find my way back to the place that I yanked out my head when I got on that broken down minibus and left my village months ago" (92).

Rather than just seeing a dead infant in front of her, the narrator strives to make sense of it, understanding its presence as a sign as she interprets the situation from within a Vodou episteme. At first, the narrator is wary of the infant, afraid that she might be a *"wanga,"* a trick; this reaction seems justified given the recent circumstances that have brought her to the city to work as a servant. Eventually, however, the narrator interprets Rose as a gift from her kinswomen: "I always knew they would come back and claim me to do some good for somebody. Maybe I was to do some good for this child" (95). Searching for meaning through the infant, the narrator reads this gift as evidence of her kinswomen wanting to reduce the pain she has experienced through her multiple miscarriages.

Within the narrative frame Danticat intentionally positions the reader to occupy the perspective of this Vodou believer, to see the world through her eyes. In so doing, she demystifies the religion as "black magic" and instead represents it as what it is: a way of understanding, a way of making sense of the world. While Danticat is certainly not the first to decolonize narratives surrounding Vodou epistemes, it is significant that she does so through the first-person narration of an underclass woman servant whose life perspectives would otherwise remain invisible. Indeed, after Danticat has established the readers' affinity with the character, we hear her employers cruelly mocking her for her beliefs: "'She is probably one of those *manbos*,' they say when my back is turned. 'She's probably one of those stupid people who think that they have a spell to make themselves invisible and hurt other people. Why can't none of them get a spell to make themselves rich? It's that voodoo nonsense that's holding us Haitians back'" (95).

The classist, regionalist comments made by her employers reflect a bourgeois mentality that positions poor, rural Haitians and their belief systems as a barrier to Haitian progress. Through these juxtaposed perspectives, Danticat illustrates how culture is a constant site of negotiation between people who see the world in fundamentally different ways, and how one's social position and aspirations significantly affect one's worldview.

Ideas of Vodou as mere "silliness" are not always addressed in such hostile ways by Danticat's characters. In "Caroline's Wedding," for instance, the Haitian American narrator pokes fun at her mother for thinking that her bone soup can "cure" her sister, Caroline, of her love for her fiancé, Eric. The sisters joke about their mother's belief that the soup can affect anything, and an exasperated Caroline humorously suggests that "if she keeps making this soup . . . I will dip my head into the pot and scald myself blind. That will show her that there's no magic in it" (160). Caroline's mother, for her part, retorts, "You think you are so American . . . You don't know what's good for you. You have no taste buds. A double tragedy" (160).

These intergenerational relationships—marked by negotiations between American and Haitian belief systems frequently played out between mothers and daughters—while at times strained from their inability to see life from another perspective, nonetheless demonstrate a lightheartedness and generosity that allows the characters to lovingly put up with each other's differing worldviews. In many cases, the younger generations who at first understand their mothers' abidance to Vodou as ignorant come to a place of respect for, if not belief in, Vodou themselves. For the daughter in "Caroline's Wedding" this takes the form of recognizing Vodou as rich cultural folklore.

Other characters undergo a significant shift in their worldview. For instance, in the story "Nineteen Thirty-Seven," the narrator visits her imprisoned mother in Port-au-Prince. The story is laden with Vodou symbols of the Madonna figure (a symbol of the spirit Erzulie). The prison guards think the mother has been taken over by an *lwa* (a spirit who takes over a human body). From the removed way the narrator discusses "accusations" of her mother being inhabited by an *lwa* and the river ceremonies her mother performed as she was growing up, it is clear that the daughter is uncomfortable with such ideas. In the second half of the story, however, we recognize a definite shift in perspective when she asks her mother, "Manman, did you fly?" (43). To which her mother responds, "Oh, now you talk . . . when I am nearly gone. Perhaps you don't remember. All the women who came with us to the river, they could go to the moon and back if that is what they wanted" (43).

The intimacy of this exchange between mother and daughter highlights the importance of the oral in passing down stories, knowledge, and beliefs from generation to generation, particularly between women. The daughter's cautious question bespeaks her desire to understand her mother's life from her mother's perspective—not just from the perspective of the male authorities who jail her mother for her beliefs—and yet her mother's melancholic response speaks to the limited knowledge she can pass on to her daughter this late in life. Still, as the daughter leaves, she is flooded with repressed memories of the river ceremonies that were so central to her mother, and she in turn performs an aspect of this ritual when a woman claiming to know her through these river rituals brings news of her mother's death. The shift in the daughter's perspective about what constitutes knowledge fundamentally alters the way she understands the "accusations" of her mother as ridden by an *lwa*. Whereas earlier she dismisses the guards' claims that her mother could fly, upon hearing of her mother's death she uninhibitedly responds, "Let her flight be joyful" (49). The narrator's desire to understand her mother's life beyond the limited perspective of the legal gaze and western bias suggests that this shift in perspective will influence how she understands not only her mother's life but also her own.

As explored through Danticat's "fake-lore," the polyvocal testimonial quality of *Krik? Krak!* reinforces the importance of interpretive communities and shows how the fragmented perspectives gleaned through interpersonal relations necessarily complicate one-dimensional claims to historical truth. It is through the social heterogeneity and resulting internal tensions articulated through her richly textured storyscape that Danticat reinforces the plurality of truth and suggests that all social truths come from a historically and politically situated somewhere. The multiple competing perspectives that come to be voiced in the collection produce a similar effect to feminist polyvocal activist testimonios, and importantly complicate essentialized notions of "Haitian culture." By firmly occupying the "tenth department," Danticat allows room for diverse readerships to learn from her representation-based analyses, in which metronormative and classist Haitian views, as well as US imperial policies and racialized economies, are critiqued with clarity and bite. Further, insofar as Danticat offers critiques *of* social inequities, so does she perform painstaking memory and dream work to carve out rich representational paradigms that forge epistemic bridges. The next chapter turns attention to Danticat's *Behind the Mountains* and *Brother, I'm Dying* to discuss how she recognizes the necessity of working across not only linguistic and epistemic registers, but also narrative registers.

CHAPTER 9

Diasporic Consciousness and Realism in *Behind the Mountains* and *Brother, I'm Dying*

> Looking around, I kept thinking the same thing I did the first time I went to Port-au-Prince with Manman. How can some people live in a small village in the mountains with only lamps for illumination and others live in a city where every street corner has its own giant lamp? It made the world seem unbalanced somehow.
>
> —EDWIDGE DANTICAT, *BEHIND THE MOUNTAINS*

> I suspect that my uncle was treated according to a biased immigration policy dating back from the early 1980s when Haitians began arriving in Florida in large numbers by boat . . . Was my uncle going to jail because he was Haitian? This is a question he probably asked himself. This is a question I still ask myself. Was he going to jail because he was black? If he were white, Cuban, anything other than Haitian, would he have been going to Krome?
>
> —EDWIDGE DANTICAT, *BROTHER, I'M DYING*

DANTICAT IS WELL KNOWN AS A FICTION WRITER, BUT SHE HAS also come into her own as a trusted voice on Haitian politics, regularly writing columns for mainstream news publications, including the *New York Times*. Her topics include anything from the arts, to Haitian American cultural issues, to the Haitian earthquake, to immigration, a topic she continues to take up with increasing fearlessness and force. For instance, her March 2012 op-ed, "Detention Is No Holiday," markedly deviates from her metaphor-filled narratives as she speaks forthrightly about the inhumane treatment of immigrants in US immigration policy, specifically citing the dismissive and officially titled hearing "Holiday on ICE" (Immigration and Customs Enforcement) as a case in point:

> The flippant title of the hearing shows a blatant disregard for the more than 110 people who have died in immigration custody since 2003. One of them was my uncle Joseph, an 81-year-old throat cancer survivor who spoke with an artificial voice box. He arrived in Miami in October 2004 after fleeing an uprising in Haiti. He had a valid passport and visa, but when he requested political asylum, he was arrested and taken to the Krome detention center in Miami. His medications for high blood pressure and an inflamed prostate were taken away, and when he fell ill during a hearing, a Krome nurse accused him of faking his illness. When he was finally transported, in leg chains, to the prison ward of a nearby hospital, it was already too late. He died the next day.

This short passage succinctly documents a family situation that Danticat explores at length in her 2007 memoir, *Brother, I'm Dying*. While Danticat embraces news outlets as an important part of her political and cultural work for reaching the broadest audience possible, she addresses the expressive limits of such forums in *Create Dangerously: The Immigrant Artist at Work*, where she gives a tongue-in-cheek account of the media attention she received immediately following the January 12, 2010, earthquake in Haiti: "And even before the first aftershock, people were calling me asking, 'Edwidge, what are you going to do? When are you going back? Could you come on television or on the radio and tell us how you feel? Could you write us fifteen hundred words or less?'" (18).

Danticat did indeed take it upon herself to respond to these media requests, and she was emotionally distraught while doing so. Repeatedly, white male journalists were asked for their analysis, while she was repeatedly asked to *feel*: How do you feel? What are your people feeling? The patriarchal, racialized, and imperial divisions established between the questions she was asked versus the questions posed to white journalists was stark; her critical insights were dismissed in a fetishistic focus on the presumed "raw material" of her affective response. And yet, there was a simple truth that remained: if she did not respond to and accept the role of the "face of Haiti," Haiti would once again be overwritten by the Pat Robertsons of the world. While an imperfect, overdetermined forum through which to deliver her perspective, it remained a necessary one.

In truth, any form of representation comes with its own overdeterminations. This is why Danticat utilizes multiple genres and forums through which to articulate parallel analyses of US immigration policies and the experiences of Haitian Americans in different representational registers. While the use of memoir in *Brother, I'm Dying* allows her to make more straightforward structural critiques than her fiction affords her, alternately, her young adult first-person *Behind the Mountains* testifies to the daily challenges of immigrant life through the perceptual register of the diary of an adolescent girl, importantly broadening her representational reach. In many ways the "absent polyphony" these texts elicit is in line with the traditional genre formula of testimonio, in which the narrative "I" is representative of the experiences of the many.

Behind the Mountains is a fictional epistolary account of a young rural Haitian girl, Celiane. The narrative, recorded in a diary Celiane's teacher gave her, takes place between October 2000 and March 2001, a time period involving drastic changes in Celiane's world. On a personal level, Celiane finds herself moving from the rural area of Beau Jour to the nation's capital, Port-au-Prince; she then travels with her mother and brother to New York, where her father has been living. In the postscript Danticat discusses how she wanted to show "how many young people who move to the United States these days go through two kinds of migration: one from the rural areas to the Haitian capital, Port-au-Prince, then from Port-au-Prince to a major American city" (164). The personal details of Celiane's journey are held in close tension with the turbulence of Haiti's political backdrop, which at this time was marked by Aristide's second presidential election.

Brother, I'm Dying is a memoir that won the National Book Critics Award; it documents the interdependent webs of relation between Danticat, her father, and her father's brother, the uncle who raised her for the first several years of her life. The narrative focuses on her uncle's untimely death due to the inhumane treatment of US customs and immigration officers who withheld the medication he took for his throat condition. The memoir also relates her own father's illness and death, and the birth of her daughter: "I found out I was pregnant the same day that my father's rapid weight loss and chronic shortness of breath were positively diagnosed as end-stage pulmonary fibrosis" (3). The surrealism of this circle of life and death is offset by Danticat's strikingly realist tone. Indeed, the "fake-lore" that has come to define her writing is markedly absent within this work, replaced with a plethora of historical facts, contexts, and details documenting US imperial connections to Haiti.

Like *Behind the Mountains*, *Brother, I'm Dying* holds in close tension the microcosm of personal relations with the macrocosm of national and global politics; yet its critique takes a more documentarian form. This realist framing gives Danticat the opportunity to more directly evoke a testimonio ethos:

> I write these things now, some as I witnessed them and today
> remember them, others from official documents, as well as the
> borrowed recollections of family members. But the gist of them was
> told to me over the years, in part by my uncle Joseph, in part by my
> father. Some were told offhand, quickly. Others, in greater detail. What
> I learned from my father and uncle, I learned out of sequence and in
> fragments. This is an attempt at cohesiveness, and at re-creating a few
> wondrous and terrible months when their lives and mine intersected
> in startling ways, forcing me to look forward and back at the same
> time. I am writing only because they can't. (25)

Here Danticat's words strongly resonate with Carolyn Steedman's notion of memory work, in which pieces of one's past and present are reworked to transform them into social knowledge. Danticat utilizes these "fragments" to arrive at more complete understanding of her father's and uncle's individual histories and their relation to structures of power, particularly as connected to US-Haitian relations and immigration policies. In this way the narrative corresponds with the deliberative strand of testimonio; she exposes the seams of her knowledge and performs a polyvocal ethos by focusing on their intersecting histories.

While both *Behind the Mountains* and *Brother, I'm Dying* are laden with historical references and contextualization, the ways in which they deliver such information varies. Early on in *Brother, I'm Dying*, Danticat provides straightforward historic contextualization: "The hill in Bel Air on which the house was built had been the site of a famous battle between mulatto abolitionists and French colonists who'd controlled most of the island since 1697 and had imported black Africans to labor on coffee and sugar plantations as slaves. A century later, slaves and mulattoes joined together to drive the French out, and on January 1, 1804 formed the Republic of Haiti" (29). Aware that much of her audience will be uninformed about the geopolitics of Haiti, Danticat claims the right to both entertain and inform through the narrative world she constructs.

This approach in *Brother, I'm Dying* is appropriate for adult readers who have no doubt come to her work via the *New York Times* or other mainstream avenues, but it might prove intimidating for a younger audience. Her *Behind the Mountains* contains historical material, but it is delivered in a modified way suited to a younger readership. The epistolary voice allows Danticat a narrative device through which to call attention to important cultural and historical dates via journal entry dates in clear, simple language. For instance, within the opening pages readers are met with their first cultural lesson: "I learned from my geography lesson that the name of this country, Haiti, comes from the Arawak Indian word *ayiti*, which means "mountainous land" or "land on high." There is also a proverb that says, "Behind the mountains are more mountains." This is certainly true because our house is on a mountain, but not the tallest one. Some mountains are bigger and taller still" (4–5). This short passage delivers young readers lessons in precolonial history (the continuing presence of the Arawak people), cultural forms of communication (the proverb "behind the mountains"), and topography (the mountainous terrain of Haiti) all at once.

Behind the Mountains explores immigration in ways a young readership can relate to. For instance, in the second half of the collection Danticat devotes much attention to Celiane's nervousness around starting a new school, complete with her feelings of shyness about meeting new friends, and even getting lost on her bus ride home: "I understand now what Manman meant when she talked about being lost in the city. I felt as though I was looking both for my new home as well as for myself. After all, who was I, here without my family, without the father who had sent for me and the mother and brother I had come with?" (108). Here, her search for self as an immigrant lost in a new city is coupled with an adolescent search for self.

While Danticat utilizes the trope of adolescent peer pressure and draws upon the confusion we all feel when inhabiting a new social space to create empathetic bridges between readers and Celiane, she also moves to address the particularities of Celiane's situation, and how her own situation might differ from that of her readers'. Language, of course, is one of the main ways in which Danticat accomplishes this: "Papa said that I would be in a special class for students just like me, who had recently come from Haiti and did not yet speak English. The lessons would be in Creole" (100). Here Danticat at once addresses a central pragmatic issue of immigration—the acquiring of a new language—and how it comes to mark social difference. Imagine, she asks her readers, if beyond the "typical" teenage things you worry about, you were also learning a new language and moving from a country that few people had heard of. By contextualizing the theme of "not belonging," Danticat at once connects with dominantly positioned young audiences while challenging them to think beyond themselves. Simultaneously, this maneuver connects with other socially marginalized, although differently situated, readers by providing a narrative that may allow them to better articulate their own sense of cultural nonbelonging.

In staying true to her claim of occupying Haiti's "tenth department," Danticat delivers a comparative perspective on the overlaps and departures in Haiti and the US. For instance, Danticat utilizes the stressful home life of Celiane's New York friend, Immacula, to comment on the US racialized, gendered, and classed service economy: "Immacula is back . . . I overheard her and Faiherbe talking about Immacula's mother, who, it seems, spends a lot of time working as a home attendant for other people and very little time at her own home, which leaves only Immacula to take care of her younger sisters" (119). Through this informal observation—qualified with "overheard" and "it seems"—Danticat positions Celiane to deliver an analysis of how structural inequities play out in the crevices of people's daily lives, creating cyclical and intergenerational inequalities and unfairly impacting the lives of children. Pages later, Celiane comments on a letter she has received from her cousin Thérèse: "Thérèse's mother, like many poor mothers in the provinces, has decided to send her to live with a family of a man her mother sometimes sells vetiver to in the market in Léogâne . . . This doesn't sound good. Most girls who end up in this kind of arrangement never go to school . . . Tante Rose was very lucky. Perhaps Thérèse will be, too. But for every story like Tante Rose's, there are thousands of girls who end up alone in the city with nothing" (123).

Through this passage we not only see Celiane's sad and reluctant realization of how her cousin's educational opportunities are being taken from her, but also a comparison of Immacula's and Thérèse's stories in terms of their national and regional locations; for both, life possibilities are prematurely stunted due to the structural effects of sexist, classist social policies. The qualification "for every story like Tante Rose's, there are thousands of girls who end up alien in the city with nothing" confronts myths of upward mobility and meritocracy. Danticat suggests to her young readership that while Thérèse and Immacula might in fact prove to be the exceptions to the rule, statistically speaking, this is unlikely.

Danticat also addresses the challenges that cross-continental families face, from the pragmatics of letter writing and the shipping of pre-recorded audio messages, to the hassles of visa approval, to the growing pains they face when reunited. Specifically, Celiane's older brother, Moy, and her father develop a tumultuous relationship once they are reunited. After several arguments, her father asks Moy to leave his house and Moy all too gladly moves out. Within this dynamic, Celiane finds herself torn, with strong emotions for both her father and her brother. It is finally in a letter that the wise-beyond-her-years Celiane helps her family to bridge this rift: "I know we cannot return to the past and be the way we were in Beau Jour, but whatever family meant there and whatever it means now, I know we can be that, too" (150). *Behind the Mountains* also addresses the lighter side of the contradictions of diasporic consciousness, as when Celiane informs us, "We heard on the Haitian radio station that there would be a big snowstorm tomorrow" (98). Considering that snow is a foreign concept in Haiti, meteorologically speaking, this tongue-in-cheek inclusion reminds the reader of the between-worlds space Celiane and her family, like other immigrant families, inhabit on multiple levels, some of them more lighthearted than others.

This theme of snow, as a symbol of the different worlds that Haitian nationals and their diasporic counterparts inhabit, is also taken up in *Brother, I'm Dying*: "'What does snow feel like?' Tante Denise's oldest brother, George, asked. My father didn't talk about how cold and damp snow could be or how slippery and dangerous it could become when gelled and frozen. He didn't talk about the beauty of the individual flakes or how a few feet of them could look like a pasty rug over a lumpy bed. The only thing we have to compare it to, he simply said, was hail" (92). Of the different ways that her father could have translated the sensory aspects of snow, he chooses a literal, understated comparison. This descriptive and conceptual rift is a telling reminder for readers housed outside of Haitian and Haitian American politics of how incomplete our own understanding of Danticat's narrative may be—the limits of epistemic translation. It is probably for this reason, then, that she grounds *Brother, I'm Dying* in a realist framework. While simple in its form of address, it performs a straightforward social commentary that does not allow things to get lost in translation.

It is one of the main ironies of *Brother, I'm Dying* that it is through Danticat's self-conscious steering away from her trademark orally laden poetic language that leaves a pronounced emotional impact on the reader. The first section of the book is marked by descriptive prose—for example, the description of the horror of her uncle Joseph's run-in with US Customs and Immigration and his subsequent death, while the final section turns to facts and figures. While earlier stories are spun from oral tale-telling and recollections, for this last part of the narrative she finds herself completely reliant on official US documents to piece together what happened. As a master storyteller, Danticat utilizes bureaucratic, factual language to good aesthetic effect:

My uncle was now alien 27041999. He and Maxo [his son] had left Port-au-Prince's Toussaint Louverture Airport on American Airlines flight 822. The flight was scheduled to leave at 12:32 p.m., but was a bit delayed and left later than that . . . Once they got off the plane at around two thirty p.m., my uncle and Maxo waited their turn with a large group of visitors in one of the long Customs and Border Protection lines. When they reached the CBP checkpoint, they presented their passports and valid tourist visas to a CPB officer. When asked how long they would be staying in the United States, my uncle, not understanding the full implication of that choice, said he wanted to apply for temporary asylum. He and Maxo were then taken aside and placed in a customs waiting area. (214)

The only clause in which Danticat performs the role of interpreter in this paragraph, rather than mere relayer of information, is when she says that her uncle did not understand the "full implication of that choice." The full implication, it turns out, is that this choice to be truthful would lead to his death. As Danticat reflects, "I can only assume that when he was asked how long he would be staying in the United States, he knew that he would be staying past the thirty days his visa allowed him and he wanted to tell the truth" (215). These interpretive clauses aside, the facts and figures of the seemingly mundane events that led to her uncle's death serve a larger purpose: to highlight the senselessness of the events, and how despite her professional role as interpreter, memory worker, and storyteller who relies on oral accounts just as often as she draws upon official documents, she cannot *understand* how this happened.

Danticat's fact-ridden and figure-obsessed prose (which does retransition back to her more affectively laden language in the final chapter, aptly titled "Transition") illustrates Strejilevich's claim that while official state documents might get at objective knowledge of the facts, they are inadequate for cultivating social understanding; that the only worthwhile understanding of history lies in its interpretation. She strengthens this point by juxtaposing her fixation with the facts (as readers we sense that she has poured over these details, reading and rereading them to find some sort of meaning hidden amid their concreteness) by alternately posing several questions and speculations that she is left with:

> I don't know why my uncle had not simply used the valid visa he had to enter the United States, just as he had at least thirty times before, and later apply for asylum. I'm sure now that he had no intention of staying in either New York or Miami for the rest of his life . . . Had he acted based on someone's advice? On something he'd heard on the radio, read in the newspapers? Did he think that given all that had happened to him, the authorities—again those with the power both to lend a hand and to cut one off—would have to believe him? (215)

Surely, Danticat's futile attempt to make meaning where she cannot find any resonates with anyone who has lost anyone to seemingly senseless circumstances, violent or otherwise. Her rhetorical phrasings mimic her continued cognitive attempts to piece the situation together: "documents . . . indicate," "according to the transcript," "again no further explanation or details were requested" (216–18).

Her inability to understand her uncle's death is paralleled by her inability to understand what she finds within the documents she gains access to. For instance, she learns that while he was in New York for his throat surgery in 1984, a file was opened and closed, granting her uncle the "alien" file number 27041999 (220). She learns that he was fed only chips and soda regardless of the length of time he was detained (221). She reads the "Discretionary Authority Checklist for Alien Applicants"; under the question "Would the applicant be admissible if s/he had a valid passport and/or visa?" Officer Reyes, the officer in charge of his case, checked, "Yes," a response Danticat responds to with the narrative interruption, "My uncle had both" (224).

The most disturbing information she learns is how her uncle's medication—which would have saved his life—was taken from him, accompanied by a patronizing medical note: "Patient uses a traditional Haitian medicine for prostate & says if he doesn't take it he pees blood & has pain" (226). As Danticat bluntly adds, "Russ Knocke, a spokesman for U.S. Immigration and Customs Enforcement, would later derogatorily refer to my uncle's traditional medicine as 'a voodoolike potion'" (227). Danticat's choice to name names, to identify for her readers the specific officials and doctors who held her uncle's life in their hands, and who failed their human contract to him in the service of a national project, marks the anger, outrage, and disbelief that has led Danticat to transition from "fake-lore" to the nightmare of her realist account.

The straightforwardness of Danticat's critique in the narrative's final pages carries so much weight precisely because this direct commentary is not a register that Danticat typically utilizes in her creative work, and it accumulates much more force than 1,500-word maximum media articles provide her. *Behind the Mountains* and *Brother, I'm Dying* express powerful perceptual and structural critiques of US immigration and the diasporic experiences of Haitian Americans; Danticat is able to reach across audiences through a self-conscious employment of multiple narrative frameworks, languages, and epistemes.

Listening Differently: Confessions
of an Uninformed Reader

In relation to my reading Danticat's work as a dominantly positioned US social actor, I often think specifically about, in the words of bell hooks, "the moment of not understanding as a space to learn" (299). My reason for this has everything to do with my own first experience with Danticat. I first encountered *Breath, Eyes, Memory* as a student in a strikingly homogenous classroom of white, middle-class, New England students. We were divided into small groups to discuss Danticat's book without an understanding of the sociohistorical complexities of Haiti or US-Haitian relations. My own group discussion centered on the "testing" done by the narrator's mother to see if she was still a virgin, a discussion that served the purpose of having the group decide that "we" (US nationals) were lucky not to be "them" (Haitians).

A few years later, I again encountered Danticat's work in a classroom setting, and the framing of Danticat and her work could not have been more different. This time we were assigned her (then) new collection *The Dew Breaker*, which explores the psychic and material affects of the Duvalier regime on generations of Haitians and Haitian Americans. In our first discussion of the book (a full two weeks was allotted to the text), the professor came armed with numerous maps to familiarize us with Caribbean, and specifically Haitian, geography. She delivered a brief historical lecture on Haitian history and US-Haitian relations, choking up halfway because of the political passion that drove her message. She did not claim to know everything about Danticat or Haiti, and yet her commitment to modeling an active engagement—and her desire to pass that commitment on—was clear. It was in this context that I began to more fully make sense of the discomfort I experienced upon first encountering Danticat in such a radically decontextualized manner. If that initial engagement felt "wrong" or confusing at the time, this juxtaposition of learning experiences proved productive in thinking through what it means to encounter art and literature through a grounded, sociohistorical, social lens that shows how literature allows us an epistemic opening into another world.

In addition to these classroom encounters, I have continued to wrestle with Danticat's work in my individual reading practices. When first reading *Breath, Eyes, Memory* as an undergraduate I was pulled in by the story, yet I found Danticat's language usage to be sparse and unsatisfying. I also found this true on first reading *The Dew Breaker*. As someone who understands that *how* a story is constructed is intimately connected to the meaning that is derived from it, I could not understand how I was so pulled in—but not quite. Well versed in neither Haitian history nor French or Creole, I was not able to hear the historical resonances or how Danticat's phrasing patterns allow the French or Creole speaker to hear echoes of Haitian sayings and sentiments embedded within the English. It certainly did not occur to me that you *could* make language do such things. Listening more productively to Danticat's writing voice has taken time, patience, and the ability to move from the knee-jerk sentiment "I don't like" to the more honest "I don't fully understand."

It has been through the process of not understanding—of wanting to understand—that I have continued to read Danticat's works, and to seek out articles and interviews with her speaking about her work. Through this slow, uncertain process, Danticat as "storyteller" has emerged from my once rigid definition of her as "writer," and I have been able to recognize that the "lack" I initially read into her work had everything to do with my own inability to see and understand her project. Reading Danticat's corpus has been a pedagogical encounter in active listening and of learning to un-know those worldviews that have sedimented themselves into my understandings of literature, culture, and truth.

hooks's seemingly obvious phrase "the moment of not understanding as a space to learn" (if we already knew everything, what would there be to learn?) seems particularly relevant for connecting my personal experiences with Danticat's work with a reading praxis that facilitates an active engagement on the part of the reading audience while maintaining a respectful distance from that which our social positionings have not enabled us to know. This distancing, as we have already explored, is masterfully utilized in Danticat's work, in which the spaces between what is told become placeholders that invite some readers a moment of shared intimacy while simultaneously safeguarding a space that makes visible the power asymmetries at play for a non-Haitian audience reading her work.[1] In other words, aware of the ways her work may come to be thought of as representative of a monolithic, unchanging Haitian culture, Danticat at once opens a space for dialogue and cross-cultural understanding while refusing to play the role of native informant.[2] In her own words: "I hope to inspire the readers to learn more about their connection to the material they're reading. I hope to spark their interest and send them on that quest for more information" (Capshaw Smith 203), and in my case, it worked. In addition to safeguarding a space from which to speak and not be consumed, Danticat's purposeful fissures pique the interest of the uninformed reader to a point of active engagement, thus shifting the power dynamic between author and audience to one of storyteller and listener, a far more embodied and reciprocal relationship that potentially enables a willful and ethical engagement premised on mutuality and recognition.

In any cross-cultural exchange there are bound to be moments of "silence," gaps in knowledge, clashing beliefs, references and concepts failing to translate.[3] By writing across linguistic systems, epistemes, and narrative registers Danticat performs a writing praxis that asks readers not to gloss over these inevitable moments but to rather understand them as an opportunity for honest reflection, as a space to learn. This, I think, is at a profound level what Danticat means through her powerful statement, "Create dangerously, for people who read dangerously. This is what I've always thought it meant to be a writer. . . . Creating fearlessly for people who see/watch/listen/read fearlessly" (*Create Dangerously* 10, 148). Danticat's own fearlessness in brashly traversing different linguistic, cultural, and material worlds—all of which come with their own racialized, geopolitical, and class-based risks—and bringing these worlds to mainstream US reading audiences through her writing praxis, serves as a challenge to spark the reader's own interpretive fearlessness. Her work is consciously situated at the nexus of memory work and dream work by bringing history to bear on contemporary Haitian and US landscapes, while challenging us to open ourselves to the possibility of new social scripts that are not dependent on hierarchical social orders. It is not a naïve hope that guides this practice. Rather, by rooting her narratives in an array of racialized class locations and geographies attentive to the social categories that situationally serve to bridge and divide, Danticat demands that readers be attentive to their own social locations, without ever fixing what these social locations mean, or foreclosing the possibility of us forging new social scripts through our interpersonal relationships.

POSTSCRIPT

Countering Restriction with Expansion
Cultivating Kaleidoscopic Counterpublics

> What is always needed in the appreciation of art, or life, is the larger perspective. Connections made, or at least attempted, where none existed before, the straining to encompass in one's glance at the varied world the common thread, the unifying theme through immense diversity.
>
> —ALICE WALKER, *IN SEARCH OF OUR MOTHERS' GARDENS*

> There is something quite profound about not knowing, claiming not to know, or not gaining access to knowledge that enables us to know that we are not the sole (re)producers of our lives. But we would have to apprehend the loss that comes from not knowing and feel its absences in an immediate and palpable way in order to remake ourselves enough, so that our analyses might change. We have to learn how to intuit the consequences of not knowing, to experience their effects in order to reverse some of the deeply embedded deposits on which an imperial psyche rests.
>
> —M. JACQUI ALEXANDER, "WHOSE NEW WORLD ORDER? TEACHING FOR JUSTICE"

I RECENTLY DELIVERED A DEMO TALK ABOUT THIS PROJECT AS part of a public speaker series in Vermont. I created a slideshow with the title, "How Literature May Make Us Better Global Citizens" and gave a twenty-minute gloss on how literature allows us to look at the world from multiple perspectives, providing us with opportunities to understand beyond our own worldviews. I qualified the lived importance of the talk by incorporating recent Harvard studies documenting decreased empathy levels in students who report that their parents have taught them to prioritize financial gain over the well-being of others. I discussed how after teaching global literature for years I noticed that students often either distance themselves from the truth claims being made by the narrative ("This is too far from my experience," "I am not the proper audience," "I'm so glad I'm not them") or overidentify with the narrators by erasing the very real material and ideological differences between them ("I totally get where she's coming from," said the student whose father works on Wall Street about the narrator in *Breath, Eyes, Memory*). I even provided a short passage from Chimamanda Ngozi Adichie's *Americanah*, which openly engages with the predominant strain of Vermont liberal color blindness when the main character, Ifemelu, visits a boyfriend's aunt in the southern part of the state.

After these attempts to ground my project in "the real," a committee member asked me what impact I hoped my work would have. Not missing a beat, I reiterated that due to its solitary nature, reading is a safe place for us to be confronted with our own biases and sites of ignorance, and that if we are more mindful of our reading practices and open ourselves to doing the internal work, these interpretive exercises can affect how we engage with those we perceive as "others." I reminded the committee that Burlington, Vermont, is a sanctuary city boasting twenty-six spoken languages in the public school system. I suggested that living in a Burlington neighborhood with many New American families could influence how I engage with my neighbor, or perhaps determine *if* I engage with my neighbor. That as an educator such a reading practice can come to influence how I interact with students of different backgrounds within my classroom. How as a parent of a student at a magnet school, such a practice might affect how I interact with my child's friends and families, how I come into contact with service workers, how I occupy space, how I interact with a coworker. I received an email shortly thereafter informing me I was not chosen because my topic was "too academic."

If I'm honest with myself, I knew that would be the outcome even as I stood there presenting. I could actually feel the all-white committee's defenses going up and the gaping epistemic chasm growing between us. I could have proposed some other fun, poppy topic, but I felt like I would not be living up to my epistemic responsibility as a Vermont-based educator who both understands the liberal colorblind ideology that defines the state and has learned how to see beyond it. Here I was, ten years from when I first began collecting the pieces of this project, confronting the very same questions that haunted me then: *How do I enable them to hear the epistemic contributions of marginal experience narratives and understand how their own processes of becoming more fully human are inextricably linked with the truths they put forth?*

It was a failed attempt with them, dear readers, and I hope that these closing reflections on epistemic failures—on national, local, and personal levels—enable you to see why the ideas discussed in this book are not the sole domain of academics or activists. Rather, in a Sandovalian spirit, I hope these words reach the ears of sleeping "citizen activists" (184).

Linking the Global with the Local

On July 6, 2016, Philando Castile was killed by a Minnesota police officer in the Twin Cities region after being pulled over for his taillight being out. His girlfriend and her four-year-old daughter were in the car while the officer fired seven shots, point blank, at Castile, who after fulfilling his obligation to inform the officer that he had a legal permit to carry and a gun on his person, was slowly reaching for his license when he was shot. On June 16, 2017, the Hispanic officer who shot and killed Castile, Jeronimo Yanez, was acquitted by the mostly white jury of second-degree manslaughter and two counts of intentional discharge of a firearm that endangers safety. The day following the verdict, the video of the police dash cam was released. Uproar over the verdict and video ensued, mainly focused on the all-too-familiar reality of black bodies dying at the hands of police officers who are later acquitted by white juries.

This nationally covered case caught my attention because the Twin Cities region is one of the communities that nurtured me as an adult and a home that I now carry within me. I am literate in the racial politics of the space. I did not watch the video to try to determine whether the officer should have been convicted. I already knew he should have been. In fact, I didn't *want* to watch the video at all. But I did watch it because I wanted to know what the jury saw—and didn't see, epistemologically—that allowed them in all good conscience to arrive at a not-guilty verdict.

Here I was, putting my budding kaleidoscopic consciousness to good effect. While watching the video I was able to view it from multiple simultaneous perspectives: the implicit racist gaze of a faction of my extended family soundly steeped in their white epistemes; the white liberal apologist arguing we can't know if it had anything to do with race; the lens of a black academic friend pulled over so many times under the auspice of a taillight being out she is afraid to have a glass of wine when out to dinner; as a mother of a four-year-old child; through the eyes of a four-year-old.

Although I never internalized the racist gaze of some of my extended family members, who unquestionably believe that their white cultural values and perspectives are "true" and "right," through proximity and listening to them over the years, I have learned how they see the world. When the verdict was delivered, I deeply empathized with and understood the outrage in the black community, but because of my proximity to this racist episteme, could only think "of course." The nearly all-white jury voted "not guilty," because in their epistemic world, they *are* the officer.[1] The black man killed in the car? He does not even register to them as a complex person with feelings and dreams and family.

What I imagined while watching the video was where the white juror's attention went in terms of the narrative being delivered. It certainly was not on the faceless black man whose life was abruptly taken at the beginning of the video. Rather, it was of the extended aftermath, in which the officer continuously repeated "Oh my god, oh my god" and was visibly distraught that he had just acted out of cultural fear rather than protocol and killed a man in the process—over a taillight. What I imagine the jury saw—in their imaginations, as influenced by their epistemic worldview—was the officer's family, maybe his daughter and wife, going to visit him in jail. The guilt and shame and embarrassment he must be feeling in the aftermath. They didn't think about the little girl in the backseat. They didn't think of the dead man's body bleeding out on the street. They only thought, "That could be me," and that empathic bridge between themselves and the officer was strong enough to cancel out any other strains of empathy. Strong enough to make the murdered man a side character in their psychic drama.

It disturbs me that I can "try on" and inhabit this perspective so completely. That all it took was one viewing of the video to know with certainty the reason he was acquitted. But after years of trying to turn it off (which is something different from identifying with it), I realize that even this is an epistemic resource if used to good effect. This is not to say that it is an epistemically "true" or "valuable" perspective, but it *is* a perspective held by dominant social groups who empathize with those in power. What it means is that when I teach racial justice issues in my classroom at my predominantly white college, I am able to *anticipate* how many white students will respond. I know, because I was once peripherally groomed within such logic, and because of that knowledge, I am able to formulate counterarguments that disarm such modes of defensive disengagement—to meet them where they are.[2]

All of this was playing in my mind just recently as I was driving home with my child on an ordinary fall evening in Vermont, just after dark. As I went to turn off a main road by the University of Vermont I noted a visual cacophony of flashing lights interrupting the flow of traffic. It took me a moment to realize it was two police cars pulled along the side of the road and a newish white Cadillac SUV pulled over just in front of them. Both officers standing out of their cars were white, and I pleaded silently that the driver of the Cadillac not be black. But of course he was. A midtwenties black man looking very nervous and making sure he had his paperwork together for when the officer(s) came up to the car. My first response was sheer rage—and to pull over—to let the officers know that someone was holding them accountable for their actions. Perhaps that is what I should have done. But I also wondered what a lone white woman pulled to the side of the road would accomplish. I later posted about this on social media, raging, asking how do we hold officers accountable— what do we do from our social locations when we witness situations like this? What actions do we take? I wanted to do so much more than use it as a teachable moment for my child on institutional racism. Predictably, a white liberal man with whom I attended high school informed me that I was being racist by presuming the officers had ill intent "without knowing all of the details"—even as my explicit critique was on the privilege of discretion: if it had been a white man driving a new Cadillac SUV, would it take two police cars to pull him over? Would it be done in such a public manner?

This recent local incident solidifies why stories matter—and why nationally "boosted" stories have epistemic relevance to the local contexts we find ourselves within. If I had not been paying attention to the national political landscape, perhaps I would have thought nothing of it. Perhaps I would have rendered it invisible by subconsciously registering it as a routine traffic violation and remaining oblivious to the racial dimensions of the stop. Perhaps I could have done the same even if I was paying attention because that is a more comforting narrative—to reinforce my worldview and my sense of justice in the world. But because I do pay attention, I did look—with suspicion, with curiosity, and with an awareness that "isolated" incidents often match up with national patterns. If we are paying attention, connecting the dots, as polyvocal feminist testimonios ask us to do, then we are better able to see how these structural inequities play themselves out in the crevices of our daily lives, no matter how seemingly mundane or isolated. These moments create opportunities for dialogue, consciousness building, and localized action. At the very least they crack open our sedimented worldviews.

For instance, just a couple of months ago I answered a phone call from a white friend who was outraged that the mother of one of her Mexican students had been arrested on the street, in front of a convenience store in the center of town, by ICE officials. The family had lived in this small, working-class upstate New York town, just north of Saratoga Springs, for almost fifteen years, and until recently had run a very successful Mexican restaurant. Due to the Trump administration's witch hunt against undocumented immigrants, this family, like so many others, was targeted and has since been torn apart. More recently, an article went viral on the arrests of fifteen more undocumented Mexican workers in the area and the closing of the restaurant due to lack of workers.

These raids took place in a conservative part of New York that is predominantly white and Republican, where a majority of people voted for Trump either out of political allegiance or because, as many said and believed, "The election didn't affect them." As soon as I saw the article I knew that these same people would be upset about the closing of the restaurant, not out of concern for the family—the children being ripped from their parents, those not yet arrested living in fear of deportation—but because now they won't be able to eat there on the weekend or get a free tequila shot with their dessert. These are the same people who will no doubt be upset when they head to the horse-racing track at Saratoga and find it closed for the day due to another ICE raid. They will not make the connection that the fulfillment of Trump's "Make America Great Again" campaign promise will only serve to highlight how many "others" their own lives are dependent on. They will not see how their vote for Trump "because it won't affect me" *does* affect them, as well as their economy. They do not understand why they should care for people who occupy different epistemic worlds.

I can see this epistemic logic, because I am of this place. I was groomed by a white, middle-class, Irish-Catholic family who registered Republican due to the party's "strong morals" and "family-friendly policies." No matter how many clicks I make in my own kaleidoscopic perspective, the ability to register such cultural logic does not disappear. At the same time, just because I am *of* that place does not mean that I am unable to travel to new epistemic worlds and distance myself from the biased logics that swirled around me as a child—or hold them in epistemic friction with each other, generating a new epistemic perspective. While my friend was giving me the details, I found my "progressive" self internally frustrated with her: *You're only just now upset? Haven't you been paying attention?* But then I had to take a step back and see it from another perspective: my friend had grown. She was not calling to myopically complain about the restaurant closing. She was calling because a family that she had built a relationship with was suffering. She was mad. She was scared for them. She was connecting the dots.

My friend didn't go to graduate school and read books on structural injustices and Marxist theory and progressive politics. She didn't have the same educational opportunities as I did to see outside of her epistemic bubble. But whatever opportunities she has had, she has taken. While I have moved around and traveled, coming into contact with people of multiple epistemes, she has continued to live and work in the same small town I was raised in. The relationship she built with this family allowed her to see beyond her epistemic blinders: she didn't vote for Trump. She has been active in efforts to raise money for this family's legal fees. She is crossing an epistemic bridge, and I had to back away from my own arrogant perception (Lugones) to see it.

To circle back to the social landscape of my current home in Vermont, I recently accompanied my child to the home of a school friend to pick her up for a race they had trained for together. Aside from her name, I know that she is black and Muslim—these are the only visible, contextual pieces I have. I do not know how long her family has been in Vermont, or where they lived before. I infer that they are New Americans, but I do not know for sure.

Two days prior, while picking my child up from the after-school program, I introduced myself to her friend to let her know what time she could expect us. She took the opportunity to introduce me to her mother, who has also there for pickup. Without thinking, I blurted out, "Hi, I'm Quinn's mom," and promptly stuck my hand out to shake her hand. Mid-action, and while registering her hijab, I watched her momentarily hesitate and look down at my hand. In that hesitation it occurred to me that I had made a cultural faux pas. I began to internally panic: *Was it against her religion for her to shake hands? Or her culture? Did I extend the wrong hand?* I suddenly felt very American in the worst sense of the word—completely ignorant about the different worlds bringing us to that moment. After that brief hesitation, she reached out and shook my hand.

When we went to my child's friend's house to pick her up for the race, her mother opened the door and invited us into the living room, where there were five active children thoroughly enjoying their Saturday morning and a decor that felt very distant from my own, despite us living two blocks apart. Tapestries and framed religious figures covered the walls and windows, and ornate pillows covered the couch. As we stood there I said that we would love to have her daughter over to swim during the summer. Again, as soon as I said it, I felt the sentence hang thick in the air: *What were their religious or cultural rules about swimming and girls covering their bodies? Were there rules? If so, did those rules apply to such a young child?* With language and cultural barriers playing out between us, we parted with a smile.

I narrate these brief final anecdotes because they are such ordinary examples of the everyday border crossings we find ourselves encountering in a globalized world, as well as to suggest that no matter how much we may work toward a kaleidoscopic consciousness, there will always be moments when we falter.

In truth, ten years ago, despite my interest in learning about other epistemes, I would have berated myself over these exchanges, disgusted that I found myself in a moment of utter ignorance. Or, alternately, I would have immediately gone home to google anything and everything about Muslim social codes so as to "master" a parallel social interaction should one arise. The thrust behind these actions would not have been to learn—it would not have come from a place of curiosity or desire to grow. It would have come from the desire to save face and not act "wrong." To gain control of a social situation in which I found myself utterly ignorant.

But in those situations I instead found myself just noticing the questions that arose, to be present and curious, and making a note in my head to try and find answers. Because truthfully, even a google search wouldn't provide the definitive answers I was looking for. How would google know the lived truth of her family? How devout they are? Or how their primary culture blends with their religion and "americanness"? How they may have chosen to inhabit new social worlds since coming to Vermont? Or how the parents manage their own observation of their faith and culture differently than their children's? Assuming that a static encyclopedic entry could convey the dynamic truth of a family occupying many social worlds would merely replicate the imposed assumptions I deeply resented growing up when people presumed that since I grew up in a Catholic family and attended Catholic school we knelt together each night to say the rosary.

My point is not that I shouldn't *want* to know how to respectfully engage with the family of my child's friend, but rather that if we can sit—even momentarily—with our ignorance and use it to spark curiosity in ourselves about others, we can expand our epistemic worlds rather than shrink from such growth opportunities, having the courage to move beyond our comfort zones, fear, and inherited cultural imaginaries. This story is embarrassing in its banality, but I cannot reinforce enough how much internal work it took for me to just sit with the discomfort.

Perhaps at some point my child and this little girl will become friends to the degree that I will build a relationship with her mother and feel comfortable enough to ask her these questions. I don't know—and that is OK. And I must remember that epistemic divides cut multiple ways. As a queer woman with a gender fluid child, I am sure there are many questions she has about the social worlds I inhabit!

In part, it was the work that polyvocal feminist testimonios have done on me that allowed me to stay in these moments with a sense of curiosity and a keen sense of my own epistemic limitations, rather than retreating in fear and discomfort. But while such textual preparations are epistemically useful for bringing people to *recognize* their epistemic blind spots, they cannot *replace* the importance of interacting with people from multiple epistemes and sets of experiences. As Medina argues, the cultivation of a kaleidoscopic consciousness "requires sustained *interactions* with significantly different individuals and groups (interactions that provide disruptions and diverse forms of epistemic friction)" (243). Rather than providing an "answer," the cultural work of feminist polyvocal testimonios contributes to the cultivation of a resistant imagination that is "pluralized, polyphonic, and experimentalist" (252) as a way of modeling a way *in* to this more expansive consciousness. They constitute a particular decolonial "imaginative practice" that urges us to consider how "imagination and action must go together" (253). In this way, they offer themselves as "an exercise in translocal knowledge production" that seek to aid in the cultivation of feminist counterpublics (Alvarez 16). Rather than providing abstract reflections, they are rooted in an embodied, multisensory "social erotic" ethos (Sandoval, "Dissident Globalizations" 24) that privileges oppositional consciousness, flexible coalitions, and vulnerability. In short, they demand we link heart and head, theory and practice.

While those in more privileged social positions must always be aware of how the frameworks and scripts we use to convey our life experiences can serve to consolidate narratives of privilege and power, so too do we need to open ourselves to being vulnerable, and to expose our own sites of complicity and contradiction to processes of critique and analysis in order to forge successful, reciprocal cross-border alliances. Such dialogic practice is rooted in a postpositivist realist ethos that values epistemic diversity within self-chosen interpretive communities in order to arrive at more objective social truths, and to demystify relations of power to bring about meaningful social change. Indeed, socially privileged actors committed to social change must tell the truth of how social systems have informed our own lives, even—and especially—when these truths are ugly and uncomfortable, for they contain important pieces of social knowledge that are needed to disband, undermine, and alter oppressive power structures.

Feminist polyvocal testimonios lay claim to the epistemological relevance of such entanglements and the social knowledge they afford through careful dialogic analysis. They insist that we must enter those sites of messiness—and narrate them. Such processes force us to realize our own social locatedness, whether physical or imagined, and these realizations can also serve as a necessary catalyst for self-consciously creating communities of meaning in our own life that are capable of enabling alternative forms of affiliation that counter social restriction with interpersonal expansion.

Practitioners of testimonio dare their readers to open their imaginations to the vulnerability that accompanies laying claim to the limits of their social knowledge. In these practitioners' commitment to alliance-building, they claim these knowledge limits as a space to learn, a process that is enabled through sustained dialogic interaction and a recognition of the political responsibilities that accompany the social information we have learned. They insist that it is only when we open ourselves to a dialogic interpretive process wholly, honestly, and humbly that the subjective limits of partial perspective can be felt as a source of strength rather than threat. It is through the intentional working through of such social vulnerabilities that a fierce and lasting politics of hope and social equity is forged.

Notes

Preface

1   Paula M. L. Moya asks similar questions in *The Social Imperative* (2016) in regard to how a sociohistorical approach to literature can enact more ethical and culturally literate social perspectives.

2   José Medina's *The Epistemology of Resistance* (2013) was published after a nearly finished draft of this book was completed. While our projects therefore were constructed independently of each other, his book provides useful vocabulary for articulating many of the central ideas of my own work on the epistemic importance of polyvocal feminist testimonios, and I reference his terminology throughout the book.

3   Linda Martín Alcoff's "The Problem of Speaking for Others" (1992) and Gayatri Spivak's "Can the Subaltern Speak?" (1988) both address the inherent epistemic violence at play when a socially privileged voice speaks "on behalf" of a marginalized social group.

Introduction: An "I" That Is "We"

1   Larry Rohter's "Tarnished Laureate" was published on December 15, 1998, heading off the availability of Stoll's book in print.

2   One particular "lie" that garnered much attention was Stoll's accusation that Menchú did not witness the murder of her brother, as her text suggests. When later interviewed about this, Menchú calmly and freely names her mother as the eyewitness, framing her act of narrative substitution as a form of protection since her mother could have faced serious consequences for speaking out (Aznárez 111). Menchú further contextualizes her decision by adding, "Today I can tell you all these things because nobody will be assassinated tomorrow because of it" (114).

3   My utilization of the terms "Global North" and "Global South" does not narrowly refer to hemispheric locations. Rather, I use them to refer to unequal power relations on the global stage, especially in regard to

racialized, classed, and economic positionings. I understand these terms as necessarily unstable and acknowledge the contexuality of any and all power relations. Indeed, I find the concept of "worlds within worlds" a useful reminder on how even within a given geopolitical site there are "many norths" and "many souths" that correspond with the locational power relations at play.

4   A central rhetorical tactic of feminist testimonio is to "traffic" in the language of liberal individualism through the employment of first-person narration in order to gain intelligibility within first world circuits, while operating in excess of these very same paradigms.

5   Working against a purely documentary interpretation and toward an intentionally crafted perspective of Menchú's account alternately rubs up against western notions of "art for art's sake" given her activist role. As bell hooks argues, a "covert form of censorship is always at work when writing that is overtly espousing political beliefs and assumptions is deemed less serious or artistically lacking compared to work that does not overtly address political concerns" ("Women Who Write Too Much" 19).

6   "Practitioners" is a term that I use to refer to the writers and speakers of feminist testimonio. I use this term as a way of calling attention to the self-conscious rhetorical shaping of life stories the authors employ in order to interrupt dominant representational scripts. More so than "authors," "writers," or "speakers," the term "practitioners" highlights this mode of storytelling as a methodology and as a practice in which the narration of life stories is performed in the service of social justice efforts.

7   For more on postpositivist realism, see, for example, the chapter by Mohanty et al. in Alcoff et al., *Identity Politics Reconsidered* (2006).

Chapter 1: Situating Testimonio

1   See Barbara Harlow's *Resistance Literature* (1987).
2   Cuba's Casa de las Américas publishing house added a separate literary prize category for testimonio in 1970.
3   See Leigh Gilmore's *The Limits of Autobiography* (2001) for an in-depth discussion of how testimonio has successfully challenged, co-opted, and appropriated the form from its Enlightenment roots.
4   Metonymy is a form of narrative substitution in which one object comes to stand in symbolically for other objects that it is relationally connected to.
5   As an interesting counterpoint, Sylvia Molloy's *At Face Value* (1991) argues that Latin American autobiography does claim itself as representing a paradigmatic life, further highlighting the representational differences between testimonio and autobiography even within the Latin American context.
6   This has become especially clear to me as an academic in the North American academy. In introducing my work on feminist testimonio,

I often find myself needing to translate it to those unfamiliar with it as "inverted autobiography." If autobiography shines the spotlight on the narrated self, I suggest, then testimonio shines a spotlight on the heterogeneous social conditions that have *produced* the narrated-I; the narrative "I" is thus always already a part of a collective. Ironically, in the act of making my project intelligible to those unfamiliar with testimonio I discursively reenact a form of epistemic violence, defining testimonio in terms of its more recognizable variation, the autobiography, thereby reinstating its privileged position as the dominant form of life writing.

7   It is important to realize that even though it was in the fictional realm of the novel that the plot structure of the bildungsroman was first employed, its plot formula was quickly integrated into autobiographical accounts. It is therefore not surprising that postcolonial feminist literary writers who self-consciously fictionalize their life narratives frequently utilize adaptations of the bildungsroman to do so.

8   Contemporary postcolonial uses of the bildungsroman by women writers also complicate its reliance on a sole protagonist in favor of exploring the importance of intergenerational relationships between women, and replace the trope of economic and social mobility with a coming-to-consciousness model in which these reworked bildungsromans become "a site of both reproduction of the individualist plot of development and the interruption of its troubling norms" (Smith and Watson, *Reading Autobiography* 129).

9   Leigh Gilmore's *The Limits of Autobiography* (2001) and *Autobiographics* (1994) also call for the range of autobiographical forms to be understood as interrelated forms of life writing rather than as marginal offshoots.

10 Here I refer to the Latina Feminist Group's *Telling to Live* (2001).

11 Medina's concept of "kaleidoscopic consciousness" is rooted in his belief in multipersectivalism, in which "the imperative to renew our perplexities and to reinvigorate our openness to alternative standpoints is the imperative to constantly expand our personal as well as shared perspectives and sensibilities, our individual and collective imaginings" (21).

12 A brief note on my terminology: In working across diverse bodies of thought, certain discursive conflicts arise. I maintain that these language differences communicate more about the audiences different theories are addressing rather than a conceptual incompatibility of the ideas they put forth. Specifically, a nonpositivist understanding of "objectivity," while productive for postpositivist realist theory's purposes, proves unproductive and largely overdetermined in conversations of testimonio, precisely because of its association with legal interpretations of witness testimony. For the purposes of this chapter, then, I frequently reframe these language differences in terms of "truth" and "truth-value." While "truth" is often narrowly interpreted to reference factual accuracy, positivism, and objectivity, I use the phrase "truth-value" to call attention its own

situatedness; while it may not get all of the facts straight, there is nonetheless valuable epistemic knowledge that can be gleaned through the knowledge claims it puts forth. As such, the "truth-value" of experiential-based narrative accounts is entwined with their situated knowledge claims.

Chapter 2: Feminism, Epistemology, and Experience

1   See Spivak, "Can the Subaltern Speak?" (1988), and Brown, "Wounded Attachments" (1993).
2   In these debates, feminist standpoint theory is often charged with a reductive biologic determinism, in which identities are considered to be pre-given and stagnant. In contrast, postmodernism recognizes all identities as socially constructed and consequently unreal—as performative costumes to take on and off. Within this logic, everyone becomes a cultural hybrid; boundaries are infinitely permeable, identities are only reactionary and limiting, and therefore the only hope for liberatory politics is to reject any and all identity claims, unless they are self-consciously and ironically adapted in order to subvert them or used "strategically" for the purposes of rights-based organizing (i.e., "strategic essentialism").
3   Paula Moya has undertaken much of the recent work on postpositivist realist theory, and it is no coincidence that much of her motivation for and application of this theory is located in a key site of intergroup encounters: the situated context of US classrooms. As Moya explains, "I agree that in theory boundaries are infinitely permeable and power may be amorphous. The difficulty is that people do not live in an entirely abstract or discursive realm. They live as biologically and temporally limited, as well as socially situated, human beings . . . A politics of discourse that does not provide for some sort of bodily or concrete action outside the realm of the academic text will forever be inadequate to change the difficult 'reality' of our lives" ("Realism" 79).
4   As these central principles illustrate, in many ways, postpositivist realist theory learns from, builds upon, and extends the core principles of standpoint theory. Concerned with pluralizing the subject positions considered to inhabit Enlightenment's universal "I" while also critiquing western science's positivist frameworks, which privilege neutrality and unmediated objectivity, standpoint theory is committed to the idea of situated knowledge. Standpoint theory claims that knowledge is always subjectively and contextually located, rather than postured as the long assumed disembodied "view from nowhere," to draw upon Haraway (1988).
5   See Moraga, *Loving in the War Years* (1983); Moraga and Anzaldúa, *This Bridge Called My Back* (1984); Anzaldúa, *Borderlands/La Frontera* (1987).

6 Strejilevich's language here resonates with the distinctions Sandra Harding makes between a "claim" or "perspective," and a more fully developed, theoretically reliable "standpoint." Nevertheless, I argue that in the collaborative activist testimonios I engage with, insofar as the "raw material" of experience is engaged with and worked through within the group, and in turn translated into a dialogic, polyvocal framework, the collective interpretation constitutes a standpoint, with all of the necessary contradictions and ambiguities associated with socially diverse women organizing around social issues they all remain committed to.

7 See Bell, *Walking on Fire* (2001).

8 The Sistren Theatre Collective was established in 1977.

9 "In Awadhi, *sangtin* is a term of solidarity, of reciprocity, of enduring friendship among women; it is used by a woman to refer to her close female companion who sees her through the trials and tribulations of life" (Sangtin Writers xxiii).

10 Abolitionist testimonial literature spanning US, English, and Caribbean contexts includes Douglass, *Narrative of the Life of Frederick Douglass, an American Slave* (2001); Equiano, *The Interesting Narrative and Other Writings* (2003); and Prince, *The History of Mary Prince, a West Indian Slave* (2000).

11 It might be argued that the application of "testimonio" to testimonial texts outside of the Latin American context overwrites culture- and place-specific writing traditions. However, I propose that the very localized resonance of "testimonio" furthers its ability to be understood as a postcolonial paradigm. In fact, the widely accepted use of the German-origin literary term "bildungsroman" to refer to first-person narratives from a range of geopolitical sites should make us wary of arguments suggesting that testimonio is not equally suited to travel, replicating arguments that western models be understood as "universal" while all others remain "culturally specific." Simultaneously, it is the decidedly non-neutral encoding of "testimonio" that confronts the inescapable contradictions involved in postcolonial modes of representation. At once a marker of Spanish colonization and coded within a language positioned as lesser in an English-dominated global culture, the linking of disparately rooted texts under the Spanish signifier becomes a bridging mechanism or tactical maneuver (Sandoval) that replicates the very hybrid, strategic, and creative ethos of testimonio itself.

12 This concept is similar to Brent Hayes Edwards's consideration of the discursive function of "black diaspora" in *The Practice of Diaspora* (2003). Edwards considers the construct "black diaspora" not as a naïve glossing of difference, but rather in terms of *décalage*, a linguistic "prop" that allows for cross-cultural exchange while making discursively visible the asymmetries and incompatibilities that accompany such dialogue; a "differences within unity" model (14).

13 Recent works such as José Medina's *The Epistemology of Resistance* (2013) and Castro and Ergun's *Feminist Translation Studies* (2017) explore this concept in depth.

Chapter 3: Constructing Feminist Transnational Bridges through Polyvocal Praxis

1 See Capshaw Smith, "Splintered Families" (2005).

2 For an overview of primary texts and criticism engaging with feminist uses of autobiography see Stanton, *The Female Autograph* (1984); Brownley et al., *Women and Autobiography* (1999); Webber and Grumman, *Woman as Writer* (1978); Smith and Watson, *Women, Autobiography, Theory* (1998).

3 Within the psychoanalytic model, the act of testifying is understood to provide therapeutic resolution and psychic closure to the testifier through the act of conveying the events to an outside party. Various truth commissions, including those enacted in South Africa and Latin America, have also utilized this framework in an effort to address human rights violations and catalyze national processes of healing. For an extended discussion of this topic see Schaffer and Smith, *Human Rights and Narrated Lives* (2004).

4 In "Beyond Eurocentrism" (2014), Stef Craps also argues that the fetishization of narrating the traumatic event reiterates a western paradigm for healing that is not attuned to culturally specific grieving processes, while also focusing on the individual psyche rather than the structural conditions that lead to such trauma (50).

5 On the function of metonymy in *testimonio*, see also Sommer, "Not Just a Personal Story" (1988); Beverley, "Margin" (2004); Zimmerman, "*Testimonio* in Guatemala" (1996). In each of the collections referenced here, the women were given the choice whether to employ a pseudonym, maintain anonymity, or be referenced by their real names. In *Lionheart Gal* (Sistren Theatre Collective, 1996), the women remain anonymous. In *Playing with Fire* (Sangtin Writers, 2006), pseudonyms are used within the narrative frame, but the work is published under the authors' real names. In *Walking on Fire* (Bell, 2001), all the women chose to use their real names except for two who also employ pseudonyms in their daily life. *Telling to Live* acknowledges the names of the women who participated in the project, but a few of the individual narratives are authored anonymously.

6 For early discussions of polyvocality see feminist theorist Kathleen Martindale's "Power, Ethics, and Polyvocal Feminist Theory" (1993) and Doris Sommer's "Not Just a Personal Story" (1988). Of course, the Sistren Theatre Collective's *Lionheart Gal* was published before both of these articles, in 1986, again suggesting that academic theories often follow "on-the-ground" practices.

7 Debra Shogan's "Polyvocal Ethics" (1997) usefully historicizes Martindale's work on polyvocal ethics.

8 This is a reference to Michael Hames-García's "Who Are Our Own People?" He considers how thinking beyond our immediate social locations counters "restriction with expansion" (126) and forces us to rethink a limiting understanding of who "our people" are. Strejilevich's inclusion of activists as perspectives coming from "the same place" provides a telling example of how one's "own people" need not be rigidly determined by social location, and can be alternately connected through self-consciously assumed political and ideological positionalities (711).

9 In "On a Critical Realist Theory of Identity" (2006), Rosaura Sánchez differentiates between the terms "social position" and "positionality." "Social position" refers to "one's social location within a given social reality" along the lines of Paula Moya's concept of imposed, ascriptive identity markers; "positionality" refers to "one's imagined relation or standpoint relative to that positioning" (38). Social positioning and positionality are necessarily interconnected, yet there may be a purposeful "out of sync-ness" between them that affects how a person lives in the world. As Sánchez argues, "Positionality is a useful diagnostic construct as it enables one to better examine and understand why individuals sharing a similar or even the same positioning do not *live* their situation in the same way" (38).

10 See Freire and Marcedo, "A Dialogue" (1995).

11 The figure of Alice was originally taken up by Satya Mohanty in "The Epistemic Status of Cultural Identity" (1993) and refers to a particular member of a feminist consciousness-raising group, as discussed in Naomi Scheman's "Anger and the Politics of Naming" (1980). This figure has since become a paradigmatic example/reference point in postpositivist realist theory.

12 Paula M. L. Moya, *Learning from Experience* (2002), argues that the experiential knowledge of marginalized people needs to be recognized as epistemically privileged precisely because of what their relations to power have enabled them to see and know (132).

13 Jamaica Kincaid's *A Small Place* (1988) is a forceful example of this.

14 In Medina's words, "A kaleidoscopic consciousness is what is needed to confront the problem of pluralism . . . it does not need to have full mastery of the different perceptual perspectives and standpoints (which is often impossible without having lived one's life in a certain way). Rather, it is sufficient to know that these different standpoints are there with their cognitive-affective powers and their cognitive-affective limitations—that is, that they have certain ways of framing that open our eyes, ears, and hearts to some things but not to others—and that there may be other standpoints that remain opaque or even invisible to us" (200–201).

Chapter 4: Activist "Co/Labor/Actions"

"Co/Labor/Actions" is a term borrowed from Alicia Partnoy, "Disclaimer Intraducible" (2009).

1   It is worth noting here that my close readings drive this section in large part because these works have not received extended critical literary attention. They are rarely, if ever, discussed in terms of the representational politics they intentionally embody. The critical literature that does exist consists mainly of reviews, in addition to some journal articles in which the texts are brought in as a passing example within a larger conversation. For example, *Playing with Fire* is mostly cited as an example in critical NGO studies. Multiauthored pieces such as *Telling to Live* occasionally have specific essays singled out and referenced for content. Out of all of the texts, *Lionheart Gal* is discussed in the most literary way, most notably by Carolyn Cooper in "Writing Oral History" (1955), with which I engage.

2   Nari Samata Yojana (NSY) is a pseudonym used by the *sangtins* to refer to a well-established NGO that operates under the banner of women's empowerment.

3   *Playing with Fire* weaves together the collective voices of nine *sangtins*, seven of which become the "autobiographers" of the narrative. This choice was made out of awareness of the significant class and power differentials existing between the seven village-level NGO workers (Anupamlata, Ramsheela, Reshma Ansari, Shashibala, Shashi Vaish, Surbala, and Vibha Bajpayee) and Richa Singh and Richa Nagar. At the time of publication, Richa Singh was a regional coordinator at NSY. Richa Nagar is a trained geographer and gender and women's studies professor at the University of Minnesota, Twin Cities.

4   While Bell's process cannot properly be called "collective," it nonetheless employs a collaborative feminist methodology in which she worked closely with the collection's storytellers to ensure that she properly transcribed their stories.

5   I do not merely "assign" the term "feminist" to describe these texts; rather, each project employs the descriptor. Still, the productiveness of women-specific organizing efforts is continually subject to debate within these works, especially within the three texts that emerge from sociopolitical spaces laden with "women and development" efforts (Jamaica, Haiti, India). The narrators of *Walking on Fire* and *Playing with Fire* explicitly express a desire for feminist initiatives to work in tandem with people's movements concerned with economic equality and land reform. As articulated by Selitane Joseph in "Chunk of Gold," "My biggest problem with some women's organizations is that they think that women alone can wage the battle. It's not true! Men are exploited as well as us. We ask men and women to band together so we can

overturn this bone-crushing system, this cursed system. We have to keep our eyes open because if women and men are divided, the place we want to go to—we'll never get there" (Bell 143). This sentiment is strikingly echoed by the Sangtin Writers, who ask, "Can real equality be achieved in our society if we isolate gender difference from all other differences and base all our strategies and conversations on the gaps between women and men? When we know that the nature and form of gender differences cannot be comprehended in any context without connecting them with caste and class differences, then the inability to raise questions about classism in our own organizations gives our work the shape of an animal who uses one set of teeth to show and another one to chew!" (116). Such single-issue platforms make little sense indeed. More than signaling a gender-specific focus, then, this qualifier more importantly signals an egalitarian and politically motivated mode of inquiry that is evidenced in feminist testimonio's use of nuanced collaborative methodologies attentive to the possibilities and foreclosures of differently positioned women coming together to work around collectively defined sets of social issues.

6   A brief note on my own methodological style in this chapter: in an attempt to extend the dialogic function of polyvocal feminist testimonio, the structural format of the rest of this chapter is to work across texts by theme in an effort to interweave individual contributions and place them into direct conversation. Like polyvocal feminist testimonio itself, this mode of analysis works to bring the texts into dialogue with each other without forcing them into false resolution, therefore more readily highlighting their overlaps and departures. As Chandra Mohanty has argued, working through difference allows us to more fully theorize commonalities (226).

7   Ford-Smith, interview, July 2, 2011.

8   This information about the cover illustration is provided in *Lionheart Gal*.

9   Bell also includes a photograph of Florencia Pierre, which seems especially poignant since this is the closest she can get to incorporating the corporeal element of dance in written form.

10 In "Writing Oral History" (1995), Carolyn Cooper explores these points more thoroughly, arguing that Ford-Smith's decision to write the introduction in standard English undermines the language politics she argues for. Cooper presents a compelling counterargument by writing the second half of her academic article in Jamaican Creole.

Chapter 5: Resisting Representational Stasis

1   In *Walking on Fire* the *istwas* of *griyos* Yannick Etienne, Lelenne Gilles, Maries Josee St. Firmin, Josette Perard, and Lise-Marie Dejean all perform this function.

2   As a critic looking for examples of polyvocal feminist activist collaborative testimonios, I initially came to this text full of skepticism. On the cover page Bell—not the *griyos*—is listed as the author. Many of the interviews come from women she just met, and she decides to represent their ideas in English and market them to a US reading audience. It was not until I came to this definition of resistance that my impression began to change. While her solely authored introduction certainly does not challenge the hierarchy of knowledge production, she does productively use her academic background to instruct her readership on how to encounter the Haitian women's narrative outside of the "bare life" paradigm too often perpetuated by international accounts of the nation.

3   Perhaps because of the relative privilege of its contributors and their assumptions about readership, *Telling to Live* places more emphasis on explaining the methodology and theory behind their collection of life narratives than on directing the reader through decoding processes.

Chapter 6: "Sometimes My Geographies Get Jumbled"

1   In contrast to the activist testimonios, the works discussed in this section have received a fair share of critical literary attention. However, most scholarship on the Argentine pieces is confined to traditional discussions and debates on testimonio, including the representational ethics, practices, and contradictions of trauma narratives, the ethical components of the genre through the lens of human rights violations, the gendered dimensions of these women-authored texts, and the critical importance of historical memory. While these discussions have all contributed to important conversations on testimonio, given the primary focus of this book in stretching contemporary discourses surrounding testimonio, I do not engage with them at length. It is worth noting that more has been written on Alicia Partnoy's *The Little School* than Strejilevich's *A Single, Numberless Death* and Alicia Kozemeh's *Steps under Water* combined, and that there is a dearth of critical scholarship on Kozameh's work, in particular. For further reading please see Breckenridge, "Taking the Stand" (2003); Detwiler, "The Blindfolded (Eye)Witness in Alicia Partnoy's *The Little School*" (2000); Feal, "Latin American Feminist Criticism and the 'Realm of the Real'" (1994); Ghiggia, "Play in Memories of State Terror in Argentina" (2012); Kaminsky, "Body/Politics" (1993); Partnoy, "Cuando vienen matando" (2006); Sternbach, "Re-Membering the Dead" (1991); Treacy, "Double Binds" (1996). For further reading on Mootoo, see Busse, "Who Is a Victim? (2012); King, "Re/Presenting Self and Other" (2008); Hong, "A Shared Queerness" (2006); May, "Dislocation and Desire in Shani Mootoo's *Cereus Blooms at Night*" (2004); May, "Trauma in Paradise" (2006); Warnock, "'Soul Murder' and Rebirth" (2007); Wesling, "Neocolonialism, Queer Kinship, and Diaspora" (2011).

2 Tyler's racial ambiguity is significant given the racial and ethnic landscape of Trinidad, where relationships between Afro- and Indo-Trinidadians are strained due to colonial tensions. Racially marking Tyler's body would have altered the ways in which readers interpret the power dynamics between Tyler and Mala; Mootoo sidesteps this representational impasse by leaving his ethnicity undetermined.

3 Kozameh, interview, March 28, 2008.

Chapter 7: Cultivating Community through Creative Communication

1 This is in part why Medina argues for a "connectedism" rather than "collectivism," which the co-narrational and polyvocal structures model.

2 Through a series of essays linking anticapitalist and nationalist critique, the contradictions of feminist, queer, and critical race studies, and a transnational agenda, Alexander lays the groundwork for an embodied notion of intersubjective living that imagines "the human" as interdependent (6), accountable to both the self and the collective (18), and consistent with ways of being that "do not always already mobilize an 'other'" (109). As Alexander's work suggests, working toward a model of positive interdependence need not mean that we subscribe to an overly idealistic notion of overcoming our social differences through interconnection. Rather, through a self-conscious working through of our social interdependencies we can put to use such imposed relationships to collectively combat the unequal power relations that have produced them.

Chapter 8: Retransmissions

1 Indeed, shortly after the 2010 earthquake in Haiti several mainstream media sources interviewed Danticat in their search for "expert" perspectives. The ways in which Danticat was framed on several of these shows limited the knowledge and insight of the author to a tokenized "voice" for the Haitian people.

2 It is also important to note that through continual processes of cultural intermixing and the massacring of native Caribbean peoples, there is no coherent originary language or culture accessible to Danticat that predates the French colonial influence. Furthermore, as an immigrant writer publishing in a country dominated by English, Danticat must also consider her audience and point of entry.

3 Chicana feminist scholars such as Gloria Anzaldúa have explicitly taken up this stratification of linguistic codes. The interlingual language negotiations Anzaldúa refers to certainly speak to the forms of code switching that I understand as underpinning Danticat's use of English.

4 Similarly, fiction writer Assia Djebar is said to "arabic-ize" her use of French. See Anne Donadey's "The Multilingual Strategies of Postcolonial Literature" (2000).

5 In *Create Dangerously*, Danticat suggests that the most frequent criticism she receives from Haitian nationals is that her fictional works "lie" about Haitian cultural experiences (as manifested by the *Breath, Eyes, Memory* "testing" scandal). "'You are a parasite and you exploit your culture for money and what passes for fame,' is the second most common type of criticism I get from inside the community," Danticat writes (33).

6 Indeed, Danticat's position as migrant is far less privileged than that of Rushdie. With her extended Haitian family living in the rural, impoverished conditions of Bel Air and her father assuming the position of taxi driver in their Brooklyn neighborhood, Danticat's class positioning has not granted her the same migrant luxuries as those extended to postcolonial figures such as Salman Rushdie or Edward Said.

7 N'Zengou-Tayo suggests that this Creoleness-of-phrase is most evident in dialogue with implied or specified Creole speakers, which allows for their life experiences to enter into historical purview (136). For example, in "The Missing Peace" in *Krik? Krak!*, the granddaughter informs the Haitian American visitor that "intelligence is not only in reading and writing" (Danticat 111). N'Zengou-Tayo reads this as an English translation of the Creole "Pale franse pa vle di lespri," which she translates back into English as "Speaking French does not mean intelligence" (136). N'Zengou-Tayo reads Danticat's slight alteration of the phrase as an example of cultural translation that "shifts the issue on the illiteracy problem in the Haitian countryside and allows for a better understanding of the social gap" (136–37). The obvious critique of the cultural capital that French continues to hold in a neocolonial Haitian social order is lost on English speakers unfamiliar with Creole, but the phrase allows Haitian readers an added level of meaning and social critique.

8 Danticat's edited volume of Haitian American writings, *The Butterfly's Way*, certainly speaks to this point.

9 I'm struck by how Ngugi wa Thiong'o's description of the third interpreter in "The Allegory of the Cave" resonates with Fulani's description of Anancy taking the stories back to his village for the community to share. I see Danticat as a third interpreter, giving back to her community through her writing. In addition to the points Fulani makes, I think that Danticat's excitement over the French translation of *Krik? Krak!* and the Creole renditions of her work on Haitian radio (Candelario 84) speaks to her desire to have her words reach and affect Haitian audiences.

10 Closely connected to the concept of "oraliture," Glissant defines "oral literature" as "a text that was meant first and foremost to be read aloud and that could benefit from the techniques of oral expression" (188).

11　This sentiment is directly voiced in Barbara Christian's "The Race for Theory" (1987).

12　The term "kitchen poet" is a nod to kinswoman Paule Marshall, whom Danticat deems "the greatest kitchen poet of all" (*Krik? Krak!* 227).

13　This exchange also eerily echoes the experiences of the enslaved crossing the Atlantic in the Middle Passage as the young lover flees Haiti via boat to avoid political persecution.

14　In an interview with Bonnie Lyons, Danticat stresses the importance of place to identity in rural Haitian families. She suggests that when someone from the city is asked where he or she is going when headed to see family, a typical response is, "I am going to my country." Danticat tells Lyons that "the rural area is like a country within a country" wherein everybody "traces his or her family to some particular village" (*Krik? Krak!* 186). As such, Danticat's representation of the centrality of village and ancestry to Haitians furthers the importance of her juxtaposing stories of extreme displacement with a number of stories centered on Ville Rose in different time periods in *Krik? Krak!*

15　These connections highlight the centrality of intergenerational and familial relationships in Danticat's work. It is also through this strategy that we come to know more about the characters than the individual stories allow for, adding further roundness to their lives.

16　One notable exception to this is the story entitled "Nineteen Thirty-Seven," which centers on the Trujillo massacre, which violently expelled all Haitians from the Dominican Republic. The exact historical location of this narrative thus establishes a time frame from which to further understand when the other stories are taking place.

17　Guinin represents a spiritual place in Vodou, an Africa (as homeland) under the ocean. As Danticat describes it, Guinin " stands in for all of Africa, renaming with the moniker of one country in an ideological continent which, if it cannot welcome the returning bodies of its lost children, is more than happy to welcome back their spirits" (*Create Dangerously* 134).

18　For an excellent discussion of the ways in which Danticat both incorporates and retells aspects of Haitian folklore and Vodou, see Evans Braziel, "Défilée's Diasporic Daughters" (2004).

Chapter 9: Diasporic Consciousness and Realism in *Behind the Mountains* and *Brother, I'm Dying*

1　This notion of spacing as placeholder brings to mind Brent Hayes Edwards's notion of the "prop," which allows for cross-cultural exchange while making discursively visible the asymmetries and incompatibilities that accompany such dialogue. See Edwards, *The Practice of Diaspora* (2003).

2 Danticat has spoken elsewhere of the importance of representations in overcoming stereotypes (Capshaw Smith 203) as well as the danger of writers from "smaller groups" being thought to portray an "authentic" account of their culture from which foreign readers can absorb their "insight" (Lyons 190).

3 Denise Shaw also importantly suggests that the "veil of silence" that imbeds itself within Danticat's fiction is in part due to the traumatic histories her work addresses; the (willful?) "not telling" becomes as important to her stories as what is told (3).

Postscript: Countering Restriction with Expansion

1 I contend that it made no difference that the officer was not white, since the power of the position holds more signification than individual identity. Ta-Nehisi Coates makes a parallel argument in *Between the World and Me*. In other words, the body of a police officer symbolizes power and enforcer of law and power, and white juries are most likely to identify with whoever holds that power, regardless of race.

2 Linda Martín Alcoff's *The Future of Whiteness* (2016) discusses whether an anti-racist white consciousness is possible and what "whiteness" might mean when separated from a racist episteme.

References

Adichie, Chimamanda Ngozi. *Americanah*. New York: Anchor, 2013.

Agamben, Giorgio. *Homo Sacer: Sovereign Power and Bare Life*. Trans. Daniel Heller-Roazen. Stanford, CA: Stanford University Press, 1998.

Ahmed, Sara. *The Cultural Politics of Emotion*. New York: Routledge, 2004.

Alcoff, Linda Martín. "The Problem of Speaking for Others." *Cultural Critique* 20 (Winter 1991–92): 5–32.

———. *The Future of Whiteness*. Malden, MA: Polity, 2016.

Alcoff, Linda Martín, Michael Hames-Garcia, Satya P. Mohanty, and Paula M. L. Moya. *Identity Politics Reconsidered*. New York: Palgrave Macmillan, 2006.

Alexander, M. Jacqui. *Pedagogies of Crossing: Meditations on Feminism, Sexual Politics, and the Sacred*. Durham, NC: Duke University Press, 2005.

Alvarez, Sonia E. "Enacting a Translocal Feminist Politics of Translation." *Translocalities/Translocalidades: Feminist Politics of Translation in the Latin/a Américas*, edited by Sonia E. Alvarez, Claudia de Lima Costa, Verónica Feliu, Rebecca J. Hester, Norma Klahn, and Millie Thayer. Durham, NC: Duke University Press, 2014.

Anzaldúa, Gloria. *Borderlands/La Frontera: The New Mestiza*. San Francisco: Aunt Lute Books, 2007.

Aznárez, Juan Jesús. "Rigoberta Menchú: Those Who Attack Me Humiliate the Victims." *The Rigoberta Menchú Controversy*, edited by Arturo Arias. Minneapolis: University of Minnesota Press, 2001.

Bambara, Toni Cade. "The Lesson." *Gorilla, My Love*. New York: Random House, 1972.

Behar, Ruth. *Translated Woman: Crossing the Border with Esperanza's Story*. Boston: Beacon Press, 1993.

Bell, Beverly. *Walking on Fire: Haitian Women's Stories of Survival and Resistance*. Ithaca, NY: Cornell University Press, 2001.

Beverley, John. "The Real Thing." *The Real Thing: Testimonial Discourse and Latin America*. Durham, NC: Duke University Press, 1996.

——. "Introduction: Testimony and Empire." Testimonio: *On the Politics of Truth*. Minneapolis: University of Minnesota Press, 2004.

—— "The Margin at the Center: On Testimonio." Testimonio: *On the Politics of Truth*. Minneapolis: University of Minnesota Press, 2004.

Boler, Megan. "A Feminist Politics of Emotion." *Feeling Power: Emotions and Education*. New York: Routledge, 1999.

Braziel, Jana Evans. "Défilée's Diasporic Daughters: Revolutionary Narratives of Ayiti (Haiti), Nanchon (Nation), and Dyaspora (Diaspora) in Edwidge Danticat's *Krik? Krak!*" *Studies in the Literary Imagination* 37.2 (2004): 77–96.

Breckenridge, Janis. "Taking the Stand: Examining the Testimonial Process in Nora Strejilevich's *Una Sola Muerte Numerosa*." *Confluencia* 19.1 (2003): 42–49.

Brown, Wendy. "Wounded Attachments." *Political Theory* 21.3 (1993): 390–410.

Brownley, Martine Watson, and Allison B. Kimmich, eds. *Women and Autobiography*. Wilmington, DE: SR Books, 1999.

Bueno, Eva Paulino. "Race, Gender, and the Politics of Reception of Latin American Testimonios." *Going Global: The Transnational Reception of Third World Women Writers*, edited by Amal Amireh and Lisa Suhair Majaj. New York: Garland, 2000.

Busse, Cassel. "Who Is a Victim? Difference and Accountability in Shani Mootoo's *Cereus Blooms at Night*." *Studies in Canadian Literature* 37.1 (2012): 82–99.

Candelario, Ginetta E. B. "Voices from Hispaniola: A Meridians Roundtable with Edwidge Danticat, Loida Maritza Pérez, Myriam J. A. Chancy, and Nelly Rosario." *Meridians* 5.1 (2004): 69–91.

Capshaw Smith, Katherine. "Splintered Families, Enduring Connections: An Interview with Edwidge Danticat." *Children's Literature Association Quarterly* 30.2 (2005): 194–206.

Castro, Olga, and Emek Ergun, eds. *Feminist Translation Studies: Local and Transnational Perspectives*. New York: Routledge, 2017.

Christian, Barbara. "The Race for Theory." *Cultural Critique* 6 (Spring 1987): 51–63.

Chungara, Domitila B. de. *Let Me Speak! Testimony of Domitila, a Woman of the Bolivian Mines*, translated by Victoria Ortiz. London: Monthly Review Press, 1979.

Coates, Ta-Nehisi. *Between the World and Me*. New York: Spiegel and Grau, 2015.

Cooper, Carolyn. "Writing Oral History: Sistren Theatre Collective's *Lionheart Gal*." *Noises in the Blood: Orality, Gender, and the "Vulgar" Body of Jamaican Popular Culture*. Durham, NC: Duke University Press, 1995.

Craps, Stef. "Beyond Eurocentrism: Trauma Theory in the Global Age." *The Future of Trauma Theory: Contemporary Literary and Cultural Criticism*, edited by Gert Buelens, Sam Durrant, and Robert Eaglestone. New York: Routledge, 2014.

Danticat, Edwidge. *Breath, Eyes, Memory*. New York: Vintage, 1994.

——. *Krik? Krak!* New York: Vintage Books, 1996.

———. *Behind the Mountains*. New York: Orchard Books, 2002.

———. *The Butterfly's Way: Voices from the Haitian Diaspora in the United States*, edited by Edwidge Danticat. New York: Soho Press, 2003.

———. *The Dew Breaker*. New York: Alfred A Knopf, 2004.

———. *Brother, I'm Dying*. New York: Vintage, 2007.

———. *Create Dangerously: The Immigrant Artist at Work*. Princeton, NJ: Princeton University Press, 2010.

———. "Detention Is No Holiday." *New York Times*, March 27, 2012.

Deleuze, Gilles, and Felix Guattari. "Introduction: A Thousand Plateaus." *A Thousand Plateaus: Capitalism and Schizophrenia*. Trans. Brian Massumi. Minneapolis: University of Minnesota, 1987.

Detwiler, Louise A. "The Blindfolded (Eye)Witness in Alicia Partnoy's *The Little School*." *Journal of the Midwest Modern Language Association* 33/34 (2000): 60–72.

Donadey, Anne. "The Multilingual Strategies of Postcolonial Literature: Assia Djebar's Algerian Palimpsest." *World Literature Today* 74.1 (2000): 27–36.

Douglass, Frederick. *Narrative of the Life of Frederick Douglass, an American Slave: Written by Himself*. New Haven, CT: Yale University Press, 2001.

Edwards, Brent Hayes. *The Practice of Diaspora: Literature, Translation, and the Rise of Black Internationalism*. Cambridge, MA: Harvard University Press, 2003.

Elenes, C. Alejandra. *Transformando Fronteras*: Chicana Feminist Transformative Pedagogies." *Qualitative Studies in Education* 14.5 (2001): 689–702.

Equiano, Olaudah. *The Interesting Narrative and Other Writings*. New York: Penguin, 2003.

Evans Braziel, Jana. "Défilée's Diasporic Daughters: Revolutionary Narratives of Ayiti (Haiti), Nanchon (Nation), and Dyaspora (Diaspora) in Edwidge Danticat's *Krik? Krak!*" *Studies in the Literary Imagination* 37.2 (2004): 77–98.

Feal, Rosemary Geisdorfer. "Latin American Feminist Criticism and the 'Realm of the Real.'" *Letras Femeninas* 20.1/2 (1994): 149–61.

Ford-Smith, Honor. "My Experience in the Theatre Collective Sistren." *Fighting on Two Fronts: Women's Struggles and Research*, edited by Maria Mies. The Hague, Netherlands: Institute of Social Studies, 1982.

Franco, Jean. "Obstinate Memory." *The Decline and Fall of the Lettered City*. Cambridge, MA: Harvard University Press, 2002.

Franklin, Benjamin. *The Autobiography of Benjamin Franklin*. New York: Dover, 1996.

Freire, Paulo. *Pedagogy of the Oppressed*. New York: Continuum, 1993.

Freire, Paulo, and Donald Marcedo. "A Dialogue: Culture, Language, and Race." *Harvard Educational Review* 65.3 (1995): 377–403.

Fulani, Ifeona. "Caribbean Women Writers and the Politics of Style: A Case for Literary Anancyism." *Small Axe* 9.1 (2005): 64–79.

Ghiggia, María. "Play in Memories of State Terror in Argentina: *The Little School* by Alicia Partnoy." *Journal of the Midwest Modern Language Association* 45.2 (2012): 187–215.

Gilmore, Leigh. *Autobiographics: A Feminist Theory of Women's Self-Representation.* Ithaca, NY: Cornell University Press, 1994.

———. *The Limits of Autobiography: Trauma and Testimony.* Ithaca, NY: Cornell University Press, 2001.

Glissant, Edouard. *Caribbean Discourse: Selected Essays,* translated by J. Michael Dash. Charlottesville: University Press of Virginia, 1989.

Gordon, Avery. *Ghostly Matters: Haunting and the Sociological Imagination.* Minneapolis: University of Minnesota Press, 1997.

Grewal, Inderpal. "Autobiographic Subjects and Diasporic Locations: *Meatless Days* and *Borderlands.*" *Scattered Hegemonies: Postmodernity and Transnational Feminist Practices,* edited by Inderpal Grewal and Caren Kaplan. Minneapolis: University of Minnesota Press, 1994.

Gugelburger, Georg M., ed. *The Real Thing: Testimonial Discourse and Latin America.* Durham, NC: Duke University Press, 1996.

Hall, Stuart. "Encoding and Decoding." *Culture, Media, Language,* edited by Stuart Hall, Dorothy Hobson, and Paul Willis. London: Hutchinson, 1980.

Hames-García Michael. "'Who Are Our Own People?' Challenges for a Theory of Social Identity." *Reclaiming Identity: Realist Theory and the Predicament of Postmodernism,* edited by Paula M. L. Moya and Michael R. Hames-García. Berkeley: University of California Press, 2000.

Haraway, Donna. "Situated Knowledges: The Science Question in Feminism and the Privilege of Partial Perspective." *Feminist Studies* 14.3 (Autumn 1988): 575–99.

Harding, Sandra. *Whose Science? Whose Knowledge? Thinking from Women's Lives.* Ithaca, NY: Cornell University Press, 1991.

Harlow, Barbara. *Resistance Literature.* New York: Routledge, 1987.

Henze, Brent R. "Who Says Who Says? The Epistemological Grounds for Agency in Liberatory Political Projects." *Reclaiming Identity: Realist Theory and the Predicament of Postmodernism,* edited by Paula M. L. Moya and Michael R. Hames-García. Berkeley: University of California Press, 2000.

Hirsch, Marianne, and Valerie Smith. "Feminism and Cultural Memory." *Signs* 28.1 (2002): 1–19.

Hong, Grace Kyungwon. "'A Shared Queerness': Colonialism, Transnationalism, and Sexuality in Shani Mootoo's *Cereus Blooms at Night.*" *Meridians* 7.3 (2006): 73–103.

hooks, bell. "'This is the oppressor's language / yet I need it to talk to you": Language, a Place of Struggle." *Between Languages and Cultures: Translation and Cross-Cultural Texts,* edited by Anuradha Dingwaney and Carol Maier. Pittsburgh: University of Pittsburgh Press, 1995.

———. "Women Who Write Too Much." *Word: On Being a [Woman] Writer,* edited by Jocelyn Burell. New York: Feminist Press, 2004.

Kaminsky, Amy. "Body/Politics: Alicia Partnoy's *The Little School.*" *Reading the Body Politic.* Minneapolis: University of Minnesota Press, 1993.

Kaplan, Caren. "Resisting Autobiography: Out-law Genres and Transnational Feminist Subjects." *Women, Autobiography, Theory: A Reader*, edited by Sidonie Smith and Julia Watson. Madison: University of Wisconsin Press, 1998.

Katz, Cindi. "On the Grounds of Globalization: A Topography for Feminist Political Engagement." *Signs* 26.4 (2001): 1213–34.

Kincaid, Jamaica. *A Small Place*. New York: Farrar, Straus, and Giroux, 1988.

King, Rosamond S. "Re/Presenting Self and Other: Trans Deliverance in Caribbean Texts." *Callaloo* 31.2 (2008): 581–99.

Kingston, Maxine Hong. *The Woman Warrior: Memoirs of a Girlhood among Ghosts*. New York: Vintage, 1989.

Kozameh, Alicia. *Steps under Water: A Novel*, translated by David E. Davis. Berkeley: University of California Press, 1996.

Latina Feminist Group. *Telling to Live: Latina Feminist Testimonios*. Durham, NC: Duke University Press, 2001.

Lugones, María. "Playfulness, 'World'-Travelling, and Loving Perception." *Making Face, Making Soul/Haciendo Caras: Creative and Critical Perspectives by Feminists of Color*. San Francisco: Aunt Lute Books, 1990.

Lyons, Bonnie. "An Interview with Edwidge Danticat." *Contemporary Literature* 44.2 (2003): 183–98.

Maier, Linda S. "Introduction: The Case for and Case History of Women's Testimonial Literature in Latin America." *Woman as Witness: Essays on Testimonial Literature by Latin American Women*, edited by Linda S. Maier and Isabel Dulfano. New York: Peter Lang, 2004.

Martindale, Kathleen. "Power, Ethics, and Polyvocal Feminist Theory." *A Reader in Feminist Ethics*, edited by Debra Shogan. Toronto: Canadian Scholars' Press, 1993.

Matthews, Irene. "Translating/Transgressing/Torture . . ." *Frontline Feminisms: Women, War, and Resistance*, edited by Marguerite R. Waller. New York: Routledge, 2001.

May, Vivian M. "Dislocation and Desire in Shani Mootoo's *Cereus Blooms at Night*." *Studies in the Literary Imagination* 37.2 (2004): 97–122.

———. "Trauma in Paradise: Willful and Strategic Ignorance in *Cereus Blooms at Night*." *Hypatia* 21.3 (2006): 107–35.

McCormack, Donna. *Queer Postcolonial Narratives and the Ethics of Witnessing*. New York: Bloomsbury, 2014.

Medina, José. *The Epistemology of Resistance: Gender and Racial Oppression, Epistemic Injustice, and Resistant Imaginations*. Oxford: Oxford University Press, 2013.

Menchú, Rigoberta. *I, Rigoberta Menchú: An Indian Woman from Guatemala*. London: Verso, 1983.

Minh-ha, Trinh T. "Reflections from the Writing-Mirror Box." *Making Face, Making Soul/Haciendo Caras: Creative and Critical Perspectives by Feminists of Color*. San Francisco: Aunt Lute Books, 1990.

Mohanty, Chandra Talpade. *Feminism without Borders: Decolonizing Theory, Practicing Solidarity*. Durham, NC: Duke University Press, 2003.

Mohanty, Satya P. "The Epistemic Status of Cultural Identity: On *Beloved* and the Postcolonial Condition." *Cultural Critique* 24 (Spring 1993): 41–80.

Molloy, Sylvia. *At Face Value: Autobiographical Writing in Spanish America*. Cambridge: Cambridge University Press, 1991.

Moraga, Cherríe. *Loving in the War Years*. Cambridge, MA: South End Press, 2002.

Moraga, Cherríe, and Gloria Anzaldúa, eds. *This Bridge Called My Back: Writings by Radical Women of Color*. New York: Kitchen Table Press, 1984.

Mootoo, Shani. *Cereus Blooms at Night*. New York: Perennial, 2001.

Moya, Paula M. L. "Postmodernism, 'Realism,' and the Politics of Identity: Cherríe Moraga and Chicana Feminism." *Reclaiming Identity: Realist Theory and the Predicament of Postmodernism*, edited by Paula M. L. Moya and Michael R. Hames-García. Berkeley: University of California Press, 2000.

———. *Learning from Experience: Minority Identities, Multicultural Struggles*. Berkeley: University of California Press, 2002.

———. "What's Identity Got to Do with It? Mobilizing Identities in the Multicultural Classroom." *Identity Politics Reconsidered*, edited by Linda Martin Alcoff, Michael Hames-García, Satya P. Mohanty, and Paula M. L. Moya. New York: Palgrave Macmillan, 2006.

———. *The Social Imperative: Race, Close Reading, and Contemporary Literary Criticism*. Stanford, CA: Stanford University Press, 2016.

Muñoz, José Esteban. *Disidentifications: Queers of Color and the Performance of Politics*. Minneapolis: University of Minnesota Press, 1999.

Nagar, Richa. *Muddying the Waters: Coauthoring Feminisms across Scholarship and Activism*. Chicago: University of Illinois Press, 2014.

Nagar, Richa, and Amanda Lock Swarr. "Introduction." *Critical Transnational Feminist Praxis*, edited by Amanda Lock Swarr and Richa Nagar. Albany: SUNY Press, 2010.

Nance, Kimberly A. *Can Literature Promote Justice? Trauma Narrative and Social Action in Latin American Testimonio*. Nashville: Vanderbuilt University Press, 2006.

N'Zengou-Tayo, Marie-José. "Rewriting Folklore: Traditional Beliefs and Popular Culture in Edwidge Danticat's *Breath, Eyes, Memory* and *Krik? Krak!*" *MaComère* 3 (2000): 123–40.

Oliver, Kelly. *Witnessing: Beyond Recognition*. Minneapolis: University of Minnesota Press, 2001.

Panjabi, Kavita. "Probing 'Morality' and State Violence: Feminist Values and Communicative Interaction in Prison *Testimonios* in India and Argentina." *Feminist Genealogies, Colonial Legacies, Democratic Futures*, edited by M. Jacqui Alexander and Chandra Talpade Mohanty. New York: Routledge, 1997.

Partnoy, Alicia. *The Little School*, translated by Alicia Partnoy, Lois Athey, and Sandra Braunstein. San Francisco: Midnight Editions, 1998.

———. "Cuando vienen matando: On Prepositional Shifts and the Struggle of Testimonial Subjects for Agency." *PMLA* 121.5 (2006): 1665–69.

———. "Disclaimer Intraducible: My Life/Is Based/On a Real Story." *Biography* 32.1 (2009): 16–25, 293–94.

Personal Narratives Group. *Interpreting Women's Lives: Feminist Theory and Personal Narratives*, edited by Personal Narratives Group. Bloomington: Indiana University Press, 1989.

Prince, Mary. *The History of Mary Prince: A West Indian Slave*. New York: Penguin Books, 2000.

Randall, Margaret. *Cuban Women Now: Interviews with Cuban Women*. Toronto: Women's Press, 1974.

———. *Sandino's Daughters: Testimonies of Nicaraguan Women in Struggle*, edited by Lynda Yanz. Vancouver: New Star Books, 1981.

———. "Reclaiming Voices: Notes on a New Female Practice in Journalism." *The Real Thing: Testimonial Discourse and Latin America*, edited by Georg Gugelburger. Durham, NC: Duke University Press, 1996.

Rege, Sharmila. *Writing Caste/Writing Gender: Narrating Dalit Women's Testimonios*. New Delhi: Zubaan Publishing, 2006.

Rohter, Larry. "Tarnished Laureate." *New York Times*, December 15, 1998.

Rushdie, Salman. *Imaginary Homelands: Essays and Criticism, 1981–1991*. New York: Penguin, 1992.

Saadawi, Nawal el. *Woman at Point Zero*, translated by Sherif Hetata. New York: Zed Books, 1983.

Said, Edward W. *The World, the Text, and the Critic*. Cambridge, MA: Harvard University Press, 1983.

———. "Traveling Theory Reconsidered." *Reflections on Exile and Other Essays*. Cambridge, MA: Harvard University Press, 2003.

———. *Humanism and Democratic Criticism*. New York: Columbia University Press, 2004.

Sánchez, Rosaura. "On a Critical Theory of Identity." *Identity Politics Reconsidered*, edited by Linda Martín Alcoff, Michael Hames-García, Satya P. Mohanty, and Paula M. L. Moya. New York: Palgrave Macmillan, 2006.

Sánchez-Casal, Susan, and Amie A. Macdonald. "Feminist Reflections on the Pedagogical Relevance of Identity." *Twenty-First Century Feminist Classrooms: Pedagogies of Identity and Difference*," edited by Amie A. Macdonald and Susan Sánchez-Casal. New York: Palgrave Macmillan, 2002.

Sandoval, Chela. *Methodology of the Oppressed*. Minneapolis: University of Minnesota Press, 2000.

———. "Dissident Globalizations, Emancipatory Methods, Social Erotics." *Queer Globalizations and the Afterlife of Colonialism*, edited by Arnaldo Cruz-Malave and Martin F. Manalansan. New York: New York University Press, 2002.

Sangtin Writers, and Richa Nagar. *Playing with Fire: Feminist Thought and Activism through Seven Lives in India*. Minneapolis: Minnesota University Press, 2006.

Satrapi, Marjane. *Persepolis*. New York: Pantheon, 2004.

Scarry, Elaine. *The Body in Pain*. New York: Oxford University Press, 1987.

Schaffer, Kay, and Sidonie Smith. *Human Rights and Narrated Lives: The Ethics of Recognition*. New York: Palgrave, 2004.

Scheman, Naomi. "Anger and the Politics of Naming." *Women and Language in Literature and Society*, edited by S. McConnell-Ginet, R. Borker, and N. Furman. Westport, CT: Praeger, 1980.

Scheppele, Kay Lane. "Foreword: Telling Stories." *Michigan Law Review* 87.6 (1989): 2073–98.

Schlau, Stacey. "Introduction: The Use of the Word." *Spanish American Women's Use of the Word*. Tucson: University of Arizona Press, 2001.

Scott, Joan W. "The Evidence of Experience." *Critical Inquiry* 17.4 (1991): 773–97.

Shank, Sofia, and Richa Nagar. "Retelling Stories, Resisting Dichotomies: Staging Identity, Marginalization and Activism in Minneapolis and Sitapur." *Rethinking Feminist Interventions into the Urban*, edited by Linda Peake and Martina Reiker. Oxford: Routledge, 2012.

Shaw, Denise R. "Textual Healing; Giving Voice to Historical and Personal Experience in the Collective Works of Edwidge Danticat." *The Hollins Critic* 44.1 (2007): 1–13.

Shea, Renee H. "The Dangerous Job of Edwidge Danticat: An Interview." *Callaloo* 19.2 (1996): 382–89.

Shogan, Debra. "Polyvocal Ethics." *Resources for Feminist Research* 25.3/4 (1997): 60–63.

Sistren Theatre Collective, with Honor Ford-Smith. *Lionheart Gal: Life Stories of Jamaican Women*, edited by Honor Ford-Smith. Kingston: University of West Indies Press, 2005.

Smith, Sidonie, and Julia Watson. *Women, Autobiography, Theory: A Reader*. Madison: University of Wisconsin Press, 1998.

———. *Reading Autobiography: A Guide for Interpreting Life Narratives*. 2nd ed. Minneapolis: University of Minnesota, 2010.

Sommer, Doris. "Not Just a Personal Story: Women's *Testimonios* and the Plural Self." *Life/Lines: Theorizing Women's Autobiography*, edited by Bella Bordzki and Celeste Schenck. Ithaca, NY: Cornell University Press, 1988.

Sosnowski, Saúl. "Foreword: Of Memory's Literary Sites." *Steps under Water*, translated by David E. Davis. Berkeley: University of California Press, 1996.

Spivak, Gayatri Chakravorty. "Can the Subaltern Speak?" *Marxism and the Interpretation of Culture*, edited by C. Nelson and L. Grossberg. Basingstoke: Macmillan, 1988.

———. "The Politics of Translation." *Outside in the Teaching Machine*. New York: Routledge, 1993.

———. "Three Women's Texts and Circumfession." *Postcolonialism and Autobiography*, edited by Alfred Hornung and Ernstpeter Ruhe. Atlanta: Rodopi, 1998.

Stanton, Domna C., ed. *The Female Autograph: Theory and Practice of Autobiography from the Tenth to the Twentieth Century.* Chicago: University of Chicago Press, 1984.

Steedman, Carolyn Kay. *Landscape for a Good Woman: A Story of Two Lives.* New Brunswick, NJ: Rutgers University Press, 1991.

Sternbach, Nancy Saporta. "Re-Membering the Dead: Latin American Women's 'Testimonial' Discourse." *Latin American Perspectives* 18.3 (1991): 91–102.

Strejilevich, Nora. *A Single, Numberless Death*, translated by Cristina de la Torre. Charlottesville: University of Virginia Press, 2002.

———. "Testimony: Beyond the Language of Truth." *Human Rights Quarterly* 28.3 (2006): 701–13.

Stoll, David. *Rigoberta Menchú, and the Story of All Poor Guatemalans.* Boulder, CO: Westview Press, 1999.

Stone-Mediatore, Shari. *Reading across Borders: Storytelling and Knowledges of Resistance.* New York: Palgrave Macmillan, 2003.

Thiong'o, Ngugi wa. "The Allegory of the Cave: Language, Democracy, and a New World Order." *Penpoints, Gunpoints, and Dreams: Towards a Critical Theory of the Arts and the State in Africa.* Oxford: Clarendon Press, 1998.

Tissot, Damien. "Transnational Feminist Solidarities and the Ethics of Translation." *Feminist Translation Studies: Local and Transnational Perspectives*, edited by Olga Castro and Emek Ergun. New York: Routledge, 2017.

Treacy, Mary Jane. "Double Binds: Latin American Women's Prison Memories." *Hypatia* 11.4 (1996): 130–45.

Viezzar, Moema. "Methods of Oral Testimony." *Fighting on Two Fronts: Women's Struggles and Research*, edited by Maria Mies. The Hague, Netherlands: Institute of Social Studies, 1982.

Vigil, Ariana E. *War Echoes: Gender and Militarization in U.S. Latina/o Cultural Production.* New Brunswick, NJ: Rutgers University Press, 2013.

Warnock, Jeanie E. "'Soul Murder' and Rebirth: Trauma, Narrative, and Imagination in Shani Mootoo's *Cereus Blooms at Night*." *Adventures of the Spirit: The Older Woman in the Works of Doris Lessing, Margaret Atwood, and Other Contemporary Women Writers.* Columbus: Ohio State University Press, 2007.

Webber, Jeannette L., and Joan Grumman, eds. *Woman as Writer.* Boston: Houghton Mifflin, 1978.

Wesling, Meg. "Neocolonialism, Queer Kinship, and Diaspora: Contesting the Romance of the Family in Shani Mootoo's *Cereus Blooms at Night* and Edwidge Danticat's *Breath, Eyes, Memory*." *Textual Practice* 25.4 (2011): 649–70.

Zimmerman, Marc. "*Testimonio* in Guatemala: Payeras, Rigoberta, and Beyond." *The Real Thing: Testimonial Discourse and Latin America*, edited by Georg M. Gugelburger. Durham, NC: Duke University Press, 1996.

Index

A

academics, xiii, 21, 103, 211;
benevolent, 32; and debates on
testimonio, 10; Latina, 47, 88, 99,
100; North American, 7
academy, xiv, 38, 40, 43; northern, 4,
48; US, 88, 110, 118
activism, 78, 91, 114; nonhierarchical,
92; rights-based, 41. *See also*
connected activism
Adichie, Chimamanda Ngozi, 210
Agamben, Giorgio, 145, 151, 191
agency, 46, 113, 125, 152; collective,
114; critical, 184; denial of, 124;
individual, 70
Ahmed, Sara, 58
Alexander, M. Jacqui, xiii, 162, 209
alliances: building, 86, 91–92, 96,
219; coalitional, 62, 79, 119, 132;
commitment to, 219; cross-
border, 61, 76, 218; political, 62;
possibilities for, 73; and power, 75
Anzaldúa, Gloria, 43–44, 177
audience(s), 53, 73, 120, 147; academic,
7; and active reading, 148; activist,
50; authorial directive for, 94;
broad, 102, 197; connecting with,
7; and Danticat, 182, 200, 201, 205,
207–8, 210; different, xiii, 8, 10,
90, 109; disparate, 106, 175, 180;

diverse, 107; dominantly
positioned, 78; and feminist
testimonio, 80; first-world, 6,
26, 106; Haitian-based, 182;
international, 79; linkages
between, 175; multiple, xi, 8, 57,
77, 106, 131, 174, 176; non-Haitian,
207; northern, xi, 20; and power
relations, xii, 73, 208; privileged,
8–9, 61, 75, 132; questions of, 106;
reaching across, 205; reading,
60–62, 91, 111, 120, 207; registers,
109; relationship with text, 91; and
truth-value, 5; US, 102, 180, 208;
US anglo, 175; young, 200–201.
See also reader(s); readership(s)
autobiographical practices, 57
autobiography, 4, 23, 43; acts of, 22,
23; *Autobiography of Ben Franklin*,
22; Beverley on, 21; bildungsroman
as, 22; fictionalized, 41; liberal,
24–25; as life writing, 5, 8, 23; and
Menchú, 4–6; reframing, 22–23;
and "self-made man," 5; Smith
and Watson on, 22–23; Sommer
on, 21; studies of, 9, 11, 21; and
testimonio, 4, 5, 17, 21, 23; and
women writers, 22
Awadhi (language), 87, 89, 102, 106

B

Baca, Colorado, 89, 99, 111, 112; border-crossing ethos, 112

Bambara, Toni Cade, ix–x

bearing witness, 26, 60, 113, 144

Behar, Ruth, 3, 8, 23

Bell, Beverly: agency, 125; authorial directives, 94, 98; class, 118–19; editorial decisions, 94, 100, 102, 104–5, 119, 124–25; *griyo/istwa* paradigm, 88, 94, 105, 183; Haitian folklore, 53, 104; interviews, 88, 94, 102, 105, 111; linguistic choices, 53, 100, 102, 104; multiple audiences, 131; photography, 100; representational framing, 88, 100, 110, 125, 127–30; resistance, 124, 152; solidarity, 131; *Walking on Fire*, 11, 55, 59, 69, 86, 88, 102, 123–24, 152; writing prompt, 113. See also *Walking on Fire*

Beverley, John, 21, 48, 49, 50, 86, 137; "The Margin at the Center," 18–19, 25, 48; "The Real Thing," 48, 49

bildungsroman, 22; autobiographical, 23; postcolonial, 23, 64; and women, 22

Black Lives Matter, 40

black vernacular English, ix

Boler, Megan, 61; collective witnessing, 61

border crossings, 95, 97, 112, 118, 119, 176, 216

Brown, Wendy, 32, 72

Bueno, Eva Paulino, 7

C

Caribbean studies, 9

Casa de las Americas, 50–51

Castile, Philando, 211–12

Cereus Blooms at Night (Mootoo), 9, 12, 59, 137, 139–41, 149–50, 156–59, 160, 163–67, 183; alternative kinship, 141, 164; cereus plant, 149, 163–64; creative communication, 159–60; decolonizing interpersonal relations, 166; embodied listening, 157; epistemic bridging, 165; epistemic multiplicity, 164; interdependence, 141, 156, 160, 163, 165; listening differently, 157–58; nonverbal communication, 156; overidentification, 166; relationality, 165; self-reflexivity, 156; shared queerness, 60, 156, 167; trauma, 157

chained action, 50

Christian, Barbara, xiii

citizen activists, 211

citizen body, 5

coalitional alliances, 119; building, 86, 91–92; cross-border posture of, 95; feminist, 86, 92; horizontal, 62; modeling, 79; practices of, 96; spirit of, 132; and women, 119

coalitional politics, 66, 72

coalitions, small-scale, 70, 116

co-conversation, 24, 77

collaboration: across difference, 70, 116; artistic, 114; commitment to, 116; feminist, 94; feminist polyvocal activist, 69; Latina Feminist Group, 89, 98, 115; praxis and, 86; processes of, 98, 108

collective approach, 66, 87, 108–9, 114, 116; individual, 17–18, 24, 70, 85, 95, 97, 113, 155, 185–86; as chorus, 20; decision making, 93; dialogue, 116, 119–20, 129; efforts toward, 116; emotional labor, 117, 123; ethos, 18; feminist methodology, 85; goals of, 70, 72, 114–16; knowledge production, 96; Latina Feminist Group, 88, 96, 99,

102, 112, 119; marginalized knowledge claims, 47; meaning-making, 72, 79, 86, 93, 96–97, 184–85; and meetings, 111–12; methodologies, 85, 92, 109, 112; necessity of, 154; prompts and, 113–14; Randall and, 108; regional differences, 112; relationality and, 95; resonance of, 20, 65, 93; resources, 71; Sangtin Writers, 87, 95, 98, 106, 126, 129; Sistren Theatre Collective, 87, 96, 99; and storytelling, 45, 94, 126; and testimonio, 17–19, 115, 186; and witnessing, 61–62; and women, 88, 93, 100, 117; in writing, 48

collective conscience, 132

collective histories, 18, 72

collective "I," 101

collective memory and memory work, 6, 58, 137, 142

collective unconscious, 185

communication: creative, 153, 156, 159–60; cultural, 200; dialogic modes of, 74; modes of, 156; nonverbal, 149; "real", 159; subjective modes of, 35

community: epistemic value of, 170; interpretive, 68; of knowers, 68–69, 160–62; of meaning, 69, 72, 219; and Menchú, 4–5; and nation-states, 59–60; oppressed or repressed, 4, 112; practice of, 112; romanticization of, 183; truths of, 4; of women, 183, 185;

community consciousness, 140

co-narration, 97, 106; framework, 136; practice, 140; strategies, 11

connected actions, 92

connected activism, xi, 11, 117, 132

consciousness: critical, 16, 37; decolonizing, 148; diasporic, 202; expansive, 218; linguistic, 179; oppositional, 140, 218; political,

160; rebel, 88; relational modes of, 161; and trauma, 148–51. *See also* kaleidoscopic consciousness

consciousness raising, 43, 62

Cooper, Carolyn, 103

counternarratives, 17, 29, 58, 74, 146

countertestimony, 4, 31

countertopographies, 9, 52, 74

Creole, 103; Danticat and, 173, 175, 177–82, 191, 201, 207; Haitian, 53, 88–89, 102, 104–6, 201; Jamaican, 53, 87, 89, 102–3, 105, 118

critics and critique, 23, 62, 75, 88, 95, 218; autobiography studies, 20–21; cultural, 6; feminist, 22, 74; Latin American, 20–21; literary, 23; macrosocial, 8, 11, 15, 44, 51; and Menchú, 8; microsocial, 27; postcolonial, 22; social, 42, 45, 51, 88, 127, 129; and testimonio, 31, 136

cross-border work: and alliances, 61, 76, 218; coalitional posture of, 95; and cultural work, 176; dynamics of, xii; and solidarity, 75

cultural imaginary, xi, 12, 27, 56, 57, 81, 217

cultural production, 23, 57

cultural translation, 80, 179

cultural work, xi, 57, 74, 100, 176, 197, 218

cultural workers, xii, xiii, 12, 100, 182

D

dalit, 51, 87

Danticat, Edwidge, 9, 12, 55, 57, 69, 174; Anancy, figure of, 181; *Behind the Mountains*, 12, 180, 195–202, 205; between-worlds-space, 176; *Breath, Eyes, Memory*, 22, 174, 180, 206–7, 210; *Brother, I'm Dying*, 12, 195–200, 202, 203, 205; *The Butterfly's Way*, 69, 176; collective meaning-making, 184–85;

feminist (as label), 55–56

feminist activist polyvocal testimonio, 53, 61, 64–65, 86, 97; backstage preparations for, 90–91, 114; collaborative, 11, 69; defined, 55; direct address, 122, 126–27; extraliterary, 108–9; methodologies, diologic, 117, 132; methodologies, self-reflexive, 119; methodologies, story-based, 114; methodology sections, 108–10, 130–31; as performative, 90–91, 114; and power relations, 131; and Randall, 92; and representational strategies, 92; structures of, 65; and women's collectives, 93

feminist counterpublics, 12, 218

feminist literary criticism, 33, 73–74

feminist literary testimonio, 65, 135–37, 143, 152, 162, 170; alternative kinship, 161; co-narrational framework, 136; defined, 55; empathetic bridges, 147; interdependence, 161; interpersonal connections, 170; memory work, 140, 143, 151; role of art in, 141; stuctures, fragmented, 145; structures, polyvocal, 160–61; temporal disruption, 143; trauma, 147–48

feminist polyvocal testimonio, xi, 53, 67, 72, 89, 96, 101, 214, 217; contextual relationships, 72; cultural work, 218; decolonial ethos, 12; defined, 7; dialogic interaction, 69; epistemic importance, 10; epistemic strategy, 20, 120; fragmented narratives, 64; frameworks, 66; as lens, 10; partial perspective, 65, 85; and postpositivist realist theory, 72; structures, polyvocal, 65, 96

feminist standpoint theory, 29, 30, 31, 33, 36, 64, 66

feminist testimonio, 8–11, 23–24, 54–81, 108, 116. *See also* feminist activist polyvocal testimonio; feminist literary testimonio; feminist polyvocal testimonio

feminist theory, 11, 31, 33, 99. *See also* feminist standpoint theory

first-person plural, 8, 15, 19, 51, 52

folklore, 39; and Danticat, 187, 194; Haitian, 53, 99, 110, 175; Jamaican, 53, 99, 103, 110

Ford-Smith, Honor, 45, 87, 102–3, 110, 112, 132; coalitions and collaboration, 70, 116; collective creative process, 114; dialogic processes, 116; story-based paradigms, 122

Franco, Jean, 58

Freire, Paulo, 37, 62, 69–72, 116

G

gaze: anthropological, 77; legal, 195; Mala's (in *Cereus Blooms at Night*), 157; narrated-I, 25; racist, 212; of readership, 25; "widened," 125

gender essentialism, 31, 94; strategic, 31

Glissant, Edouard, 182

globalization, 54, 80, 95, 126, 218

Global South, xii, 5, 20

Gordon, Avery, 24

grounded theory, 90

Guatemala, 3–4, 6

Gugelberger, Georg M., 48

H

Hall, Stuart, 73

Harding, Sandra, 36, 47

Henze, Brent E., 43, 70–71, 79

heteroglossia, 20

knowledge production, 108, 111, 170; in the academy, 38; as collaborative endeavor, 71; collective, 96; democratic, 10, 77, 105; dominant flows of, xi; dominant paradigms of, 98; elitist, 90, 101; linguistic modalities of, 100; official, 38; oppositional, 34; politics of, 7, 11, 89; power differentials in, 56; resistant modes of, 43; social, 10, 42; subjective truth claims of, 8; terrain of, 9, 10, 86, 90, 107; translocal, 218

L

labor, 116, 117; "backstage," 114; emotional, 115, 117, 123; gendered division of, 110; in *Playing with Fire*, 115; processes of, 109, 120, 115; representation of, 114, 120; and *Telling to Live*, 115; and unions, 132; visibility of, 109
language registers, 10, 101, 174
Latin America: context, 48, 86; literary critics, 18, 20, 75; social landscape, 50; social movements, 52; studies, 9, 11; testimonio, 15, 51, 52, 146
Latina Feminist Group, 9, 11, 70, 86, 88, 96, 98–99, 105, 112, 115–19, 121; language choices, 102, 105; members of, 94. See also *Telling to Live*
Latinas: deconstruction of, 117; diversity of, 98, 115; experiences of, 116; feminist academics and scholars, 48, 88, 99; identity, 95; as pan-ethnic, 88, 114; as pan-Latina, 98. *See also* Latina Feminist Group
latinidades, 89, 107
Let Me Speak! Testimony of Domitila, 47

life narrative, 23, 28, 40, 107–9, 116, 122–23; forms of, 21; of Menchú, 5; uses of, 40
life writing, xi, 5, 22–25, 28, 40–44, 50, 51, 57, 96, 113; and alternative paradigms, 8; forms of, 5, 18, 21; hybrid, 8, 43; practices of, 8, 20; resistant, 8
"limit situations," 72
Lionheart Gal (Sistren Theatre Collective), 9, 11; authorial directive, 94; decoding, 126; dialogic process, 127; direct address, 129–30; language choices, 53, 101–4; narrative framing, 69, 86–89, 96, 99; methodologies, storytelling, 45, 122, 125–26; methodology section, 108, 110, 112, 114, 116–18; politics of recognition, 114; polyvocality, 99; rhetorical questions, 129–30; as working-class, 125
The Little School (Partnoy), xii, 12, 137, 141, 145, 152–54, 160
los desaparecidos, 50

M

Maier, Linda, 18
Maier and Dulfano, 47
marginal experience narratives, 11, 39, 40, 42–44, 66, 73, 86, 211
McCormack, Donna, 157
Medina, José, xiii; chained action, 50; connected activism, xi, 11, 117; epistemic arrogance, 76; epistemic counterpoints, 93; epistemic friction, 56, 76; epistemic humility, 72; epistemic privilege, 37; epistemic responsibility, 11; epistemologies of resistance, 34; imagination, 57; kaleidoscopic consciousness, 11–12, 29, 62, 80, 177, 218; whiteness, 76

memoir, 5, 25, 41, 174; *Brother I'm Dying*, 197–98

memory, 28; archive of, 46; collective, 6; experience of, 170; experiences based on, 39; historical, 121, 135; interpersonal, 64; living, 151; and Menchú, 6; personal, 21, 46; reflections on, 136; subjective, 28, 65; terror of, 145; and testimonio, 44; and truth, 7

memory work, 46, 58–60, 115, 146; active, 151; act of, 143; collective, 137, 142; creative, 140, 145; Danticat and, 195, 204; historical, 160; intentional, 151, 199, 208; and Sangtin Writers, 117–18; story-based models of, 132

Menchú, Rigoberta, 4–5, 55, 130; controversy, 3–9, 21, 41, 64, 136; *I, Rigoberta Menchú*, 3, 6, 27, 47, 108

metaphor: Anzaldúa and, 43–44; chorus of voices, 96–97; culturally resonant, 53, 89, 103–4; cultural trauma, 148, 152; Danticat and, 196

methodology: collaborative, 65, 116; collective, 92; collective feminist, 85; deliberative, 121; dialogic, 66, 70, 108, 117, 132; epistemically responsible, 11; feminist, 100; and folklore, 103; of the oppressed, 16, 48; participant focused, 100; Randall on, 63; representational, 8, 10; sections about, 91, 107–9, 112, 114, 116, 122–23, 126, 130–31; self-reflexive, 119; story-based, 45, 66, 107, 114; storytelling, 44–45, 107; testimonio as, 11, 15, 28, 51, 66, 89, 101, 113, 132

metonymy, 19, 63

migration, 110, 126; Danticat and, 174–75, 177, 196–201, 203, 205

Minh-ha, Trinh T., 15, 57

Mohanty, Chandra, 52, 74–75, 95, 117; common differences, 96; comparativist framework, 75

Mohanty, Satya P., 30, 34, 36, 37

Mootoo, Shani, 9, 12, 55, 59, 137, 139–40, 149, 156, 163–67, 185. See also *Cereus Blooms at Night*

Moraga, Cherríe, 43, 66; theory in the flesh, 66

Moraga and Anzaldúa, 43

Morales, Aurora Levins, 47, 90, 184

Moya, Paula, xiii, 11, 34–36

Muñoz, José, 64, 139, 157

N

Nagar and Swarr, 62, 71, 75

Nance, Kimberly, 6–7, 20, 25, 31–32, 75–78, 130; deliberative testimonio, 9, 64, 78, 120–21, 128–29, 130; forwarding, 75–76; fusion, 76, 79

Nanny of the Maroons, 103, 125

narrative frames, 19, 62–63, 66, 69, 89–90, 92, 127, 130, 141, 193

narratives: and ambivalence, 121; bourgeois, 5, 16; *dalit*, 51; dominant, 11, 26, 65, 140; experiential, 10, 28, 31, 38–39, 42, 66; first-person plural, 8, 15, 52, 19; fragmented, 64, 69, 136; frameworks of, xi, 11, 12, 41, 63–64, 66, 71, 78–79, 96–97, 101, 135, 139, 141, 144, 160, 162, 164, 205; historical, 31, 88; legal, 41; life, 5, 21, 28, 32, 40, 107–9, 116, 122–23; marginal experience, 11, 39, 40, 42–44, 66, 73, 86, 211; multiplying of, 65, 88; performativity of, 21; personal, 92; and perspective, 39, 64, 69, 79; registers of, 195, 208; social, 30, 31, 46; story-based, 42, 66; strategies of, 187

national trauma, 136, 137, 141, 146
nation-state, xii, 59
native informant, 9, 208
New Americans, ix, 210, 216
NGOs, 48, 85, 87, 98, 110, 102, 106, 110, 113, 118
novels: historical, 23; of development, 22; testimonial, 64
Nunca Más, 138, 142

O

objectivity, 5, 20, 27–28, 42; fact-based, 28; and postpositivist realist theory, 68; strong, 36, 47; unmediated, 28, 40
Oliver, Kelly, 60
oppositional consciousness, 44, 49, 218
organizing, 87, 96, 111, 121, 132; egalitarian, 85; feminist, 106; social justice, 119; transnational feminist, 131

P

Panjabi, Kavita, 51–52
papelitos guardados, 89
paradigms: academic, xiv, 71; activist, 117; alternative, 45, 92, 157; connected, 117; dominant legal, 41; dominant narrative, 25, 26; dominant western autobiographical, 5; heteronormative, 167; individualist, 155; interpretive, 34; interrelational, 155; knowledge production, 98; liberal, 26; life-writing, 8; locationally distinct, 104; racial, xii; representational, 43, 91, 92, 195; Smith and Watson, 23; social, 44; trafficking in, 17, 77, 109; witnessing, 20; witness-testifier, 60–62
partial perspective, 10, 11, 35, 65, 219

Partnoy, Alicia. See *The Little School*
pathos, 25, 56, 122–23, 128–29
Personal Narratives Group, 65
platforms: abolitionist, 51; aesthetic, 16; coalitional, 72; diverse, 40; liberatory, 16; political, 16, 26; social justice, xi, 11, 40, 52, 56
Playing with Fire (Sangtin Writers and Richa Nagar), 9, 11, 53, 59, 69, 104–11; caste, 117–18; direct address, 129–30; emotional labor, 123; framing, 85–90, 126; gender, 95; interpretive codas, 122, 126; labor, 114–15; language choices, 101–2, 105–6; memory work, 117; metaphors, 104; methodology sections, 108–10; middle-class respectability, 126; Nari Samata Yojana, 111; place-based ethos, 110–11; polyvocal framework, 94–98; prompts, 113–14; *Sangtin Yatra*, 131; rhetorical questions, 129
political economy, 54
politics: Ahmed on, 58; coalitional, 66, 72; epistemic, 162; geo-, 200; global, 199; Haitian, 187, 196, 203; of hope, 219; hybrid textual, 16, 52; identity, 19, 72; intersectional, 54; of knowledge production, 7, 11, 89; language, ix, 102, 180; of location, 55, 73; progressive, 215; racial, 211; of recognition, 91; of representation, xi, 174; of subjective truth claims, 8; transformative, 77; transnational feminist, 10; without guarantees, xii, 80
politics of difference, 56, 64, 86, 91–92, 94–96
polyglot effect, 23
polyphony, 20, 63, 94, 98, 187, 218; absent, 19, 20, 92, 136, 198; as frame, 69

polyvocal feminist testimonio. *See* feminist polyvocal testimonio

polyvocality, 100, 139–31, 138, 174; commitment to, 64; decolonial affect, 64; and deliberative methodologies, 121; deployments of, 131; discussions of, 62; epistemic function, 68; epistemology of, 170; as ethos, 199; in feminist testimonio, 64, 68; as framework, 63–64, 66, 91, 106, 119, 121, 161, 170; in literary testimonios, 64; and *Playing with Fire*, 89, 95, 97; representational practices of, 80; as strategy, xi, 73, 91, 120, 187; as structure, 63, 65, 86, 94, 96, 97, 160, 162; as tactic, 136; and testimonio, 69; uses of, 65. *See also* feminist polyvocal testimonio

positionality, 18, 79

positivism: and counterevidence, 31; and evidence, 5, 109; frameworks, 39; and postpositivist realist theory, 10–11, 29, 33, 35–37, 39, 41–42, 46, 66, 68, 72, 79

power, 92, 123–24; analyses of, 28; asymmetries of, 8, 71, 75, 78, 170, 181, 207; balance of, 26; bidirectionality of, 17, 60, 62; contestations of, 32; decentralized, 63, 120; differentials of, 25, 56, 60, 71, 96, 118; dominant, 26, 106; dynamic nature of, 37; dynamics of, 7, 16, 39, 45, 160; emotional, 123; flows of, 17, 63; formal, 16; geopolitical, 8; global, 61; ideological, 45, 49; of the imaginary, 140; imbalances of, xii; of interpersonal exchange, 117; interpretive, 60; of language, 141; macrosocial, 27, 17, 86; margins of, 124; narratives of, 218; negotiations of, 75, 123–24;

objective reality of, 42; and powerlessness, 16, 17, 87, 125; as privilege, 119; relations of, 31, 34, 37, 58, 72; relationship to, 36, 37; as service, 119; social, 55, 118, 127; speaking to, 16–17; structures of, 15, 27, 32, 37, 39, 44, 55, 64, 160, 199, 218; systems of, 24; transnational flows of, 52

power relations, xi–xii, 6, 37, 38, 101, 131, 170, 187, 218; between audience and author, 208; between audience and text, xii, 6–8, 73, 91

praxis: collaboration as, 86; critical, 132; dialogic, 11, 62, 71, 75; feminist, 73; feminist criticism as, 54, 74; feminist testimonio as, 64, 108; Freire and, 71; hybrid textual, 16; linguistic, 105; literature as, 54; reading, 207; resistant, 45; textual, 16, 52, 120; transnational feminist, xi, 70, 74; writing, 29, 79, 208

privilege, 118; epistemic, 11, 37; geopolitical, xii, 73, 118; narratives of, 218; questions of, 108; racial, xii; of reading audiences, 8, 20, 61, 73, 75, 77, 80, 109, 120, 132, 136; as responsibility, 119; social, x, 88, 99, 119, 218; white, 76

process-based approach, 11, 108, 114, 130–31

public intellectualism, xiii

publishers, northern, 26

R

racialization, xii; and class systems, 35, 128, 208; and colonial subjectivities, 156; and national landscapes, 160; and privileged readers, 8, 56, 61, 73, 75, 77, 107, 109, 120, 136

radical humility, xiv

Randall, Margaret, 48, 63, 69, 78, 92–94, 96, 108; *Cuban Women Now*, 78, 92; *Sandino's Daughters*, 78, 92–93

reader(s): accountability of, 17; adult, 200; affective identification of, 76; assumptions of, 66; consciousness of, 57, 100, 168; construction of, 121–22; cross-border alliances with, 61; and direct address, 130; dominantly positioned, 77; ego of, 76; empathetic bridges with, 147; first-world, 60; grooming, 121; ideal, 76; as interpretive outsider, 25; interpretive power of, 60; interpretive processes and, 76, 79, 89, 122, 208; invitation to, 25, 56, 71, 77, 90, 97, 122, 131; as listener, 67; positionality of, 79; privileged, 73, 75, 77, 80, 109, 120, 136; as privileged friend, 129; and processes of exchange, 62; recruiting, 57; response(s) of, 77, 123; responsibility of, 76, 80; risk of, 80; and text, 74, 141; uncommitted, 128; uninformed, 208; willful ignorance of, 80; as witness, 12, 26; worldview of, 57, 81; young, 181, 200. *See also* audience(s); readership(s)

readership(s): access to, 175; affective appeal to, 25; consciousness of, 110; cross-border, 17; diverse, 136, 195; gaze of, 25; horizontal, xii; imaginative capabilities of, 122; invitation to, 71, 122; northern, xi, 6, 25, 26, 75; privileged, 120, 136; recognition of, 61; US, 119, 174, 175, 190; as witness, 26; young, 200, 202. *See also* audience(s); reader(s)

reading practice, 210; consumptive, 175; epistemically responsible, 10;

individual, 206; mindful, 210; neocolonial, 175

rebel consciousness, 88

recognition, 17, 21, 39, 60–61, 114; competing for, 180, 187; factual, 145; legal, 50, 149; vs. misrecognition, 6, 136, 146, 180; and mutuality, 208; politics of, 91

Rege, Sharmila, 51–52

registers, 45; affective, 11, 15; epistemic, 29, 195; interpretive, 40; knowledge, 43; language, 10, 101, 106; microsocial, 15, 44; multiple, 126, 174; narrative, 195, 208; representation, 198; social, 178; subjective, 28, 39

relationality, 9, 74, 155, 162, 165, 186; egalitarian, 160; intersubjective, 165; models of, 137, 160; modes of, 141, 164

relationships: contextual, 72; dialogical, 62; horizontal, xi, 132; human, 164, 168; intergenerational, 194; interpersonal, 208; between memory and truth, 7; neocolonial, 187; South/South, xi; spatial, 91; racial and geopolitical, 7; reader and audience, 91; reorganization of, 168; to language, 188; vertical, 132

representation: and accuracy, 114; alternative, 143; and Caribbean cultures, 181; conscious uses of, 91; cultural, 174, 185; discursive, 114, 120; diversifying, 97, 114; effectiveness of, 98; efforts toward, 140; essentialist, 94; fluidity and, 182; forms of, 101; and gendered subjectivity, 8; impasse embedded in, 9; interventions in, 86; lack of, 100; linguistic, 179; literary, 174; methodologies of, 8, 10; modes of, 4; monolithic models of, 88, 107;

social knowledge (*cont.*)
experiential-based, 32; of Haitian women, 184; less false, 11; life stories and, 28, 123; limits of, 219; limits of memory and, 64; multiple forms of, 100; narratively coded forms of, 33; past and present, 199; pieces of, 218; reliable, 10, 31, 40, 42; representation of, 105; sources of, 67; storytelling and experience, relationship to, 27; transforming, 62; women's experience and, 36

social location as epistemic resource, 161

socially lived theory, 8

social pact: bidirectional, 12; reciprocal, 20, 26, 136

social responsibility, 20, 186

social truth(s), 10, 40, 45, 101, 104, 122, 127, 195, 218; "bear witness" to, 26; coexisting, 64, 71; multiple, 63; objective, 39, 42

solidarity, 59, 95, 188, 123; and alliances, 62; appeals to, 75; bidirectional, 131; commitment to, 115; cross-border, 75; efforts toward, 70, 88, 92, 131–32; feminist, 96; group, 96; international, 49; poetics of, 85; political, 17, 119; postcolonial, 52; and relationality, 162; *sangtins*, 87; sense of, 156; transnational network of, 111, 131–32; utopic notion of, 167–68

Sommer, Doris, 21, 24

South/South relationships and trajectories, xi, 52, 73

speech acts, 77; self-referential, 23

Spivak, Gayatri, 3, 8, 19, 32, 179; ethical translation, 179

standard English, 101, 103–5, 118; bending, 102; decolonizing use of, 89

standard French, 104

standpoint theory. *See* feminist standpoint theory

Steedman, Carolyn, 37, 45, 46, 199

Steps under Water (Kozameh), 9, 12, 20, 137–38, 140–41, 146–49, 154–55, 160–63, 167–69; alternative forms of kinship, 162; compañeras, 155, 163, 167–68; dialogic exchange, 162; interdependence, 163; polyvocality, 161

Stoll, David, 4–6

Stone-Mediatore, Shari, 33, 38, 40, 42, 43

storytelling, 39–41; collective, 94; culturally specific, 104; distrust of, 41; epistemological relevance of, 27, 184; experiential-based, 42; in *Krik? Krak!*, 182; methodologies of, 42, 44–45, 69, 107–9; oral, 104, 184; political work of, 183; power of, 44; practice of, 44, 104; purposeful, 127, 129; questions of, 10; as resistant mode of praxis, 45; as survival, 183; as tool, 10

Strejilevich, Nora, 9, 12, 19, 27–28, 46, 58, 60, 67–68, 185, 204; polyvocality, 161. See also *A Single, Numberless Death*

subaltern(s), 6, 18, 32; voices of, xii

subjectivity, 42; asserting, 153; claims to, 155; concepts of, 170; connected, 70; embodied, 54; enacting, 101; gendered, 8; imagined, 24; individual, 97; inter-, 162; linguistic, 105; new modes of, 160; relationship with objectivity, 42; theories of, 5; undoing, 155

subject position(s), 36, 63, 65, 71, 74, 76, 91, 93

subjects: archival, 38; authentic, 8–9, 65; diasporic, 176; disadvantaged,

37; dominant, 37, 78; gendered, 90; interviewing, 93; marginalized, 8, 36–37, 51, 77; oppressed, 113; postcolonial, 22; privileged, xiii; racialized, 88; situated, 175; social, xi, 38, 139; third world, 4, 9; women as, 36

T

Telling to Live (Latina Feminist Group), xii, 9, 11, 47, 53, 86, 107–9, 121, 130; Chicana feminist thought, 110; dialogue, 70, 115–17; direct address, 130; framing, 88–90; labor, 115; language choices, 101–2, 105; methodology section, 107–9; place-based ethos, 111–12; polyvocality, 94–96, 98–100; prompts, 113–14; *testimoniadoras*, 89, 99, 102, 105, 113, 115

testimonio: affective, 47; antiliterary, 18; collective ethos of, 18; as culturally resistant writing project, 15, 56; defined, x; deliberative, 64, 76–77, 121–22, 128–29, 130, 199; dialogic function of, 92; epistemic value of, 53; extraliterary, 18; historical archive of, 17; Latin American, 15; methodology, 15, 20, 48, 66, 86; as "out-law genre," 18; pedagogical function of, 20; polyphonic, 20, 63; as resistance literature, 17; rhetorical framing in, 25; socioliterary, 18, 27, 110; textual practice of, 44, 52; traditional, 23, 63; translocalized utilizations of, 53; and witness paradigm, 26. *See also* feminist activist polyvocal testimonio; feminist literary testimonio, feminist polyvocal testimonio

transnational feminism and feminists, xi, 110; activists, 120; critique, 74; organizing efforts, 131; politics, 10; politics of location, 73; praxis, xi, 70, 74; solidarity efforts, 131–32; theory, 74; thought, 9

traveling theory, 49, 50

trauma studies, 60

tropes: dialogue, 120; dominant, 26; imaginative, 8; narrative, 26, 44; rhetorical, 11; process, 120; recognizable, 77; of withholding information, 130

truth claims, 5–6, 8–9, 100, 210; embedded, 62; as embodied knowledge, 100; fragmented, 63, 65, 94; and Menchú, 4–5; multiple, 64, 96; socially situated, 9; subjective, 8; trust in, 120; unmediated, 91; unproblematized, 64; women's, 36

truth(s), 4, 8–9, 66, 42, 211; coexisting, 93, 94, 120; epistemic, 121, 122; juridical model of, 5; and literary testimonio, 170; narrative, 74; objective, 39, 218; partial, 16; situated, 72, 117; social, 10, 39, 40, 42, 45, 63–64, 71, 101, 104, 122, 195; and Truth, 65–66, 72; uncomfortable, 218; women's, 186

truth-value, 5, 28–29, 41, 42, 44, 46, 66, 79; collective, 94; of experience, 38; social, 40

U

United States: academy and academics in, xii, 88, 89, 110, 118; anglo audience in, 175; audiences and readerships in, 119, 174, 175, 102, 180, 208; borders of, 174, 180, 187; context of, xii; cultural imagination of, 190; culture of, x,

United States (*cont.*)
105; and Danticat, 175, 178, 188; and Haiti, 102, 187–88, 190–91, 199, 201, 206; and Haitian coup, 188; and immigration, 174, 197, 198, 203, 205; landscape of, 208; Latina scholars and, 48, 99; imperial policies of, 195, 199; military of, 191; print media in, 180; publishing market of, 174, 181; and women-of-color feminisms, 54, 185

Uttar Pradesh, 85, 87, 102

V

Viezzar, Moema, 42

Vigil, Ariana, 52, 64

violence, 145; class, 183; epistemic, xiii, 32, 75, 191; intimate partner, 88, 110, 126; of power relations, xii; sexual, 59; social, 60; state-sponsored, 110

W

Walking on Fire (Bell), 11, 53, 55, 86, 94, 96, 183; Anacaona, tale of, 104; bidirectional solidarity, 131; culturally specific storytelling, 104–6; dialogic process, 70, 116, 120; direct address, 127; framing, 69, 130; *griyo/istwa* paradigm, 105–6; interviews, 98–100, 111; knowledge production, 89–90; language choices, 89, 101–2, 104; methodology, 108, 110–11; middle-class voices, 119; multiplying the narrative, 88, 114; pathos, 128–29; place-based ethos, 111; polyvocality, 94, 99–100; prompt, 113; reader as friend, 130; resistance, 123–24, 152; social function of hope, 59; women's oral storytelling, 104

whiteness, xiv, 76

willful ignorance, xii, 80

witness-testifier paradigm, 60–62, 91, 141

witness testimony, 18, 27

women-headed households, 110

women's issues, 48, 88, 98

worldview(s), 6, 8, 28, 36, 39, 75, 214; accepted, 61; altering, 81, 186; challenged, 75; competing, 67, 75; center-periphery, 56; Danticat and, 178; decentering, 72, 75; destabilizing, 77; in dialogue, 79; differing, 194; epistemic, 212; internalized, 56; learning to un-know, 207; one's own, 81, 193, 209; readers', 57, 121; shift in, 194

DECOLONIZING FEMINISMS
Piya Chatterjee, Series Editor

Humanizing the Sacred: Sisters in Islam and the Struggle for Gender Justice in Malaysia, by Azza Basarudin

Power Interrupted: Antiracist and Feminist Activism inside the United Nations, by Sylvanna Falcón

Transnational Testimonios: The Politics of Collective Knowledge Production, by Patricia DeRocher